Lydia

The Journey Home

A True Story

by

Elsie Loewen

Edited by Marion Kraaikamp
Cover Design by Jeff Bellmont
Copyright© 2000 Elsie J. Loewen
ejloewen@telusplanet.net

National Library of Canada Cataloguing in Publication Data

Loewen, Elsie.
Lydia

ISBN 0-7795-0001-6

1. Oushal, Lydia, 1919- 2. Russian Germans--Alberta--Biography. 3.
Immigrants--Alberta--Biography. I. Title.
FC3700.R9L63 2001   971.23'0049171'0092   C2001-910639-4
F1080.R79L63 2001

PREFACE

Framed portraits line the walls of her home, a gallery of relationships both past and present. Some of the smiling faces now live only in cherished memory, each a poignant reminder of another time and place.

Lydia Oushal knows the joy and security of a closely knit family. She also knows the pain of severed ties through death, decree, and personal tragedy.

I travelled with her in retrospect through more than eight decades of change, experiencing vicariously the drama and danger of textbook history unfolding, with its devastating impact on the lives of ordinary people. I shared the hope and struggle of each new beginning — and the crushing disappointment of promise unfulfilled. Both laughter and tears permeate her memories, offered candidly without reserve.

Her story embraces many facets of grief with its often overwhelming sense of isolation, abandonment and despair. It is also about miracles. About hope and forgiveness. About the triumph of her spirit, faith-propelled beyond mere survival, to know joy and to celebrate life with family and friends.

I am honored to share this journey with her and to recount it in a written portrait of a remarkable life well-lived, guided and protected by the One "*...who comforts us in all our troubles so that we can comfort those in any trouble with the comfort we ourselves have received from God.*" *(II Cor. 1:4 NIV)*

Elsie Loewen

Our Everything

She'd heave and hack,
give the shirt off her back,
and brighten your day with a smile.
She's generous and kind,
keeps everyone in mind,
she'd walk the extra mile.
She'd do anything grand,
lend her helping hand,
it's just the way she was built.
She'd pray for each friend,
broken hearts always mend,
her love will never wilt.
Her beauty and grace
could catch any face,
she's the only pea in her pod.
When it's her time and she dies,
to heaven she'll happily rise,
She's touched by the hand of God.

She's our Oma,
Our Grandma,
Our Mum,
And our Friend.

She's our Everything!

- by Christine Kesler, great-granddaughter

DEDICATION

The story I am about to tell you is a gift from my heart, which I share as I saw it, lived it, and heard it from family, friends, and authorities.

During the Second World War, I put my life in God's hands and learned that the Christian life is a totally loving, trusting relationship with God in all circumstances.

There is no easy explanation for the hurt, the pain, and the many tears I have cried. I was among hundreds of thousands of people whose lives and families were torn apart. It is impossible to write everything as it was; the book would be the size of the Bible.

I wish to dedicate this book, first to my loving daughter Lilia, and also to the precious memories of my other children: Stanley, Yuri and Alla. Their love and trust, even through the pain of separation and loneliness, gave me the will and determination to live one day at a time, to keep believing when hope was gone.

I also dedicate this story of my life to my grandchildren: Debbie, Danny, Jason, Monti, Danielle, Raelyn, Sergey and Sasha. And to my great-grandchildren: Christine, Luke, Anthony, Adam, Samson, Shay-Ann, Roman and Dennis.

These are the love of my heart and I thank God for each of them.

And so, thank you Lord for yesterday, today, and all the tomorrows you give me.

I Love You!

Lydia Oushal

PROLOGUE

"By the time you get this letter, Yuri may be gone from this world."

The flimsy paper suddenly grew heavy in my hands and I sank into the nearest armchair under its weight. A striped blue and red airmail envelope lay on the floor at my feet and I tried to recapture the anticipation I felt each time I saw the familiar stationery in my mailbox. Maybe if I concentrated, these past few moments could be undone. I would read news about the new baby. And my other grandchildren. Raisa would tell me that Yuri was feeling much better, that the new medicine was healing his skin problem. That he was back to work at the factory.

"By the time you get this letter, Yuri may be gone from this world."

The message was the same. My son's condition had deteriorated. She was preparing me for the worst. I glanced at the postmark, noting that it had taken several weeks to reach me.

I had to know. Without regard for the difference in time zones between Alberta and Russia, I dialed the overseas operator in Montreal. *Please, dear Lord, let the call go through right away.* Indifferent Russian operators and their outdated equipment made telephone communication a challenge from outside the country. I chafed inwardly at each unanswered ring, mentally reviewing Yuri's previous letters as I waited. They described weeks of ineffective hospital treatment interspersed by periods of home rest. The difficulty in obtaining medication. The brave, but unconvincing attempts to reassure me that he really was feeling better.

A connection at last! In my impatience, I hardly greeted my daughter-in-law.

"How is Yuri?" Perhaps if I phrased the question in the present tense, I could avoid the answer that I dreaded most.

Raisa's voice at the other end trembled. "He's gone, Mom."

It was July 15, 1995. My world shattered. Again.

A soul-numbing chill crept through my body as I sat rooted to the chair, my face buried in my hands. *Yuri was dead?* It seemed only yesterday that I had found him again, our joyful reunion briefly erasing years of pain and longing. Now he was gone. Forever. Tears welled from deep inside, released in a flood as sobs tore from my chest until I could scarcely breathe.

It was nearly midnight — too late to call my daughter — but I desperately needed to talk to someone. *Stanley!* He would be in his truck, perhaps even now nearing Calgary. My trembling finger could scarcely press the numbers for his mobile phone.

Hearing my son's cheerful voice over the engine's roar momentarily calmed me. I decided to wait until he arrived at my house in the morning to break the news of his half-brother's death. Pulled over by a highway patrol west of Banff, he had just been ordered to rest a few hours before resuming the two-hour drive to Calgary. I could hear him crunching on cheese and crackers. He refused my offer of a wake-up call in a few hours, insisting that he was fine.

We talked briefly, confirming plans for the next day when he would help his niece and her husband move from Calgary into his house in British Columbia. I heard a new happiness in his voice and hoped that the on-line static would mask the tears in mine.

"God bless you Mom. I love you!" The receiver clicked.

I fell into a troubled sleep, wakened by the doorbell at 7:00 a.m. Hastily pulling on a robe, I rushed to the door. A policeman, not my son, waited there.

"Are you Lydia Oushal?"

"Yes." Why was this officer at my house so early in the morning? I stood back as he stepped inside.

"Is Stanley Oushal your son?"

"Yes." The look on his face brought a sudden weakness to my knees.

"I wish I didn't have to tell you this." He paused, searching for words as his eyes sadly met mine. "Your son is dead."

1

"We have a baby girl and her name is Lydia! She will be our guardian angel."

Papa's pronouncement became the first entry in the diary Mama started for me, a faithful record of all my childhood milestones: first tooth, first steps, first words. She had hoped for a son but Papa was proud and delighted to have a daughter. He named me after a little angel figurine presiding over our house from the mantel, its porcelain base inscribed *Lydia*.

I was born Nov. 2, 1919 in my parents' home in Nikolevka, one of six German colonies in the Russian Republic of Caucasus. Mama, worn out from two days of strenuous labor, hardly left her bed for the next week. Neighbours took over the household chores as well as looking after my nine-year-old brother, Reinhold.

When I was four years old, my brother Victor was born. I considered him my personal property, howling in protest when his godparents bundled him off to church the next Sunday decked in frilly white christening regalia. Whoever heard of boys wearing dresses to church! I forgot my outrage at the celebration feast following the ceremony. For such treats they could dress him in a gunny sack!

Heinrich's birth four years later completed the family roster. Papa sent my brothers and me to visit friends so that Mama's screams would not frighten us. When we eventually returned home, a neighbour lady met us at the door, hushing us with a finger to her lips. We tiptoed into the bedroom to look at the tiny baby boy sleeping in a basket beside Mama. Pale and exhausted, she tried to smile at us from her nest of down pillows. Damp tendrils of hair fanned across her forehead, spilling onto the lacy coverings.

The novelty of a new baby brother paled in comparison to ongoing preparations for Easter festivities. At Grandmother's traditional holiday feast, I announced that the Easter bunny had sent him as an extra delivery, nearly as exciting as the basket of brightly colored eggs and chocolate treats waiting for me. The adults smiled knowingly at one another over my head but no one argued.

Papa, known to others as Augustine Mueller, was born in Berlin and conscripted into the German army as a young man. Captured during World War I, he arrived in Russia as a prisoner, forced to remain there even after the war ended. Many Russian soldiers died on the battlefield, resulting in a serious shortage of farm laborers throughout the country. My father, recruited to help along with other prisoners, was sent to work in a Nikolevka vineyard. He came to Grandmother's house.

Maria Barbara Mueller, or *Marbara* to her friends, was a German widow with eleven sons. Except for Jacob, her second youngest, all of them had either been killed in the war or sent to Siberia, leaving behind wives and families to fend for themselves. Years of hard work netted her a wealth of property, including a winery, and she desperately needed help to maintain her crops. But what did this musician-turned-soldier from the city know about getting his hands dirty? And anyone who wore a white shirt and tie at night after work deserved her suspicious watchfulness. But why complain? Times were hard and no one listened anyway.

Her daughter Christina, also a war widow, was delighted with the charming new arrival. He was polite and treated her with the utmost respect, yet sometimes his eyes met hers in a way that set her heart fluttering and her cheeks aflame. Was it mere coincidence that he often appeared magically at her side to help carry heavy water buckets or armloads of wood? She smiled as she watched her little son toddling adoringly behind him.

"He doesn't know anything except music!" Grandmother's scorn targeted the budding romance. The steely glint in Christina's eye discouraged all interference. She was, after all, a grown woman with a son. She had lived in America for a year with her older sister Mena, proving that she *could* look after herself, even though homesickness brought her back to Russia. Besides, the very shortage of men that brought Augustine to them also meant a limited supply of potential new husbands. Such opportunity, literally landing on their doorstep, must be carefully considered! He even shared the same surname, which, in Christina's mind, confirmed the suitability of the match.

Grandmother frequently reminded her that husband number one, of whom she had also heartily disapproved, was no prize. While it had seemed logical that the son and daughter of the two richest families in the area might one day marry, neither family supported the union, although for vastly different reasons. His relatives thought he should look for someone with more money; hers felt that she was too good for him. But Victor Schlegel and Christina Mueller were in love. Nothing else mattered.

Only after their marriage did she learn of his secret gambling vices, spurred on by an increasing cocaine habit. He tried to hide it from her, always shielded from his debtors by a steady supply of cash from his father. The war mercifully ended what promised to be a lifetime of conflict.

Sadder and wiser, Christina still insisted on the right to choose her next husband, with or without her mother's approval. Against all objections, she and Augustine married. Grandmother, graceful in defeat, eventually succumbed to his charm herself and often described Papa as the nicest man she had ever known.

Before the war, he had been a professional musician and a member of the Berlin Symphony. Music was his life. Now as a prisoner-of-war, even though technically freed, he was barred from performing publicly. Papa believed in finding good in every situation and, denied the concert stage, he decided to teach. I was very proud of him, certain that no one in the whole world could match the melodies that flowed through his hands to the piano, clarinet or saxophone.

His skilled fingers created equal magic with tools, transforming plain wooden boards into little tables and chairs with intricately carved designs for my very own dining room. There I served tea and cookies for hours at a time to anyone who could be persuaded to join me. Aunt Charlotte, Mama's youngest sister, was like an adult playmate, often scrunching herself into a miniature chair for a party with my babies and me. She regularly added to my doll family and I reigned over them with an iron hand.

Much as I loved my dolls, I left them at the first hint of noise or activity outside. Games with other neighbourhood children were always more fun when Papa joined us and I felt very lucky to call him *mine*.

I was usually the only girl in our yard since others my age lived too far away for after-school play. Boys, though less co-operative than my dolls when I tried to take charge, quickly learned that I could hold my own in their rough and tumble games and forgot that I was *just* a girl. My brothers staunchly defended my right to play with them and anyone who objected was told to go home. If *I* didn't like someone, I stormed into the house, refusing to return unless the offender was evicted. Usually the games continued without me.

Mama and Papa tried to explain that sometimes it was good to do what others wanted, that I could not always have everything done my way. I glared at them, arms crossed and eyes narrowed into defiant slits. They sighed and left me alone. Their angel's halo showed early signs of tarnish.

I loved to visit Grandma, sitting for hours in her kitchen with its mouth-watering smells, anxiously awaiting the next bowl or spoon to lick. She told me stories of when she was a little girl and first came to Nikolevka along with thousands of other Germans who had originally been invited by Catherine the Great to develop Russia's agricultural industry. They cleared vast areas of bush for cropland and my eyes grew wide in morbid fascination when she described killing hundreds of boa constrictors that enjoyed feasting on juicy new settlers. In total she owned four hundred hectares of flourishing vineyard and thirty-five hectares of orchards with apples, plums, peaches, pears, and cherries.

Her L-shaped house was joined to the barn by a summer kitchen, used during hot months for cooking without heating up the main living area. The rich furnishings and polished silver tea service, always elegantly displayed, made me feel like a princess in one of Mama's bedtime stories.

She also owned our home, a modern brick house with a summer verandah and tile roof. Persian carpets covered the floors and walls and in the center of the house a big round oven, fuelled by wood and coal, heated all the rooms. In winter we warmed cold hands and feet against the warm outer tiles after hours of skating or sledding. By local standards, we were wealthy.

I often wished for a sister to play with, but being the only girl in the family had its advantages. My brothers often battled for territory in the room they shared while I enjoyed having one for myself.

Papa reserved one room for his music, which we could only enter under his watchful eye lest we leave a cloud of sticky fingerprints on the shiny instruments. This was a refuge, his only remaining link to a life left behind forever. He spent hours polishing the gleaming brass, as though the familiar motions transported him to another place and time. Here he could remember the exhilaration of mastering a difficult overture. Applause thundering from distant balconies. Life before war and capture.

But wherever his solitary wistful memories might take him, we were his present — and future. Both he and Mama knew from personal experience how quickly homes and families could be disrupted by war and far-away decisions beyond individual choice and control. It was important to invest time and energy into their family *now*. The future held no guarantees.

We enjoyed a carefree childhood. Papa played baseball with us in summer and joined us on sleds and skates in winter. Mama preferred more sedate family activities, like picnics in mountain meadows with flower and mushroom-picking expeditions along the winding forest trails near Nikolevka. On weekends we visited the Turkish baths, where men and women went their separate ways for a few hours of relaxation in pine-scented pools.

We all enjoyed stories, as was evident from the many book shelves in our house. Reading aloud was an evening pastime, and it was hard to decide which of the fairy tales and animal stories was my favorite to hear over and over. Before bedtime the big Bible came down from its shelf and either Mama or Papa read to us. My brothers and I crowded close to see the colored pictures and Papa was happy to explain what they meant, even if we didn't always pay attention while he was reading. He never tired of telling us how God made the world and everything in it; how

Jesus died for all sinners and how someday we would go to be with him.

Then we prayed together. Papa taught us the Lord's Prayer and often encouraged us to keep the *Our Father* in our hearts. Sometimes I felt an urgency in his voice which I did not understand. He would put his hand over his chest and I wondered exactly how this prayer found its mystical way inside. Then he sang us to sleep. His strong baritone, softened to lullaby volume, made me feel safe and protected as I drifted off.

My parents, both raised in German Lutheran tradition, believed that our Christian training was their responsibility and that anything we learned in church should supplement what they taught us at home. Church started with a Saturday night ritual when we all brought our shoes to Papa's workbench, lining them up neatly for a weekly beauty treatment. While we slept, he buffed away the week's dust and dirt, no scuff mark spared, all the while praying for each owner and the separate paths each pair of feet would take in the new week ahead. The Muellers always arrived for the Sunday service with shoes glistening. And, as befits children of a soldier, those shoes were not permitted to shuffle, at least when Papa could see.

I loved Sundays with their delicious promise of a special day ahead, my first waking thought about which of my many Sunday dresses to wear to church. Breakfast was more relaxed on Sundays since there was no school for us or work for Papa. Mama was already busy preparing dinner, her dress covered by a white lacy apron, a sign in itself that Sunday was no ordinary day. Half an hour before the service, we joined a procession of friends and neighbours on their way to worship. My parents were the handsomest couple of them all. Papa was tall and strong and Mama always looked so elegant beside him. I was proud that they had a sense of fashion, unlike some other people who wore the same dreary clothes every week.

We always sat in the same pew and if I was careful, I could exchange signal messages with friends sitting nearby until Mama ended our fun. My mind often wandered during the sermon, and I could feel twin warning signals from either side if I fidgeted. When the singing began, I forgot everything else, even the special roast beef dinner in the oven at home. I loved music, easily learning the words to familiar hymns even before I could read. My fondest dream was to join the choir, but in the meantime I always sang loudly, though with more enthusiasm than talent.

I started school when I was eight years old. There were three other Lydias in my classroom and to avoid confusion, my teacher assigned us each a number. I was very proud to be Lydia #1, although she intended no particular importance to that designation. Mama and Papa would have preferred that I was the *last* numbered Lydia. Besides having to deal with my stubborn streak, which had grown by leaps and bounds since I started school, arrogance was an added complication.

"At least she plays with Jewish and Armenian children." My parents tried to be optimistic even though I came home day after day with stories about classmates whom I decided were unworthy of my friendship. They were pleased that ethnic differences were unimportant to me, but despaired at my unshakeable contempt for anyone who was poor, unkempt, or wiped a runny nose on a sleeve. There were no words for those who didn't wipe it at all!

"Lydia," Mama tried to reason with me, "this little girl is just like you. Maybe her mother didn't have time to wash her dress or patch the holes. Maybe she's poor. But she's God's child, the same as you." I shrugged all arguments aside. What did it matter if I chose to avoid certain children? I was not actually *mean* to them.

Mama sighed as she added another entry to the diary: "We have a two-horned bull in our house — Lydia!" At the same time, she had a few uneasy memories of her own youthful mulishness, wondering if she was reaping her own justice through me. Papa seemed especially concerned about my character. By nature sensitive to the pain and weaknesses of others, his years as a prisoner had made him even more compassionate.

"Lydia, you *must* change your attitude. Someday you will be alone and there will be no one to help you. What will you do then?" He cornered me one day after I delivered a scathing description of a little girl who dared come to school with holes in her stockings. Why was he always so serious? *Someday* was a far-off event and would take care of itself. Grown-ups, including Papa, always made such a fuss about things. As usual, I succeeded in changing the subject, teasing him into playing a game with Victor and me.

At school, I ruled the playground. If someone I didn't like was chosen as captain of a team, I refused to join the game. Despite my bossy treatment of other children, they treated me as their leader; my way was the right and only way. Highly competitive, I usually won any contest, firmly establishing my authority.

I had one very visible source of pain, exploited fully by other children when they realized how much the teasing bothered me. My hair was white, shades paler than blonde, hanging down my back in two braids. When one of the boys loudly compared it to a wild grass whose limp, silky strands waved and trembled even when the air was still, I was insulted beyond words, storming home in a tearful rage. I wanted black hair. Brown hair. Red hair. Anything but *white* hair. Mama was unsympathetic. It was time that I, who showed no remorse at my treatment of others, should finally know what it was like to be a target. "Besides," she said, hoping to teach me that there was more than one way of interpreting things, "perhaps they wish that their hair was a special color too."

As I thought about it, the idea that they were secretly envious gave me endless satisfaction. Sensing the smug change in my outlook, Mama shook her head, regretting that she had unwittingly fed my already overblown ego.

Learning to read was my most exciting accomplishment at school. Now instead of waiting until Mama and Papa had time, I could explore a whole new world of books on my own. Our comfortably carpeted outhouse was a favorite retreat from the constant interruption of little brothers, at least until someone else had urgent need of it. My doll family and its trappings gathered dust in a lonely corner of my bedroom.

2

Malaria! At age nine, I felt the terror of that word as it swept through our village, only a breath ahead of the dreaded chills and fever that wiped out entire communities. Rumored to have spread to our area via a Turkish seaport, the epidemic claimed hundreds of victims, often within twenty-four hours of the first sign of infection.

Few households escaped without at least one death. Woodworkers scarcely kept pace with the demand for coffins, many of them wrenchingly small. Grave diggers moved from one hole to the next as family after family arrived in a tragic procession to bury a loved one. Some made the sad journey two and even three times.

Although we all contracted the disease, our household was more fortunate than most. Without neglecting her own family, Mama worked tirelessly to help others in our community, cooking huge pots of soup for families too sick to look after themselves. She sat at countless bedsides, cooling brows burning with fever or comforting the bereaved.

My brothers recovered within days but despite taking massive doses of the same vile medicine, I battled the symptoms for three years. At first there were several cycles a day, first the bone-numbing chill that set my teeth chattering, followed by a few hours of fever and sweat. Eventually, it lessened to once a day, and then once a week. According to our doctor, the disease simply had to run its course, but he insisted that Mama give me only goats' milk to drink and that she remove all fruit from my diet. I dutifully choked down the medicine, which turned spoons green, followed by a generous helping of honey. Mama quietly substituted the cows' milk without telling me and I would not have known the difference but for Victor's bleating noises every time I took a drink. He appointed himself guardian of my diet, faithfully reporting any secret indulging in banned treats.

I missed fruit most of all. Except for bananas, every imaginable fruit flourished in our mild climate, much of it ripe for picking. How could I live in an area so abundantly blessed, yet be denied permission to enjoy it? I pouted in the shade of our plum tree, its branches bending under their juicy burden. It was so unfair! Who cared anyway? No matter how much medicine or goats' milk I endured, my condition stayed the same. What could it hurt? Five plums later I knew, as I brought them all back up again. Mama was very annoyed with me, more for my disobedience than for any actual harm done.

The temptation of forbidden fruit proved more powerful than Mama's wrath and a week later I did it again. This time it took ten plums to convict me. In the semi-digested evidence, Mama noticed a hard object with little hairs growing out of it like a mold. According to the doctor, this was the true culprit keeping me sick He gave me a chalky white concoction to drink which I gagged down under Mama's watchful eye. When they pumped my stomach I almost regretted discovering what was making me ill, but this was the only way to rid my beleaguered insides of residual poisons. Mama and Papa hardly knew whether to be stern about my disobedience or just relieved that I was finally on the road to recovery.

The malaria was gone but I still felt weak and lethargic. One day while playing outside I began to feel lightheaded with a strange heaviness in my arms and legs. Mama looked at my face and immediately sent me to lie down in my room.

I closed my eyes. Moments later, when I tried to open them again, I couldn't. In fact, no part of me seemed able to move. I tried to push my feet against the wooden footboard. Nothing happened. I wanted to call Mama, but my voice was gone.

I heard my brothers in the kitchen, demanding that I come back outside to continue the game but Mama sent them away, explaining that I was ill. Someone entered my room. Papa. I felt him standing by my bed even before he took first one of my hands and then the other in his own.

"Victor, go for the doctor — quickly! And send the other children away!" Spurred on by the urgency in Papa's voice, Victor for once obeyed promptly. I could hear his feet pounding down the street by the time the screen door slammed shut behind him. Papa stayed by my side, gently stroking my hand with his big strong fingers until the doctor arrived. I tried over and over to answer the questions he directed to Mama and Papa. Nothing happened. My feet strained toward the end of the bed but without contact. He checked me repeatedly for pulse and heartbeat, turning me over and back again.

"I'm sorry Augustine, she's gone." My parents stood helplessly to one side and I could hear Mama sobbing into Papa's shoulder. What had happened to me? How could they have failed to notice that something was wrong? How could it happen so quickly?

I was unable to move but what I heard struck terror into my heart. They thought I was dead! And dead people were buried!

"Don't bury me! I'm not dead!" My brain screamed the words but my lips refused all commands to speak them. Papa sat by my side, again holding my hand, and began to sing songs that I associated with death and funerals. *I'm not dead!* How was I going to keep them from burying me alive! My frightened brothers hovered near the door, waiting for an explanation that no one could give.

The strangest thing began to happen. I could suddenly see, *but my eyes remained shut.* Everything was different. Instead of furniture, I was surrounded by graves. The walls vanished like a vapor, and as far as I could see, rows and rows of gravestones marched into the distance. I had a visitor. *Standing over the graves, yet not touching them, was Jesus.* He looked down at me and held out his open hands. Was it an invitation? Then I saw angels wearing snowy white robes surrounding him, exactly as I'd sometimes imagined them. And the music! Or was it music? An exquisite sound filled the room, sometimes blending with Papa's song, sometimes its own heavenly harmony unlike anything I had ever heard.

I was taught that when someone died, Jesus took them to heaven, and here he was! Did this mean that I was going to leave Mama and Papa and my brothers? My home? I felt safe with Jesus here, as though everything would be all right. But then he faded away, and with him, the angels and their music. There was just Papa by my bed, still singing quietly as he held my hand with Mama crying beside him. I realized that they hadn't seen Jesus and the angels. They thought I was dead. *And dead people were buried!* I had to make them aware that I was very much alive!

This time when I tried to wiggle my toes, I felt movement under the blankets! No one else had seen it so I tried squeezing Papa's hand. His dirge ceased immediately. "She's alive! I felt her move!" Footsteps rushed to the door. They would not be burying me yet!

Finally I could open my eyes. A ring of teary faces surrounded my bed, all registering shock and disbelief. The doctor returned, looking as though he'd seen a ghost. He recovered enough to complete another examination.

"I don't understand it, Augustine. There was *no* pulse or heartbeat before." He shook his head, eyeing his stethoscope as though it had played a cruel trick on him.

What did it mean? Why had this happened to me? I stayed in bed for a few days, my head buzzing with questions that I was too timid to share with anyone. What would they think? Even while all this was going on, I had noticed something completely unexpected. *Mama and Papa had cried when they thought I was dead!* But tears were always discouraged, a sure sign of weakness. Sadness was kept inside so that everyone would know how strong we were. I thought that adults weren't even *able* to cry.

Finally I told Mama and Papa what I had seen in my room, describing the graves which replaced all my furniture. How Jesus stood over them, holding out his hands to me. The angels and the wonderful music. They listened carefully, without interrupting or chiding me for imagining things. When our pastor came to call, Papa asked me to tell him what I had seen and heard. His eyes never left my face as I told my story yet again, but unfortunately he had no wisdom to share with us.

"Maybe Jesus didn't take you because he knew we would miss you too much." Mama's explanation would have to suffice. Some things were too mysterious for even grown-ups, including pastors, to understand.

3

"I hope there's a war."

Mama and Papa looked at me, then at each other. Had they been too casual in discussing local rumors in front of their children? Even if the most dire predictions suggested that it could not happen before 1940, they felt that at age ten, I should understand the basic tragedy of war — that people died and families were destroyed, along with their homes. I squirmed away when Papa described battlefield horrors, preferring to dwell on thoughts of adventure and excitement. In fantasy, my role changed regularly but I was always a heroine, well-rewarded for her bravery. Mama just sighed when I talked like this and made another entry in my diary. How could she know that my brave talk was really a shield against niggling fears that hid in the bedtime darkness? Then I thought of Papa's strong, broad shoulders, and knew that nothing could hurt me as long as he was there.

Everyone in Nikolevka seemed to feel that way about Papa. He was always willing to help, whether it meant repairing a broken chair or giving advice about business or family issues. Even as an outsider, he was a natural candidate for public office, first elected mayor and then police chief for eight years. As a leader in the community, he felt responsible to keep abreast of national and international news, subscribing to several outside newspapers for a broader perspective than was available locally.

After each new batch of papers arrived, Papa became increasingly pre-occupied, his brow furrowed in concentration. At first I tried to distract him, hoping that playing a game would restore his good spirits. I soon learned that he needed this time alone and it was futile to beg. Eventually he joined our fun with more energy than ever, as though determined to enjoy each available moment with his family.

What he read deeply disturbed him. A new central government in Moscow under General Secretary Joseph Stalin headed an uneasy assortment of opposing factions, each competing for control in various parts of the country. Communism poised on the political horizon, waiting to unite all authority under what showed early signs of becoming a dictatorship.

Papa tried to place as much distance between himself and the new regime as possible, dreading a confrontation. Despite his best efforts to avoid notice, the KGB, Russia's dreaded secret police, decided that he must be a valuable source of information about allegedly subversive activities in the community. Once a month they summoned him to their headquarters for questioning about his friends and neighbours.

When Papa suddenly announced that we must move out of our spacious home into a smaller one, I accepted it without too many questions. Mama, however, was unusually quiet. Sometimes I saw her wipe her eyes when she thought no one was watching. Perhaps she was thinking about leaving her garden, the envy of our entire village. Every flower imaginable bloomed in our yard. Each windowsill sheltered a plant and she lovingly tended each one as though they were her special children.

Little by little, Russian newcomers from Moscow invaded all German communities, taking over the nicest houses with the authorities' blessing. It was not enough that they displaced families, but they took over jobs as well. People clustered on street corners, always speaking in guarded tones and hushing immediately if one of the newly imported foreigners passed by.

Moscow seemed intent on completely disrupting our lives. Nikolevka was a farming village, with all crops grown outside the residential areas. Almost overnight, farms became government communes. Farmers, now stripped of individual ownership, were assigned a specific area of responsibility, whether growing crops, raising livestock, or tending an orchard. They reported for work at a certain time and reported again when the day was over. Meals were eaten in communal trailers pulled onto the fields to minimize time spent away from the business of farming. In January, each worker's hours were tallied and payment made, both in money and produce.

Rumors abounded with frightening stories about crop seed poisoned to discourage farm workers from stealing it for their own use. Even more alarming were widespread reports of famine in which millions of people starved to death. How could this happen in a fertile country such as Russia, with fields of wheat ripening and ready for harvest? At night after Mama and Papa thought we were asleep, I overheard them discussing the situation in the next room, their voices low. I eavesdropped shamelessly, my need to know what was going on greater than my fear of discovery. Without understanding the politics behind the action, I learned that Russian grain was being sold to other countries, creating an artificial famine in the land that had produced it. Productivity declined, along with farmers' initiative. Denied ownership of the harvest, they lacked both motivation and tools to struggle with old equipment badly in need of repair.

People began to disappear. Tearful children arrived at school, whispering stories of midnight knocks at the door and fathers whisked away in a "black raven" or *chernovoran,* a long black car used by the KGB. *Would the raven ever visit our house?* Surely not! Papa's position in the community would protect us.

"Augustine! *Augustine!*"

Grandmother's shouts brought all of us rushing to the door. Hysterical and breathless, she raced toward our house as fast as her chubby legs could carry her. I watched in amazement as she puffed and panted through the gate, her dress buttons askew and hair flying behind in a tousled mane. This was the first time I had ever seen her without a thick crown of braids, each hair securely anchored. I felt a twinge of guilt for even noticing that Grandma's usual basket of treats was missing from her arm.

"Augustine, they're tearing down my house!"

Mama and Papa brought her into the house and pushed her gently onto a chair, trying to calm her sobs. I saw the glances they exchanged over her head, understanding their meaning without explanation; we too were vulnerable.

Between gasps, the story emerged. She had wakened that morning to the sound of sledgehammers slamming against wood. Government thugs had arrived at daybreak to carry out their cowardly orders, ignoring her frantic screams of protest. Hardly taking time to dress, she raced to find Papa. Surely he could make them stop.

School preparations forgotten, we all rushed to her house with Papa far ahead, hoping against hope that reason might stop this senseless brutality. It didn't. Even at a distance, we could hear the echoes of hammers on their destructive mission. Rage burned in my chest like a hot iron. Why did this have to happen? But by now I had overheard enough conversations to know the answer. Grandmother was a *kulak*, an outsider who had prospered through hard work and sound business practices. *Kulaks* were scorned by the new regime. Wealth, along with education and an ability to influence others, was reason enough to be targeted for "special treatment."

We stood helplessly by, tears pouring down our faces as we joined the silent crowd of neighbours watching in disbelief as, blow by blow, the gaping holes in the walls grew ever larger. Energized by their hostile audience, the hoodlums pillaged every room, brazenly carrying off all easily portable valuables. When they finished, Grandma was left with a single room, confronted each time she opened the door with the ruins of what used to be her home.

The authorities responsible for the growing tension in our village became a nameless, faceless *They* in my mind. *They* systematically destroyed Grandma's house and life. *They* stole anything of beauty or value. *They* broke up families, sending husbands, brothers and fathers to unknown destinations without assurance of any future contact. How I hated *Them*.

My heart broke when I visited her again, surrounded by the shattered remains of my favorite childhood retreat. Her hardy spirit, which had conquered snakes and transformed bush into farmland, was subdued and listless, lacking the determination to rebuild. I realized now that Papa's position as chief of police meant nothing to the shadowy figures that ruled over us. He understood this better than anyone. If he was powerless to prevent such senseless devastation, he felt unable to continue in a public office and begged his fellow citizens to elect someone else to replace him.

Regretfully, yet understanding Papa's reasons, the villagers voted for another chief. Once out of office, he turned his wood carving hobby into a vocation, creating decorative sculptures in a furniture factory in Pyatigorsk, a city seven kilometres away.

He also discovered that while he was *officially* forbidden to perform publicly, this rule lacked enforcement. Talented musicians were in high demand and whenever he was invited, he played his clarinet in operas, parades and dances, always waiting for the reprimand that never came. The authorities, reluctant to interfere with proud Russian cultural tradition, looked the other way.

"Children, if you can show us your God, we will believe in him, but if you cannot show him to us, then it is all fantasy."

New teachers at school gradually introduced troubling ideas into our thoughts and beliefs. How could we prove to someone who challenged us that God existed? Mama and Papa didn't try to argue with the new logic, impressing on us over and over again the same teaching from the Bible that we had heard since we were small children.

Their urgency was tempered with caution. We should not repeat at school *anything* that was said in the privacy of our home. Anonymous government informers now watched and listened for signs of rebellion against the new order. Even the most innocent remarks could have devastating effects on families, usually involving a visit from the "raven." When I heard *Siberia* mentioned in hushed adult conversations, the name sent little thrills of fear up my spine and I asked Papa to show me where it was on the map. He explained that it was very cold in Siberia and that people who were sent there often died. From then on, any word that yet another acquaintance had been taken felt like a death to me. For a while people tried to be brave, but clearly no one ever expected to see their loved ones again.

Anyone allowed to stay in Nikolevka knew that with very little notice they could be forced to give up their home. The new authorities must have the choicest accommodations available. Eventually my godmother and her three children who lived next door to us were sent away, her belongings confiscated and her beautiful house given to a Russian family.

29

To my brothers and me, the bulldog now guarding the apple tree in her backyard was symbolic of everything ugly which was happening to our community. We grew to hate its wrinkled face staring back at us and plotted revenge against our new neighbours. Our chance came one afternoon when they were away from home. With a little help from his friends, Victor lured the dog away from its post long enough for the other boys to shake every apple from the branches. We quickly gathered them up and threw them into a grassy lot nearby where they rotted in the sun. No intruder should benefit from the labor of the one who had pruned and tended the fruit into juicy ripeness.

When the people returned and discovered their empty tree, our house was their first stop of inquiry. Papa, without asking us, assured them that we would not do such a thing. We later confessed, expecting the customary punishment of kneeling in front of a window, perhaps on a layer of dried peas if we had been especially naughty, and forced to watch other children playing outside in the yard. Papa's lecture to us was stern, but without sentence. He explained that while my godmother was given no choice about leaving, these new people had not chosen to come here either. Even though they seemed to benefit from her misfortune, it was not our place to punish them. Recognizing that we needed an outlet for venting our growing anger at a system that we were powerless to change, he ended the matter there.

Mail from Siberia was rare, so we were amazed to receive a letter from our friend. It contained few details, only that she and her children were surviving. Remembering Mama's love for flowers, she sent sixteen bean seeds which apparently yielded beautiful blossoms, to be planted next spring. Mama kept them in a box on her dresser all winter like precious gems, awaiting their garden debut. It was not to be.

Growing shortages of grain affected both people and livestock. Then the authorities added a new burden: Papa must pay a new tax in the form of product, whether a live heifer, grain or whatever else might be dictated. Soon there was nothing left to buy, and we fell behind in payment. For the time being, we had dried meat and vegetables stored in the attic, but Mama used it sparingly, and I could tell that she and Papa were worried about what might follow when it was all gone.

One day in December, 1931, my brothers and I returned from school to find our home completely transformed. An ornament replaced the big Bible on its shelf. There were fewer books in the bookcase, and those remaining were strictly secular titles. The walls were bare of religious pictures, replaced with the prescribed portrait of Lenin and the ubiquitous hammer and sickle, which hung as required in the corner where we did our homework. I hated them both. The jewellery box with Mama's rings and brooches and Papa's fancy cufflinks disappeared. They were vague in answering our questions about where all these things had gone, assuring us that we must not worry about it.

A week later four policemen appeared at the door, sent in search of valuables that "rightfully" belonged to the authorities which we might be keeping for ourselves. No corner of our house went unmolested. One man searched my parents' bedroom for anything of interest, even squashing Mama's lacy pillows that were too fancy to sleep on, in hopes of discovering treasure hidden among the feathers. Rage burned inside me as I watched his beefy fingers mauling the delicately crocheted lace.

"Please don't take the beans! They come from Siberia!" I thought I might burst, unable to watch in silence as he pawed through the dresser drawers, finally latching onto the little box on top. They surely meant nothing to this man, but everything to Mama. I wanted to spare her the sadness of losing them and reached to take it away from him. He pushed me away and jammed it into his pocket, apparently enjoying his sense of power against my feeble attempts to rescue a few little seeds. I was crushed. The beans had been a tenuous link to the unknown world now inhabited by many that I knew and loved. With Mama, I looked forward to planting them and in a small way, reuniting with my godmother once again. To my twelve-year-old understanding, it seemed the only evidence that survival was indeed possible in what I pictured as a frozen wasteland. And he was taking it.

Outside, they were busy with shovels, digging random holes in the yard to see if we might have tried to outsmart them by burying valuables in the still unfrozen dirt, while another official inspected our attic for hidden booty.

"Don't stand there — you'll fall through the ceiling!" My father's urgent warning steered the man away from a straw pile sheltering our hidden winter hoard of dried fruit, corn, and smoked ham. I knew that Mama and Papa were both praying silently and I added my prayers to theirs. If God could make blind men to see, there should be no problem making seeing men to go momentarily blind!

Finally they left us alone, taking with them everything they considered to be valuable. Mama and Papa remained calm throughout the raid, later holding us tightly as we clung to them. They assured us that we could easily live without the things that were taken. Our confidence was in God, not in things, and our bedtime prayers included an extra measure of thanksgiving that we were still together as a family and that our food supply was untouched.

Christmas celebrations in 1931 were different than usual. *They* forbade us to put up Christmas trees or any festive decorations. *They* banned all concerts and carolling, gift exchanges and nativity pageants. Christmas was just like any other day. But even without all its trappings and tradition, we still found ways to celebrate. The Bible mysteriously emerged from its hiding place and Papa read the story of Jesus' birth to us from each of the three gospels. We sang the traditional carols, although more quietly than other years, ever mindful that someone might be watching and listening for an opportunity to accuse us before *Them*.

A new atmosphere of distrust in our community created wariness even between friends and neighbours. Fear of being sent away caused some to compromise their own beliefs by betraying others, hoping to protect themselves by currying favor with those in power.

Despite Mama's stringent rationing, our food supply dwindled. Even now, our stomachs rumbled loudly at the end of every meal. Beets, left in the ground in a neighbour's garden, became our steady diet, and we grew to dread the familiar odor at every mealtime. Victor and I salvaged some frozen potatoes, also left in the ground from the fall harvest. After ridding them of wintering worms, we found them to be edible, if not particularly tasty. To add variety, we picked a sour, spinach-like leaf which Mama cooked in cream from a neighbour's cow.

The remainder of our diet was unpredictable from day to day. Papa brought home bread from the factory and occasionally Grandmother gave us a chicken or rabbit. Those meals were a sweet torture. We could never eat our fill, always needing to save something for the next day. Sometimes black market meat and vegetables were available at exorbitant prices, but information about when and where to go often arrived too late to be useful. We always went to bed hungry, our dreams filled with favorite foods, always tantalizingly out of reach.

While the hated beets staved off starvation, they gave little energy for play. Heinrich, aged three, refused more than a nibble of what was offered to him, lying in his bed whimpering. From the worried looks passed between Mama and Papa, I suddenly realized that they were actually afraid that he would die. I begged him to eat — and God to keep him alive.

Heinrich lived, but many of our friends and neighbours were less fortunate. The famine lasted until the next summer's crop of vegetables was ready to harvest, with a tragic toll of hundreds of lives in our area alone. Gradually the food supply returned to normal, the authorities apparently having accomplished their intended purposes.

By government order, our church was closed just before the next Easter, stripped of its altar, organ and even the chandelier. Instead of services, it would now be used for miscellaneous meetings or theatre productions, the first of which was my school play in which I played the part of a rich man. I balked at participating. *What might God do to me for performing a secular drama in a holy place?* My friend's mother, who did not share my parents' caution, loudly denounced all those responsible for the demise of our church as devils, who would roll us in cotton batting and set us on fire.

"You have the main role, Lydia. If you don't go, they will blame us." My parents knew that anything even appearing to lack co-operation from home could have repercussions. Their absence might go unnoticed; mine would not. Momentarily fearing Siberia more than God, I reluctantly headed back to the building which I still thought of as church, little brothers in tow.

Somehow I survived the evening with no major lapses in memory despite unusually shaky knees. There was a big audience and ordinarily I would have waited to bask in the congratulations of friends. Tonight, however, I escaped immediately, running the one-kilometre distance to our house where I was sure Papa could protect me from the host of imaginary devils nipping at my heels in hot pursuit. These fears paled beside Papa's ire when he learned that my little brothers were still at the church, waiting for their big sister to brave the dark walk home with them.

4

Whatever changes the authorities made to our way of life, at least they were unable to alter the landscape. Each season was my favorite, and I spent as much time as possible outdoors with my brothers and other neighbourhood boys. We built dams across the river to create a swimming hole or formed tree tunnels by tying their tops together from either bank. Our creativity was seldom appreciated by local forest rangers.

I regularly returned home with skinned knees and shins from an afternoon of tree climbing and Mama despaired at my lack of proper feminine behavior. Surely by now some natural sense of modesty should inhibit me from swinging from the branches in a dress. I shrugged away her suggestions that this was perhaps inappropriate activity at my age. I had played with these boys all my life and they treated me just as though I was one of them. Nonetheless, Mama's voice lowered as she admonished me that I must "never, *never* let a boy touch me." I thought this a strange warning, given the vigorous play we had always enjoyed with no previous objection to tagging one another as *it* or wrestling for control of a ball. No further explanation was offered, and I dismissed it as just another incomprehensible adult quirk.

I intended no harm the day I led thirteen children up a nearby mountain, including Heinrich and Victor, aged three and seven. The day was bright and the trail beckoned, each twist and turn promising more flowers, new sights. I was always happiest in the mountains. Victor would have teased me if he'd known, but I always felt as though the forests talked to me. I could wander for hours along shady pathways by myself, with no hint of loneliness.

Every time I went for a walk I thought of the legendary hunter's dog that had chased a rabbit along these same trails, suddenly falling into a concealed hole which was really a bubbling hot spring. The unfortunate dog cooked, but its sacrifice resulted in the discovery of mineral springs and subsequent development of health spas in our area which attracted hordes of tourists, all eager to try the famous black mud beauty treatments. My "just a little furthers" took us up, up, and far away from home, the trail now a narrow path running parallel to a bottomless chasm. I felt dizzy just thinking about the abyss yawning at my feet.

"Don't look down!" My orders to everyone else seemed to invite that very action and I shuddered to think that someone's foot might slip on the unstable rocks under our feet, sending them hurtling over the edge. I realized that we had gone too far, but to continue forward felt safer than to reverse direction now. Suddenly we were at the top of the mountain — and the world! The view was spectacular, although by this time our interest in sightseeing was secondary to our hunger. An unexpected feast lay at our feet. Everywhere we looked, raspberry bushes, heavy with ripe juicy fruit, grew as though anticipating our healthy appetites.

By the time we had eaten our fill, the sun was low in the sky and I knew it was too late to begin the long trek home. Just thinking about negotiating that narrow track in the dark made me shudder. I had left home with thirteen children and preferred to return with the same number.

"We're staying here for night," I announced to my little troupe. No one minded or even gave a moment's thought to anxious families far below. Under my supervision, everybody picked armloads of long grass for makeshift beds, sheltered by rocky outcroppings. Even after the sun's rays no longer reached our little hideaway, the air and ground remained warm, a blessing for foolish children caught involuntarily in an overnight adventure. My greatest concern was about the dozens of eagles that appeared at dusk. I remembered hearing of their attacks on people and prayed that they would ignore our presence in their alpine parlor. Fortunately I forgot until later any stories of skulking wolf packs which also roamed the mountains.

We slept soundly, waking to an ocean of white fluffy clouds far below which curtained the valley from view. After a breakfast of more raspberries we basked in the sun's renewed warmth, its rays eventually burning the clouds into mere wisps of their former grandeur. It was time to go and we began our descent, stopping to chat with cow herders in a grassy meadow.

The village was in an uproar. Search parties on horseback, including the police, were scouring the bushes in the general direction where we had been seen the day before.

"Lydia should be spanked!" The mother of one of my followers glared at me as she hustled her boy away, muttering dire threats of punishment interspersed with hugs of relief that he was safely home. Papa and Mama, agreeing long ago that spanking would have no place in disciplining their children, took a calmer approach. Grateful that their prayers for our safety had been answered, they were, nonetheless, very annoyed with me for causing such worry. In addition to a stern lecture about responsibility, they sentenced me to fifteen minutes every day on my knees in front of the window. By the end of the week, I was certain that my knees would forever bear pea-shaped dimples. Mama made a new entry in my diary.

We always looked forward to the short-lived snowy part of winter. Our area, located between the Black and Caspian seas, enjoyed a moderate climate which limited significant snowfall to approximately a month. During that time, we spent every available minute outdoors, skating on the river, or better yet, sledding down the mountains. There was nothing, *nothing* that compared with the exhilaration of flying down a slope on our homemade sled as we shrieked with delight. The momentum carried us up the next slope where we'd turn around and do it all again. Sledding by moonlight was our ultimate adventure. Occasionally Mama and Papa extended our bedtime, knowing my *just-one-more-time* habit would likely push past any limits. When I returned at midnight with a little brother whose ears showed signs of frostbite, I received yet another lecture about being responsible for my younger siblings.

"But Papa, it was so bright out there — just like daylight! How could I possibly know it was so late?" He just gave me *that* look, which translated into "is she ever going to learn?"

I was shielded from much of what might be termed responsibility. Other girls my age all had chores to do around the house, and sometimes, when I heard them complaining, I felt a trace of envy. I often volunteered to polish Mama's vast collection of ornaments but she always sent me away to read or play. There would be time enough for work when I was grown up.

The kitchen was Mama's undisputed domain. She loved to create culinary masterpieces, but if I wanted to help she shooed me away. There would be plenty of time later for me to learn anything I needed to know. I contented myself with watching her shape fancy breads and pastries, especially when she baked *bapka,* the traditional Ukrainian Easter bread, and decorated it with icing roses.

Needing something to do, Victor and I decided to go into business. Commuters at the railway station on their way home from work were happy to trade ten kopecks for bouquets of wild flowers and ferns which grew in abundance nearby. Our parents disapproved of our entrepreneurism. Mama feared that we would fall under speeding trains. Papa thought people might think we were beggars. Hesitant to spoil our fun, they looked the other way, even when we added ripe, juicy apples to our wares. The details inevitably found their way into my diary.

To my dismay, crocheting did not fall into Mama's definition of *work*. After my thirteenth birthday, she and Aunt Charlotte decreed that it was time to pull me out of the treetops for a few lessons in needle skills. Some of my classmates already boasted numerous accomplishments, but while I was loath to be outdone, I could hardly sit still long enough to learn. The decision was made for me.

Under close supervision, I made delicate lace edgings on pillow shams and undergarments. I endured hours of embroidery, each project added to my hope chest, a collection of fancy accessories for my future home and husband which Mama had faithfully been stockpiling for years. I even made valiant attempts to knit, although no amount of coaching could ease my iron grip on the yarn, and the tight rows were nearly impenetrable. I thought longingly of my brothers enjoying outdoor freedom and tried to hurry so that I could join them. Thus I learned how to pick up dropped stitches.

Sewing was the last and most complicated item on Mama's agenda. I learned to create patterns from measurements and to transfer these onto actual fabric. Even so, I felt no confidence when poised over my first project, a housecoat, with scissors in hand. I truly despaired when I faced Mama's prized Singer treadle machine. It looked so easy when she demonstrated, her feet and hands in complete control as she deftly turned the fabric this way and that in the needle's path. Mine, on the other hand, suddenly became as total strangers. When my hands were ready, my feet forgot to empower the needle. When they finally obeyed my will to pump the treadle, fabric and needle took on divergent lives of their own. I spent hours ripping out crooked seams and restitching them until my efforts met with Mama's approval. To everyone's amazement, especially mine, eventually a wearable garment emerged, albeit showing premature signs of wear and tear.

Nothing prepared me for Aunt Charlotte's death.

The new farming communes brought with them heavy labor demands. For farmers, participation on the commune was compulsory, each worker assigned to a specific task. Aunt Charlotte, while of average strength, was ill-suited to lifting heavy forks of hay. After only several days of this unaccustomed strain on her body, she collapsed from massive internal injuries. Hospital treatment was unavailable, and I could tell from the helplessness on Mama's face that there was little hope she would recover. She died within two days, but not before entrusting me with a dreadful secret.

"When they burn the straw, have your mama and grandma check the ashes. You will see my children's footprints there and they will soon die too."

I was frightened. Had her mind been affected by the excruciating pain in her body? She continued, her voice weak but determined. "You must promise not to say anything about this until the straw is burned. *Promise me.*" I nodded, wishing desperately that I could share this dire premonition with someone who would assure me that it wasn't possible to know such things.

As was customary after a death, Aunt Charlotte's body was laid on a bed of straw covered with a white sheet, remaining on display in her home for three days prior to burial. She was never left alone during this time, always accompanied by a contingent of mourners singing and praying. Every time I saw her lying there so cold and still, pain tore through me until I thought I would surely die myself. I hurt for Mama too. She was the only one left here from her family, her only other sister living in America. Aunt Charlotte had been a good friend as well as a sister, and I knew Mama already missed her deeply.

Finally she was laid in a coffin on a new bed of straw covered with lacy pillows and a white cloth. Male relatives carried her to the cemetery on their shoulders and we followed in a sad little procession. The priest pronounced a final blessing, and the lid of the coffin was nailed shut. We stood by, weeping quietly as it was lowered into the grave, remaining there until the last shovel of dirt covered the hole.

It was time to burn the straw, and I could finally unburden myself of her last request. *What if no one believed me?* Mama and Grandma both listened to my story, and, while not discounting what she had said to me, suggested that perhaps she had been dreaming. Pain could, after all, affect people in unexpected ways. Nonetheless, when the ashes from the burned straw had settled, to our dismay, three distinct little footprints remained. *What could it mean?*

Three children to raise, together with the demands of the commune, made remarriage for my uncle an immediate and practical necessity. Within months of Aunt Charlotte's death, he had a new wife and nine-year-old step-daughter.

The children seemed to have difficulty adjusting to the new family. They appeared thinner every time we saw them, growing more and more listless. At first we tried to believe that it was due to the many changes in their young lives, first losing their mother and now adapting to a new family. But there were growing doubts.

"Are your children being fed?" Mama confronted their father one day when she could stand it no longer. He shrugged. As far as he knew, nothing was amiss, although work kept him away from home much of the time. Constant weariness clouded his ability to notice the subtle changes in them from one day to the next.

When she learned from the children that they were all forced to share their meager portions of food with their new step-sister, Mama was livid. "If you don't do something about this, I will take them away from you!" she threatened her brother-in-law. They both knew she had little chance of following through, however, and nothing changed. Within a year, all three children, two boys and a girl, died of starvation.

Aunt Charlotte's words repeated over and over in my mind. *How had she known that her children would follow her so soon? Had she come to get them?* There were no easy answers, and Mama and Papa reminded me of what I had always been taught about Jesus taking his children home when it was time. Perhaps he had rescued them from a sad life. It had been a long time since I'd thought about Jesus' visit to my own sickroom and how I had wondered if he would take me with him. None of that fit with what I had been learning at school. Such beliefs were old-fashioned fantasies. Until now, I had floated easily between my parents' faith and the modern views held by my teachers. As long as I did not rock either boat, life was good.

But death had not only rocked, but *capsized* my boat, forcing me to realize the lack of strong convictions on either side to call my own. I knew that I could not forever rely on Mama's and Papa's beliefs to shape my life. But I was a strong person. Surely I had everything right inside myself to cope with anything life might throw at me. Didn't I? *Could anyone ever really know?*

5

Communism now enjoyed a solid foothold in our schools and community. Any quiet discussions about the new regime moved from street corners to behind closed doors. Long-time neighbors now looked at each other with suspicion, wondering who might betray them to the authorities. We were careful to heed Papa's warning about repeating at school anything that was said at home. No one knew when an innocent remark, even if made in jest, might be reported or misinterpreted. While there were fewer reports of people vanishing, our former security was gone forever.

Despite all the adult gloom and doom, I secretly thought communism was fun. At school all our crayons, pencils and notebooks were provided free of charge. Enrollment in Young Pioneers, a club for young communists, was on a voluntary basis at first but soon became compulsory. We received a red scarf when we joined and after reciting the Pioneer Pledge, our leaders gave us a three-flame pin in honor of brave communists who died at the hands of the czar.

Every month we met for games and stories about communist heroes. My volunteer assignment was to teach old people the Russian alphabet so that they could sign their names. Many had spent most of their lives in the country, but beyond *ruble* or *kilo* refused to learn even basic Russian. My grandmother could read and write this "gypsy language" but woe to anyone who ordered her to speak it!

After the first day of my new responsibilities I returned home in tears. The man I tried to help had called me "snotty one" and refused to cooperate. Papa hugged me but insisted that I continue. He tried to help me understand how difficult it must be for someone old enough to be my grandfather to be taught by a little girl.

Summer camp was a new adventure. From six o'clock in the morning when we got up for exercises and flag-raising until the evening bonfires, our days were packed with activity: hiking, biking, dancing and singing. For the first time in my life, I was away from the family ritual of Bible reading and prayers. None of that was even mentioned at camp, except to poke fun at religion in general. Occasionally I would remember the *Our Father* as I crawled between the clean white sheets, but fell asleep before the *amen*. Soon I forgot it altogether.

Komsomol was the next stage in our training as young communists. This was an exclusive group, with some meetings closed to members who failed to meet all the criteria necessary to join. My grandmother's wealth, which the communists were happy to plunder, was nonetheless a black mark on my heritage and disqualified me from full membership. I decided that if I was only partially satisfactory to them, they were *completely* unsatisfactory to me and I refused to participate.

Membership in the Communist Party required an application supported by twelve other signatures verifying that a candidate had no incriminating family history of wealth, religion or subversive political views. Even if I had wanted to join, two out of these three conditions made me ineligible. I was content to enjoy much of what the system offered without associating too closely with it.

Communism even dictated the length of our hair: short. Mine was long. After years of letting it grow, I rebelled at the idea of *Them* telling me to cut it. By now it had lost the hated whiteness, darkening to an acceptable blonde. One by one my friends climbed into the barber's chair, silently watching their long tresses drop to the dirty floor in soft mounds. One day another girl decided that I'd held out long enough and cut a chunk of hair from the back of my head. The barber completed the job, and I now looked like the boys I'd played with all my life. That night I went straight to my room, refusing supper, a kerchief tied firmly around where my hair used to be. It stayed there all night. The next morning when Mama wanted to do my hair, Victor made sure everyone knew that I had very little of it left.

If school had consisted only of gymnastics and literature, I would have been a model student. My hunger for reading materials continued unabated, and I discovered that I also liked to write. Unlike many of my classmates, I actually enjoyed essay assignments.

"But Papa, what possible good can it do me to learn about a lot of dead Egyptian kings and their pyramids? I don't want to be a history teacher!" He ignored my wails of protest.

"It's part of your education and you need to learn it." End of discussion.

Daily sarcastic barbs from my teacher could not shame me into studying or completing the assignments. No threat of being declined by a university motivated me toward better habits. A week before the quarterly report card, I always stayed after school for an hour's tutoring, which was all I needed to achieve a passing grade. I was, however, careful that my grades stayed high enough so that I could participate in my three favorite electives: music, sports and drama. I even won prizes for good report cards, although a bird house and a towel were, in my opinion, poor rewards. After all, I had learned to make bird houses in woodworking class and could do it myself if I really wanted one. The towel was just plain dull. Mama and Papa scolded me for complaining, and told me that I should appreciate receiving *any* gift.

I represented our school in all area literary competitions. I memorized German and Russian poems with equal ease, winning awards for reciting them as well as for my essays.

Papa took an active interest in our education and always checked to make sure that we did our homework, now under the stern gaze of Comrade Lenin's portrait. I was immensely proud of my penmanship, having mastered the technique of holding the fountain pen at an exact eighty-five degree angle along my index finger. Fancy German script decorated my workbooks, a thick line on the upstroke, thin coming down.

During upper grades, athletics became my true passion in school and I spent hours after class practicing throws, jumps and balancing techniques. With each competition, more medals were added to my collection, and I proudly displayed them on my bedroom walls.

I had diligently practiced some difficult new gymnastic manoeuvres and could hardly wait to demonstrate them in the district competition. But when the day dawned, bright and sunny, I stayed in bed.

"Lydia, why aren't you up yet?" Mama's voice was sharp. She had called me earlier so that she would have time to fix my hair and uniform. Now she came into my room where I lay huddled under the blankets.

"I'm not getting up. I'm dying." I hoped my voice was calm and that Mama and Papa would not be sad for too long. I didn't want this to be any more difficult than was necessary. After it was all over, Victor would undoubtedly be pleased to have a room of his own. I hoped he would remember me with fondness. Mama stood over me, hands on her hips, wondering what responsibility I was trying to evade by staying in bed. Only last night I had been full of excitement, expecting that all my hard work and training would be rewarded. Now I was dying?

A familiar warning look on her face told me that she was quickly losing patience. Resigned to my fate, I flung back the covers to show her the red stains on my nightgown and sheets. If I'd expected sympathy, I was mistaken. In fact, she laughed at me.

"You're *not* going to die!" I stared at her. She knew that without talking to a doctor? "There's nothing to worry about — it happens to all women." At fourteen, I still considered myself a girl, not a woman, so what did she mean? Whatever it was, Mama saw no reason to change my plans for the day — or to provide more details — and in no time I was appropriately outfitted and ready to swing from the bars as planned. I was no wiser, uneasily wondering what other unpleasant "growing up" surprises lurked in the future.

I inherited Papa's love of music without any of his ability to make it. Undaunted, he decided that my education would be incomplete without learning to play the piano and, despite my strenuous objections, made arrangements for me to take lessons. Nina, the teacher, also taught a typing class. I had an idea: *Why not substitute one form of keyboard training for another?* She was uncomfortable about deceiving Papa, but agreed that my piano talents, to state it kindly, were limited.

When Papa wanted a progress report, I confessed my conspiracy with Nina. Anxious to prove that his investment, though misdirected, was nonetheless profitable, I showed him my best papers. But why hadn't I told him or Mama? He already knew the answer. What he didn't know about, he couldn't stop! I practiced on the machine in Papa's office at every possible opportunity, and he reluctantly agreed, as I knew he would, that this training would probably serve me better in the long run. He rarely refused anything I wanted.

What I lacked in musical talent, I made up for in appreciation. When Papa invited me to attend a performance of an opera for which he played with the orchestra, I was delighted. It would signal a true coming-of-age in that for the first time, a friend and I had permission to take the train to Pyatigorsk and back by ourselves. To mark my transition into adult society, Mama and Papa even let me buy my first pair of high-heeled shoes. Learning to walk on them proved more challenging than expected. I enlisted Victor and Heinrich, one on either side, to hold me up as I teetered around the house. They mimicked my wobbly stride, howling with laughter in tribute to my new sophistication. I ignored them and struggled valiantly on.

The night of the performance we were overwhelmed by the sheer elegance of the other patrons. I envied the women with their sweeping coiffures and long black gowns with jewels sparkling above plunging necklines. Their gallant escorts plied them with candy and flowers and despite my shoes, I suddenly felt very young and inexperienced, especially when the man taking our tickets told me that we shouldn't even be there! These tickets were for the *afternoon* performance and didn't I know that anyone under the age of eighteen was not to be admitted to public venues after eight o'clock at night?

I was crushed. In my excitement, I had failed to notice the time indicated on the ticket and Papa, evidently expecting me to know better, had not mentioned it. The man was smiling at me and I took heart. He knew Papa and, just this once, agreed to let us in, despite curfew regulations. When we took our place in the raised side box, I noticed that Papa looked anything but pleased to see me there.

"Where were you this afternoon?" he asked testily, coming over while the orchestra was tuning. "I waited and waited for you! You can't stay in those seats now — they belong to other ticket holders." We were prepared to move, but the people for whom they were reserved waved us to stay where we were as they found empty places nearby.

Papa's displeasure notwithstanding, we thoroughly enjoyed the drama and romance of the stage. If we were later arrested for breaking curfew, the memory of tonight would remain a happy one.

6

When my parents married, they agreed that it was best to keep Mama's former marriage a secret from my brothers and me until we were older. It was revealed one New Year's Eve, ahead of schedule and definitely not the way they planned to share such potentially disturbing information with us.

Reinhold, who attended university in Leningrad, was home for the holiday. He had just come from a party when there was a loud knock on the door. Police! To our surprise, they arrested him without explanation. Mama and Papa looked at each other but said little. Later I heard them praying in their bedroom. I tried to pray too but my mind refused to co-operate. What good did it do if, as my teachers claimed, God was only a figment of my imagination?

Reinhold had one angry question for my parents when he returned a few hours later.

"Who am I?" he demanded. At the police station they had questioned his background, telling him that he was not really a Mueller, that Papa was not really his father.

How could that be? Reinhold and Papa were so close, spending hours together like any father and son. Did that mean that he was not really my brother? I waited for my parents to say something reassuring but they could only look at him tearfully. Slowly the story emerged.

When Mama's first husband, Victor Schlegel, was killed in World War I, she was left alone with two children, a boy and a girl. Then her daughter died at age five. Reinhold was scarcely more than a baby when she re-married and Papa was the only father he had ever known.

They decided to wait until his education was complete before telling him the early details of his life. Anticipating that discussion, Mama had prepared a book with pictures of his father, some of them holding a baby boy. She gave it to him now, together with his original birth certificate. There it was — Reinhold Schlegel! She had ordered a new one in the name of Reinhold *Mueller* after she married Papa. We were all crying by this time. Realizing that Papa was not *really* Reinhold's father somehow changed everything.

When he saw Mama's care and planning in preserving the record of his past, Reinhold's anger lessened, although he still felt deceived. Their motives were protective. By waiting until he was finished the difficult university program for building train locomotives, they felt that he would not be unnecessarily distracted or lose his trust in Papa, whose name he had carried all his life.

But why should the authorities find it necessary to question his birth identity now? Or at all? Was Reinhold involved in questionable activities at university which were being monitored? They were unaware that he had a list of false identities with matching identification papers for each of them. If arrested or questioned, he could assume a name which protected certain activities conducted under a different alias.

When he completed university, I learned that he had a secret girlfriend, right there in Nikolevka. This was a new concept in my life as romance was of no interest to me, even at age fourteen. Nadia was a beautiful Russian girl with long golden hair and I could understand why he was so fascinated with her. We both knew that Mama and Papa would object; German boys should marry German girls. Sensing that I would enjoy a role in this clandestine relationship, Reinhold recruited me to convey notes between them. She worked in a silk laboratory that I conveniently passed on my way to and from school, and I made daily stops. One day I forgot, leaving the undelivered note in my pocket. Mama found it as she did the laundry.

Her reaction was predictable; nationalities should not mix. Living peacefully in the same village was one thing, but marriage was another matter! Reinhold blamed me for upsetting a satisfactory arrangement and himself for entrusting something so important to an absentminded little sister. Papa's response surprised both of us.

"If she's a nice girl and he wants to marry her, so be it." As far as Reinhold was concerned, she was, and he did, moving into the house that she shared with her father.

Their marriage faced immediate obstacles, although Reinhold took care to hide it from us. I stopped there one day after school and was horrified to see Nadia's alcoholic father sprawled across the bed in a drunken stupor, still wearing barnyard clothing and boots with traces of manure clinging to them. My finicky brother, who re-ironed his shirts after Mama was finished, lived in this mess?

I told Mama what I had seen, but she was reluctant to interfere in their lives. After their first baby was born, however, she decided it was time to act. When Reinhold travelled to Tblisi for the maiden running of the new *Stalin Engine* which he helped to build, she brought Nadia and her little boy to live at our house, much to Reinhold's surprise and relief when he returned from his trip. Soon there was another baby adding to the happy noise and commotion in our house.

Reinhold often traveled in his job, and Nadia proved that absence can, indeed, make the fond heart wander. When I stopped by the laboratory unexpectedly one afternoon, her colleagues told me she had already left for the day — with Karl, a former boyfriend from her single days. Reinhold discovered this for himself when he went to meet her there upon his return home. Again she had left early, and someone told him why.

Five hours later, when she returned home, he ordered her to pack her clothes and to move out of our house. Surprised at being found out, she nonetheless complied. "I don't have any children!" was her disacknowledgment of the two bewildered little faces left behind.

The Easter after I turned fifteen, Mama surprised me with the diary she had begun when I was born. I was thrilled and spent hours poring over the tightly written lines, re-living the events recorded, even though I remembered many of them from a rather different perspective. From now on, the responsibility to update it was mine.

Writing in my diary was a pleasant chore, especially when there was something new and exciting to report. My new part-time job as a payroll clerk in Papa's furniture factory rated an entry. He was now the manager and felt that I would benefit from the experience. While his position gave me an advantage in obtaining the job, I knew that my performance would be watched as closely as any other employee's and I vowed to give it my best efforts.

He gave me a stopwatch and told me to time a worker while he performed a particular task such as carving a wooden flower or some other design, and then to calculate his pay accordingly. Some workers resented a fifteen-year-old monitoring their work, however no one complained to Papa.

My first pay envelope contained the overwhelming wealth of forty rubles, which I planned to give to my parents. They, however, insisted that I should spend my first earnings as I wished. The world was at my feet and I invited two cousins to accompany me to Pyatigorsk. A blouse, a movie and many treats later, I returned home satisfied — and broke.

7

"What's that girl's name?"

Alexander Brusentzow often saw Papa talking with me and wanted to know who I was. Papa acted as though he wasn't sure who Alexander meant and changed the subject. He saw no reason to draw unnecessary attention to our relationship. I unwittingly raised the issue.

"What shall I get us for lunch, Papa?"

Alexander's eyebrows shot up in twin question marks. Papa ignored him. He owed no explanation where I was concerned. Only when Alexander arrived early for a New Year's Eve party at our house did Papa realize what his intentions were. He wanted permission to court me.

"I love her and want to marry her."

Both my parents stared at him in stunned silence. This man wanted to marry their daughter? Their *child!* But he was so much older than me — eight years to be exact. And what did a sixteen-year-old know about marriage? The old issue of Russian boy and German girl was raised again.

"Reinhold married a Russian girl and look what happened!" Mama's previous reservations had proved to be well founded; nothing good came of mixed marriages.

"Alexander and Nadia are completely different people." Papa liked Alexander but knew that he needed to tread carefully with Mama where her only daughter was concerned. The young man didn't drink or smoke and at the factory was very conscientious and responsible in carrying out his duties. Since completing his compulsory two-year army duty, he lived with his mother — always a good sign to an anxious parent.

Papa felt forced to compromise his highest desires for me in the face of reality. Since all but a select few Orthodox churches were closed in Russia, he knew that young men who shared his Christian beliefs were scarce. While he had always hoped that my future husband would be a man of faith, someone with strong principles who would care for me as for his own family was highly preferable to what he had observed among some of the young men in my peer group. He had taught me about God as best he could and must now leave me in his hands.

"You know that I want the best for my children and I would never agree to this if I had concerns." Papa could sense when Mama was ready to be persuaded, albeit reluctantly. However, he still had a few things to say to Alexander.

"If I let you marry her, you must promise never to stand in the way of her education. She must be allowed to study anything she wants and if you cannot agree to this, our discussion is over." Papa made it clear that if Alexander reneged on his promise, he would personally take me away from him. His daughter would not be chained to anyone's side at the expense of her own opportunity for a career and livelihood! Alexander shared Papa's educational ambitions for me and gave Papa his word.

Nobody even wondered, much less asked what *I* thought. My cousin, whose interest in romance vastly exceeded mine, made swooning gestures when his name was mentioned. As far as I was concerned, she was welcome to him!

While I had noticed Alexander's interest, I remained innocently unaware of all the negotiations conducted on my behalf. How could I know that Papa's permission for our first movie date already carried his approval for a closer relationship? He appeared stern, allowing me to go as long as I returned home at a reasonable hour.

Alexander believed in getting straight to the heart of things and after a few dates, asked me to marry him. His own certainty left him unprepared for my reaction.

"No I won't marry you! I'm too young!" Undaunted, he repeated the question at regular intervals, but my answer remained the same. Apart from being too young, I was afraid, although I wasn't sure why.

What did I know about being a wife? While I had outgrown most of the games which I had enjoyed as a child, I was far from considering any of my playmates as a husband-in-waiting. I thought of Edward, a boy from school who often hovered nearby. Did he entertain similar interests? Why was life suddenly so complicated? The diary was my closest confidante as my confusion poured from pen to page.

To my surprise, Mama and Papa remained calm when I told them of Alexander's proposal. In fact, everybody in my family wondered why I was balking at this opportunity. "He's an only child and everything he has will be yours!" What was wrong with them anyway? Did they think I could be bought with *things*? The idea offended me.

On the other hand, he really *was* very nice and I enjoyed being with him. It was hard to resist someone who so openly declared his love for me. And I secretly enjoyed the envy on older girls' faces, knowing they would gladly trade places with me. Finally I said yes, but added one condition of my own: My name would remain Mueller. He happily agreed, and the wedding wheels began to roll.

Alexander's mother came to meet me and my family, bearing the traditional salt and bread which symbolized love and acceptance. She made a special point of asking me to cut the bread. I was unfamiliar with this Russian tradition and, in response to my questioning look, she explained that this was symbolic of cutting myself off from my family and now belonging to them. *That's what you think!* The thought remained wisely silent, though my face said it for me as I dutifully sliced the loaf. If this woman expected for a moment that she *or* her son would replace my family, they were in for a surprise. The date was set for March 12, 1936, and our home buzzed with preparations. I felt strangely detached from all the excitement, as though it was happening to someone else.

With the closure of churches, the legal aspect of weddings consisted of documents issued at the town hall. Couples who wished to celebrate with pomp and ceremony arranged a separate wedding party.

As tradition dictated, I bought a new white shirt for Alexander and he purchased my wedding gown. He also arranged for a car to come to my house in Nikolevka where I was dressing, to bring me to his mother's house in Pyatigorsk. Vast quantities of food awaited the crowd of guests gathered outside enjoying the music provided by Papa's orchestra.

I felt like a queen as Nadia and our friend Paulina helped me to dress with many *oohs* and *aahs* as the elegant gown slipped over my head. There was only one thing wrong. I didn't want to be married. In fact, I agreed with a woman in the town office where we were officially wed the previous week who said I should be in school, *not* getting married. I stared at myself in the mirror, hardly recognizing this vision in satin and lace. I was a wife. I had a husband. And I didn't know what to do about either!

Outside, a crowd of my school friends waited to see me. I saw Edward standing with them and suddenly knew that I was making a big mistake. "I'm *not* going to do this," I announced, pulling the headpiece out of my newly styled hair. Nadia and Paulina exchanged worried glances, knowing quite well that I was capable, even yet, of undoing months of preparation. They rushed forward to prevent further damage.

"Lydia, think of what this will do to your parents. They have paid a lot of money for this day, together with Alexander's mother. If you don't go through with this, they will have to repay everything — double!" Their appeal to a vulnerable spot in my wilful armor had the desired result. Whatever I might want, I could not cause Mama and Papa the unnecessary expense and embarrassment by changing my mind now.

"Besides," they reassured me, sensing that my friends gathered around to whisper and stare had given me some last minute jitters, " they'll soon get married too, so there's no reason for you to wait." Assuming victory, they hastily readjusted my finery and bundled me off in the car to my wedding party. To Alexander. *My husband.* He was waiting for me, impatiently scanning the street for sight of the car. When he saw me he started to cry.

Outwardly I basked in the attention, laughing, dancing and blushing coyly through the speeches and well wishes. Dutifully enduring the tearful hugs and kisses, I was determined to ignore the growing feeling that I'd made a big mistake. No one must suspect that the happy bride was trying to forget that her life was about to change. Drastically. Forever.

Finally the last remnants of food were cleared away and the dancing stopped. The guests departed one by one with many congratulations and wishes for a happy life.

It was time for bed.

I reluctantly followed Alexander into the house, stopping short at the door to his room. My bed had been moved here to its new home but the familiar headboard looked out of place and uninviting. A deep wine-colored duvet showing through the lace overlay concealed new sheets and pillowcases, all of them emerging from my hope chest for this event. Mama could not have anticipated that, when they were finally put to use, my new husband would sleep under them by himself.

I knew that marriage to Alexander meant moving into his house, but where was it written that I had to sleep with him? I refused to enter the room. He was stunned, clearly anticipating a different ending to the day. Grunya, my new mother-in-law, quickly assessed the situation and advised him to leave me alone, seeing that I lacked all understanding of how events usually progressed. She wondered how anyone could reach my age without satisfying even a basic curiosity.

I slept little that night, wondering how I was going to deal with this situation tomorrow night. And the one after that. This must be what Mama was talking about when she cautioned me against letting boys "touch" me. While she hadn't specifically mentioned getting into bed with one, surely that was what she meant.

The morning following a wedding, the matron of honour customarily checked the bedsheets for evidence that the bride was, in fact, a virgin. When she arrived, Grunya quietly explained that this ritual was unnecessary. I had spent my wedding night in *her* bed.

In the days that followed, Alexander, blessed with unusual patience, treated me like a good friend, taking me to movies and for walks in the park. I loved hearing him play the accordion; the music reminded me of Papa and made me feel less lonely.

I agonized about how to address Grunya. *Mama* was out of the question. No amount of bread-cutting entitled anyone but my real mother to that name. At the same time, my early training about proper respect for my elders made *Grunya* stick in my throat. I became skilled in avoiding a need to call her anything. She had always longed for a daughter and was disappointed that I kept a polite distance. Rather than force me into yet another uncomfortable relationship, she tried to set me at ease.

Nonetheless, a week later I boarded a train and went home to Nikolevka, back to the comfort of everything old and familiar. Back to Mama and Papa. And I was there to stay!

"Why are you here? Did he beat you? Are you getting enough to eat?" Their questions tumbled over each other when I walked in the door.

"No, they are very kind. They treat me like a china doll." It was true. No new bride could ask for a kinder husband or mother-in-law.

"Then what is wrong?" I saw a dangerous look on Papa's face, that could only mean trouble for anyone who hurt his baby girl. I had to tell them the truth.

"I don't want to sleep with him!" There. It was finally out.

At any other time, I might have thought their quick glance at each other meant secret laughter, but their faces were serious as they turned back to me.

"Lydia, when people get married they always sleep in the same bed! That's how they have a family." What *were* they talking about? This was all I would receive in explanation but I was no closer to understanding what getting married had to do with sleeping together — or having a family. Of course Mama and Papa slept in the same bed but did that mean *all* married people did? If I had known all this earlier, I could have saved everyone the bother of a wedding! Mama had always dreaded this scene, vainly hoping that someone, somewhere would have provided the necessary information long before this.

Fortunately, Nadia was still my friend, even though she and Reinhold had separated. Later in the evening Alexander followed me to Nikolevka and called on her. They had a little visit by the river and he, embarrassed by the need to enlist her help, explained our predicament. One of my brothers was conveniently nearby and she sent him to find me, at the same time sending Alexander for a solitary walk. She wondered how I could possibly be so naive at my age.

"Lydia, there are a few things that you need to understand." Thus began my orientation to the facts of life and marriage. I listened wide-eyed as she graphically filled in the blanks of my understanding, hardly knowing what to think. One thing was certain. I loved children and if I wanted any of my own, I had to sleep with my husband, although it was becoming abundantly clear that the process had little to do with actual sleep. There was much to think about on the short train trip back to Pyatigorsk with Alexander. I could hardly look at him.

Knowledge was one thing; acting on it was quite another. To my husband's despair, I continued to sleep with his mother for another month before truly becoming his wife.

Even though my interest in God had waned considerably in the past ten years, the teaching instilled in me by my parents and their faith quietly lived out in our home, contrasted sharply with my new life. When Alexander was still a little boy, his father died of pneumonia and his brother was killed by a train, leaving only him and his mother. On her own with a small child, she earned a living by nursing rich people's babies. While the benefits of breast-feeding were sought and appreciated, it was considered unsophisticated and best left to hired help.

Occasionally her employers asked her to deliver money to the church on their behalf. She decided that if they were concerned about giving to the church, they should do it themselves and the gold rubles were redirected toward her own family's support. Whatever faith she once professed evaporated in the face of such hypocrisy, and she decided that religion had no place in her life.

The blessing, a mealtime ritual in my home, was completely absent here and I soon grew accustomed to filling my plate without that customary pause. I had long since learned to ignore the guilt of omitting bedtime prayer.

In March, 1937, Grandmother died. Mama and I visited her one day after she had spent the morning planting her flower garden. We suggested that she lie down for a nap, and to our surprise, she agreed. Sleeping in midday was, in Grandma's opinion, a lazy person's habit. She asked us to arrange all her fancy pillows around her on the bed and then sent us away for a walk while she rested. When we returned, she was dead, her hand under her cheek just as we had left her an hour ago.

Through my own grief, I tried to comfort Mama as best I could. Other than her sister in America and her brother Jacob, who lived in Pyatigorsk and rarely came to visit, Mama was all that remained of her immediate family. I tried to imagine what it might feel like to be alone, without Mama and Papa nearby. The thought was too painful and I forced it from my mind, choosing rather to focus blame on *Them*. Whatever the physical reason for her death, I fervently believed that she had died of a broken heart when *They* destroyed her home. *They* had killed her.

Grandma had left Papa instructions that there was to be only happy music played at her funeral because she was "going home" where there was no sadness. Papa found that when the time came, he simply could not comply with her wishes. She was, without a doubt, busy dancing on streets of gold but for those of us left behind, a waltz must wait for a happier occasion.

True to Alexander's promise, he encouraged me to attend university, even though it meant living apart from him in

Rostov, five hundred kilometres away. The challenges of reaching my goal to become a teacher helped to distract me from waves of homesickness that sometimes engulfed me, usually before bedtime. Shortly after the school year commenced, I became persistently ill, and all attempts to treat my apparent stomach disorder failed. The doctor initially attributed it to the disruptive changes in my life and missing my family. She was wrong; our first child was on the way. Alexander, mindful of his promise to Papa, insisted that I continue my studies.

Nonetheless, I returned home after the first semester. Nadia's support throughout my pregnancy was a constant refuge amidst all the confusing changes, both physical and emotional, that engulfed me. It was always easier to discuss such things with her than with Mama, who disapproved of our ongoing friendship but never tried to stop it.

February 27, 1938. I had come home to Nikolevka for some post-election festivities and was thoroughly enjoying the food and dancing, much to Mama's dismay. My expanded girth was still short of typical pre-birth dimensions and hardly interfered with my participation in the fun. The sharp abdominal pains, which started at my parents' house a short time later, left me breathless. Papa sent for help and immediately made me lie down.

When the doctor confirmed that my baby's birth would happen by morning, Mama immediately disappeared into her bedroom, leaving Papa to sit beside me, stroking my hand and wiping perspiration from my forehead. The doctor left, promising to return in a few hours to see how I was getting on.

"Where will it come out?" My question startled Papa who looked at me as though uncertain whether or not I could be serious. I was. He stared at the closed bedroom door. *This was a mother's territory! Where was she?* I waited for an answer and for once, Papa was lost for profound advice.

"When it comes, you'll know," was all he could manage. The pains were more rapid now and Papa knew that the doctor's "few hours" had shrunk to minutes. Unless he was prepared to become directly involved, he needed help — *now*. There had been no time to send my brothers discreetly away, and Victor was dispatched to find Paulina, whose calm nature had propelled me through the shaky moments of my wedding day.

Yuri was born shortly after her arrival and she took complete charge of cleaning him and supervising my first hours of motherhood. She and Papa discovered Mama lying in bed with two pillows pressed tightly against her ears to block the anticipated screams which she remembered so vividly from her own childbirth experiences. She could scarcely fathom such an ordeal lasting only one-and-a-half hours — and that she had a new grandson.

I stayed at home for two months, slowly gaining confidence as Yuri showed signs of surviving my awkward mothering skills. I cried when it was time to go back to university. How could I manage without a daily quota of baby gurgles and coos? He could stay in the dormitory with me like other new mothers in my class with their babies, but we all agreed that he was better off at home with his father and grandmother. I could scarcely believe in my own transformation from carefree student to mother, constantly thinking about my baby.

Once again my parents received notice that they must move, their house required for another newly arrived Russian official. It was time, Papa thought, to build his own home — their dream house — where he and Mama could live out their old age. But even as the new house took shape, he wondered if his retirement years would be as peaceful in reality as in his imagination. The communist regime kept people on edge with uncertainty. Newspapers from Moscow carried regular reports of political upheaval in Germany under Adolf Hitler. This boded no good for Russia, and there were sinister rumblings of another war. Military action against Germany's new sophisticated fleet of bombers would be far more disastrous than the war which had brought him here in the first place.

After my graduation from university in 1940, politics dealt a bitter blow to my ambitions. Even with a hard-earned certificate from the University of Rostov, I was now barred from teaching because of my German heritage. We were all branded as *fascist* by the authorities, who were concerned that people of questionable origin like me might teach wrong values to impressionable young Russian minds.

"What are they talking about? I was born and raised here! I memorized the Russian constitution! I'm as Russian as anyone in Moscow!" My stormy protests were to no avail. How could this happen? I had never even visited Germany! In fact, I was inclined to believe everything that I had heard about German soldiers, raping and pillaging their way to victory. Papa chided me for my willingness to believe every negative rumor. Each nationality had its hoodlums and I should not cast every German in an automatic role of villain. Both Mama and Papa tended to believe the best of people. *I* was more cynical.

To everyone's relief, eventually my tearful tirades subsided into moody silences, and finally reluctant acceptance of a situation beyond my power to change. Like me, Papa was disappointed that my dream of becoming a teacher was frustrated, but he understood the importance of finding another path and moving ahead. He invited me back to work in the factory, even temporarily. I agreed, without enthusiasm. Why had I spent all those months studying when my destiny as a payroll clerk seemed set in stone? Then I remembered that I was not the only one who had ever given up a dream. Papa had not chosen to become a prisoner of war. Neither had he chosen to labor in a Russian vineyard at the expense of a prestigious musical career. And if his dreams *had* been realized, I would not be here.

I sensed his pride in me for swallowing my disappointment and going on with life. Maybe his stubborn little bull was finally growing up!

War with Germany finally broke out on June 21, 1941, and Alexander was drafted two days later. There was little time for farewells. I clung to him, trying desperately to convince both of us that it would all soon be over and he could come home to us again. We promised each other that, regardless what happened, neither of us would ever marry anyone else. Fear squeezed my heart in an icy grip every time I thought about being left alone to raise Yuri and his new baby sister, Alla. My childish dreams of wartime adventure were coming true, only now I would have gladly traded them for our once safe and predictable routine. A few days later we all stood on the platform of the crowded train station, together with countless other distraught wives and mothers tearfully waving goodbye. I never saw him again.

A month later I received a letter on military paper, stiffly cold and impersonal. Alexander had disappeared. While stopping short of advising me that he was dead, his superiors felt it necessary to inform me that army records failed to place him among any of the active troops. Officially, my husband no longer existed.

Grunya and I refused to accept this notification at face value, asking repeatedly at the local army office for new information and checking every possible list of those taken prisoner or killed in action. Every inquiry ended in a shrug. Alexander had vanished without a trace. And the army was not obligated to support a non-existent soldier's family. Providing for my children was now *my* concern.

8

Russia's war against Germany fostered mass suspicion, bordering on hysteria, against everyone of German descent throughout the country, regardless of how many generations of Russian citizenship they represented. In September, 1941, official intentions became clear. The Caucasus colonies must be completely purged of German influence, and government officials conducted a name-by-name search to locate everyone fitting this description for compulsory evacuation. There must be no potential traitors left to join the advancing German army in their quest to conquer the Motherland.

Russian armies surrounded the colonies with machine guns poised. I lived in constant dread of the day when it would be our turn to receive the inevitable resettlement notice. When it came, my name was missing. My parents and three brothers were given one month to prepare all the food and clothing that they could carry. On a date to be advised, they would bring it to the train station from where they would be taken to an undisclosed location. The deliberately vague description deceived no one.

My previous fear had been for *all* of us. It had never occurred to me that someone, *especially me*, might be left behind. Fear changed to panic, then anger. How could *They* expect me to continue living here alone? I stormed the local KGB headquarters, demanding permission to share my family's fate. They raised their eyebrows in astonishment, more accustomed to pleas from those who wished to remain behind. This was a new twist! My determination to go gave them even more reason to make me stay.

"Your husband is fighting for the Motherland and you will stay here and raise your children." The matter was closed.

I raged at the injustice, hardly noticing their sudden present-tense reference to Alexander. We were all loyal, hard-working citizens of Russia, only there was no way of satisfying the ever-changing bureaucracy. I was barred from teaching because I was German. My parents were forced into exile because they were German. I must stay behind because I was married to a Russian. Why could we not just be *people* again? Where had all these artificial divisions come from? Why had I let myself be talked into marriage? Now my husband *and* my family were lost to me. How would I cope with two small children on my own? *If only.... I should have.... What if....?* My mind churned an endless refrain.

Nadia and Reinhold, though separated, were still legally married. Russian spouses in mixed marriages were usually exempt from deportation, but Nadia took no chances. She went to a judge and within twenty-four hours, the divorce was official. The judge gave her custody of the children, who until this time had lived with Mama and Papa, saying that the children were Russian and must stay with her rather than going with their fascist father. My parents, though sad about losing their grandchildren, were relieved at the decision. Whatever their destination, they knew that it was no place for little ones.

Denied the right to go with my family, I now spent every possible minute with them, helping with preparations for their journey. In our efforts to remain hopeful, Siberia was not mentioned, although we all believed it to be their destination. How would they ever survive the harsh winter conditions ahead?

Mama and Papa tried to be stoic for my sake but there were times when a look or a touch brought a flood of tears and we just held each other tightly. Each caress, every hug was a moment of warmth and comfort to store away, to savor across the cold, lonely miles that would soon separate us. We talked and talked, memories flowing unabated as though to imprint themselves indelibly in our hearts. Without any certainty of the future, it became ever more important to know that our thoughts could unite unhindered in the past.

I knew they were very concerned about me. Papa's consent to an early marriage for me had, in part, been due to a premonition that someday his role as my protector would end. Who could have known that my husband would be sent away first? Unlike me, however, Papa still believed in a God who would never leave me alone.

There were practical details to be taken care of if they were to have any hope of staying alive. Regulations permitted them to bring anything that the four of them could carry, and my parents were newly thankful for three strong sons. Families with small children needing to be held were limited in their capacity to bring food and warm clothes and blankets. We butchered pigs and cooked all the fat out of the meat, repacking it in the fat to keep it from spoiling. We bagged dried fruit and bread. The Persian carpets, which had always graced the walls of our house, were cut into strips. Papa knew better than the rest of us what would be needed, both for the journey and whatever awaited them at the other end.

They packed only items necessary for survival. She tried to hide it but I could see Mama's pain as she fingered the fine lace edging on her pillows or straightened an ornament on the dresser. Would she have another home to grace with her creative touch? Would the strangers waiting to take over this house know the pride and delight that had gone into its construction? Would they care that dreams of contented retirement with laughter of grandchildren had been destroyed with one small paper decree? Would Papa's instruments ever sing again?

Despite my desperate attempts to prolong the month by making every precious minute count for two, the time passed far too quickly. The inevitable day arrived without the prayed-for reprieve. Mama and Papa, Victor, Heinrich and Reinhold each shouldered their assigned portion of the load for the short journey on foot to the train station. Against all rules, Grunya and I helped carry as much as we could, hoping that in the confusion, no one would notice. Mama gave her cherished plants a final watering, as though taking comfort in knowing that for today at least they were alive and well. Papa stopped at the gate, looking back at his dream house and its sidewalk crafted with colorful stones, so carefully chosen and carried out of the mountains. His gaze lingered on the fence, painstakingly woven out of willow branches and bordered with rose bushes. My heart ached as he turned resolutely away, determined not to yield to the tug of mere *things* when there were more important issues at stake.

We joined other German evacuees on the dirt road to the station, all sadly silent as they looked for the last time on the village and mountains that had shaped their lives for generations. Was there any hope that they could ever return to a life here, happy and secure? I wondered how the sun could shine so brightly on this tragic little parade. Did the farmers harvesting in a nearby field know that our world was ending? I closed my eyes and willed life to be as normal as it appeared to be around me. Yuri's little hand tugging me along dispelled any illusion. Nothing was, or would ever be normal again.

Those in our neighbourhood who were, at least for now, spared this mass exodus from their homes, came to the station for a last farewell. Sympathetic tears flowed unrestrainedly as they witnessed the forced severing of ties, both family and community. Wanting to express their own sadness, they were nonetheless reluctant to intrude on precious last moments between loved ones.

This was worse than death. However sad the loss of a loved one to accident or disease, mourners could accept this as a natural part of life. It was quite another matter to know that human authority could wilfully inflict such pain.

The train awaited its human cargo, the locomotive chuffing clouds of smoke and steam into the air. Had Reinhold helped to build it? I shivered, although the day was warm. The waiting officials strutted importantly on the crowded platform, briskly checking names against a list, barking orders and gesturing impatiently as they herded people to designated areas. Prodded away from clinging farewell embraces, families with their belongings were quickly bundled into boxcars, ninety people to a car. For the second time in a matter of months, I was standing at a train station. Again, there was no time for prolonged goodbyes.

"Keep God in your heart. We will pray for you *always.*"

One last whisper choked with tears, one last tight squeeze from each of them and they were gone, hustled aboard with their precious bundles. I could barely see them through the barred window but the boys managed to secure a spot where they could wave a hanky. *Clang!* The crossbar dropped into its groove, as though sealing our separate fates. That sound would haunt me for years to come with an instant resurgence of poignant memory.

I stood there, tears pouring down my cheeks as I strained to see that little scrap of white. Soon the train curved out of sight, its plaintive whistle a mournful echo in my heart. When all was silent I still lingered, this sooty platform a shrine to all I cherished.

"Where are they going, Mama?"

Yuri's voice penetrated my pain. He didn't understand why I cried so much lately. All these people at the train station should have meant adventure, but somehow it hadn't felt like much fun. And when Grandma and Grandpa hugged him, they seemed so *sad*. Grunya diverted his attention for a few minutes while I searched for a hanky with a dry corner.

I had more questions than answers myself. How could I cope with a three-year-old's need to know, steeling myself against the inevitable "why?" that followed every explanation. Would he ever see them again? Would he remember how Grandpa bounced him on his knee and told him stories? Would he remember Grandma and all the treats that she saved for his visits? Would there be other men in his life who could wrestle on the floor with him like his uncles?

I wished that I could at least take some of my parents' belongings with me but *They* had forbidden this. Houses abandoned by official order must be left unlocked with all contents intact. Failure to comply meant certain punishment and I was reluctant to jeopardize my children by drawing undue attention to myself. Wondering if I could possibly die from the crushing sorrow in my heart, I returned to Grunya's house, carefully avoiding any route that took me close to the dear and familiar house where flowers still bloomed cheerfully in the front yard.

I debated answering the knock on my door the next day, wanting only to be left alone, but with Yuri chattering noisily beside me I could hardly pretend that no one was home. A woman, who for years had worked with Papa in the factory, waited outside. I was surprised to see her, for although I had known her nearly all my life, a visit right now was most unexpected. She held out a package to me, tactfully averting her gaze from my swollen eyes and dishevelled appearance.

"Your father asked me to give this to you after they were gone." Her voice hesitated, as though fearful of adding to my pain by any reference to my family.

I took it, wondering why Papa had enlisted a messenger. *Mama's jewellery box!* The latch resisted my fumbling fingers. What could be in here? I finally lifted the lid, nearly dropping the box when I saw its contents. There, neatly organized in typical Mama-fashion, lay all their jewellery: watches, brooches, pins, earrings, and Papa's cufflinks — a different pair for every shirt. I remembered the items from when I was a little girl but they, together with the box, mysteriously disappeared before the KGB searched our house. Now I understood why my parents had evaded all questions, never correcting my assumptions that everything was sold to buy food.

I gently caressed the gems in their gold settings, flooded with instant memories of special occasions when Mama and Papa dressed up for a concert or party. They always looked so elegant! Familiar feelings of pride mingled with overwhelming sadness as I held each item. Clearly, Mama and Papa did not expect to have any further use for exotic baubles. I was holding my inheritance. It was my parents' only way of providing for our future needs.

The box held contents even more precious than the jewels: five letters, one from each member of my absent family. I held them tightly in my hand, a new supply of tears welling up from an inner fountain that refused to run dry.

I read my brothers' letters first, hearing Victor's attempt to mask his sadness with light-hearted banter, as though my last memories of him should be of good times and laughter; Heinrich's subdued promises to think of me often; Reinhold's big-brotherly concern for my welfare.

I could hardly bear to open Mama's and Papa's letters. Their voices, now with me in memory alone, spoke gently from the neatly penned pages, each carefully chosen word of love and concern a bitter-sweet stab to my soul. They seemed so close and yet, even as I read, they were being taken farther and farther away from me. The past month's emotional tension had limited what they could express about their *real* burden for me. Their message to me as an adult was the same one I had ignored as a child: *"Change your character, Lydia. Someday you will be alone and you will be lost."* They saw that I still had much to learn about accepting people as they were, rather than how I wanted them to be

That day *had* come and I *did* feel very lost. Many people I had always disdained as being inferior now had every reason to look at *me* with scorn, or at best, pity. I had always chosen friends and companions who met my expectations. Those who failed to measure up knew that I had no time for them. I remembered Papa's frequent reminders that we were all created by God and loved equally. While I was not an ardent communist, my childhood faith in God had been replaced with belief in myself. If God existed at all, he seemed content with what I interpreted as mutual indifference. Recent events mocked any thought of his love.

I wondered if Mama and Papa had somehow known that their roles as my protectors would be short-lived. The letters showed that they still saw me as a stubborn little bull, unwilling to accept anything that interfered with my plans and ideas. They feared what might happen to me if I failed to learn what they had tried all my life to instill. Now that my worst fears of being alone were a harsh reality, I finally understood at least a little of what they meant. *But how could I change my character even if I wanted to?*

That night I tossed on my bed for hours, exhausted but unable to find even temporary relief from the turmoil inside. I felt out of control, unable to influence the events that were irrevocably directing my life.

What would happen to us now?

9

Against my will life continued, one long day at a time. The factory was conscripted into the war effort and, except for a small corner still designated to furniture, now produced military hardware.

I longed for news of my family, but despite regular inquiries to the authorities, received no information. They assured me that as soon as my parents arrived in their new home, they would undoubtedly send me an address. If I had money for a ticket, I could even join them. Eventually I gave up talking to these officials, who now spoke as though leaving Nikolevka was my parents' idea, and that I could have gone with them if I'd wanted to.

Official information about the war was heavily censored, transmitted to citizens via crackling loudspeakers mounted on houses or lamp posts. An outbreak of cholera at the front took a heavy toll on the Russian troops, adding yet another worry to families of soldiers anxiously waiting at home for word about them. One of my co-workers, a devoted communist, loudly attributed the disease to "those Germans," particularly if I happened to be within earshot, as though I was personally responsible. Another worker defended me and the comments momentarily ceased. I knew that the peaceful co-existence, which I had previously taken for granted, was over. Where a scapegoat was needed, one would be found.

Grunya also recognized the danger inherent in owning a German name like Mueller. "Change your name. Get married again." Her advice was well-intentioned but I chose to ignore it. Changing my name was to admit that *They* had won. At this very moment my family was paying dearly for our name and if I was prevented from sharing their fate, I would at least not betray them by assuming a new one myself.

In October, 1941, scarcely a month after Mama and Papa were sent away, Grunya announced that she was going away to take care of her nephew's two little boys. I was dumbfounded. How could she leave me like this! *What about your grandchildren?* I thought rebelliously. *Surely they should come first!*

She thought otherwise. My factory had adequate childcare facilities for the workers. Alla could stay in the nursery and Yuri would be in kindergarten. She was needed elsewhere.

Feeling completely abandoned, I yielded to an urge to see my parents' old home again. Perhaps I could silence forever the persistent notion that my family was where they should be, that I could walk in the front door as I had done a million times before. Mama would be stirring a pot of soup on the stove, thin broth as Papa liked it, and, as usual, would refuse my offers to help. I could almost hear Papa's saxophone in the other room moments before he came out to give me a hug.

I took the train to Nikolevka, walking the familiar blocks to the dream house, as I still thought of it. Smoke rose from the chimney, so I knew that someone lived there. Weeds choked the garden, a few flowers still blooming bravely despite the new tenants' apparent indifference. I had rehearsed a subtle excuse for being there, but very nearly forgot what it was when the door opened. I tried to keep my eyes from registering horror at the smoke-blackened walls beyond the open door. They clearly had no idea of how to operate the woodburning stove, my mother's pride and joy. Green wood protruded from the firebox, producing more smoke than flame, blanketing everything with a gritty film of soot.

I fled in tears to Nadia's house where further devastation awaited. Being a Russian had not provided her with any advantage, or even protection. Soldiers had stripped the house bare of everything, including pillows and blankets. Her little boys huddled together for warmth, their teeth chattering in the chilly room.

As payroll clerk, part of my duties included collecting union booklets from each worker on paydays. These showed records of sums deducted for union dues and had to be taken to the main office where they were checked and stamped. One day a woman I'd never seen before sat at the desk, a Russian imported to replace a German worker. She sorted through the pile of booklets, stopping when she reached mine.

"Mueller, Lydia." She paused and I held my breath, wondering what my name meant to her. I soon found out. "What is someone with a blood-sucking fascist name doing here?" She spit out the words, her voice laced with venom. "Why is a Nazi working in a Russian factory? To let the Germans know our secrets?" I remained silent until she finished examining the entire pile. Then it was my turn.

"And now, my *friend*," my voice dripped sarcasm, "*I* am Lydia Mueller and I was born here. I learned the same constitution in school and speak Russian as well as you. *I* didn't start the war and have never hurt anyone!" With that, I picked up the booklets and left her sitting there, red-faced and speechless. I felt a reckless disregard for what might happen next; it just felt good to put at least one arrogant Russian intruder in her place.

When I arrived at the factory the next day, the security guard shook his head, regretfully informing me that he had orders to keep me out. I knew whom to thank. Unwilling to accept this as the last word, I visited the superintendent, a long-time friend of my family who had worked with my father for years. He assured me that I had not been fired but was to re-locate to a smaller factory which had previously produced toys but now manufactured wooden containers for ammunition.

Steel was scarce, so the nuts and bolts holding the boxes together were made of a special hardwood, carved and shaped by machine. To my dismay, the foreman led me to one of these machines as though he actually expected me to operate it. *What did I know about machines?* I was trained in office work and boasted few mechanical skills. He explained how each piece had to be measured to strict specifications and held up to the spinning blade which cut and chiselled it to the desired shape. I watched the workers around me as they deftly turned the wood this way and that. My heart sank. No matter how often they demonstrated, I just knew that I would never master the technique. What if a fragment hit me in the eye?

I hardly noticed when Kathy, the supervisor, paused beside me. "Here," she said, "I'll show you how to do it. It's really not so bad." Her voice reassured me and the panic subsided momentarily. It looked so easy when she did it, but to my chagrin, the two hundred twenty-one pieces that I produced were all wrong. I knew that errors, even for beginners, under the present system were readily interpreted as sabotage, with grim consequences for those under suspicion.

"Never mind," Kathy whispered, "we'll figure something out." She added twenty-four of her own perfectly crafted nuts and bolts to my collection and recorded the tally in my production file, just in case anyone should check. My German name could single me out for special scrutiny at any time and while most Russians from my area did not hold it against me, some acted as though I was personally responsible for Hitler's armies and any suffering our citizens endured at their hands.

Kathy worked with me every day, and gradually my hands made friends with the machinery. It was hard to believe that Mama's treadle sewing machine, a toy by comparison, had ever intimidated me. Just when I felt that I had truly mastered nuts and bolts, the factory lost most of its manpower to the front, leaving behind a predominantly female workforce and a few elderly men well past their military prime. They transferred me to a giant circular saw used for cutting boards which were made into crates. This machine left no margin for error; one slip of the hand could have dire (and permanent) consequences! I wistfully remembered my safe duties as a payroll clerk.

One night my worst fears were realized when a piece of wood flew out of the saw and struck me in the eye. I was knocked unconscious and woke up in hospital, bruised and sore, but thankfully intact. To my relief, when I returned to work a week later, I learned that my career as a machine operator was over. From now on I was assigned the messier, but less hazardous task of painting the crates.

As a service to the workers, the factory management arranged for area farmers to bring produce for sale directly to the factory. Employees could purchase vegetables for a nominal fee after completing their shift, avoiding the inevitable queues at local markets. Staples such as oil, flour, and sugar were also available and several of us were responsible for handing out each worker's allotted portion based on seniority. This added two to three hours of unpaid time to our normal shift. My daily exhaustion acted as a shield against the constant pain of loneliness that lay in wait for an unguarded moment.

One day the lady responsible for removing me from my previous job arrived at my window. Though she clearly recognized me, she neither greeted me nor thanked me when I handed her the vegetables. I wondered if, by tomorrow, she would have found a way to continue her vengeful campaign against me.

It was early December, two weeks later, when the dreaded *chernevoran* pulled to a stop in front of the factory and several sombre-looking men emerged. *KGB!*

"Where is Lydia Mueller?" My co-workers remained silent. Few households and families had escaped the loss of friends or loved ones to the hated secret police and no one was willing to co-operate with them.

"I am Lydia Mueller." When I realized they were asking for me, I came forward.

"Be in our office at 9:30 tomorrow morning." Handing me a card with an address printed on it, they climbed back into the "raven" and sped away. I stared after them, my heart pounding.

What could they want with me? Did they have information about Mama and Papa? Alexander? Was I to be sent away as well? What about Yuri and Alla? Anxious thoughts drove away all possibility of sleep that night.

I was no wiser the next day after meeting with them. They asked me endless questions about my parents, my brothers, cousins and other relatives who had been sent away years before. Where were they? What were they doing? Did I hear from them? My standard answer to their questions was "I don't know," and "no." After all, *They* had sent my family away in the first place and surely knew more than I did. If I asked questions, they just shrugged, admitting nothing.

They wanted to know about letters addressed to Mama from America and to Papa from Germany but I was of no more help here. I was a young girl when such mail had last arrived, and even then had paid no attention to these details that now seemed so important. Besides, in 1935 all mail, in and out of Russia, had been suspended so why would anyone be concerned about it now?

One question seemed uppermost in their minds: Did I know of anyone collaborating with the Germans? *Were they serious? What could I possibly know of spy activity?* My life was complicated enough with two fatherless children to care for and a full-time job without worrying about political loyalties. If there were Nazi sympathizers in my circle of acquaintances, it was a well-kept secret.

After an hour of questions, most of them repeated several times as though to trap me in a contradictory answer, I was dismissed. On my way out of the room, a clerk handed me a *propusk,* a little piece of paper with the date and time stamped on it which was carefully inspected at the outside door by the security guard before he allowed me to pass. I went back to work.

Reflecting on the interview later, I was increasingly puzzled — and afraid. The officials had been polite and even friendly, yet there was a menacing tone that haunted me. Perhaps it was their awareness of details that I considered trivial, such as the dates of foreign letters received by my parents. They had pointedly ignored my questions about Alexander. If he was dead, perhaps my protection through marriage to a Russian was over. If I had to leave, what would happen to Yuri and Alla? Were they still considered to be Russian children?

Weeks passed without further contact from the KGB and gradually my fears faded in the busyness of juggling family responsibilities and my work at the factory. Just when I had convinced myself that they realized their error, I received another summons. A month later, yet another. The same people interrogated me. The questions were always the same. So were the answers. The men were courteous, however this did nothing to allay my fears. What did they want from me? At the end of each interview, I took the *propusk* to the security guard who glanced at it before opening the door.

The battlefront slowly moved closer to Pyatigorsk, bringing with it a steady stream of wounded soldiers and stretching the capabilities of the local supply of doctors and nurses. To offset the shortages, every girl and woman was recruited for "voluntary" hospital duty and trained by the Red Cross in basic patient care. Some of the soldiers were blind, needing assistance for everything from eating to bathroom visits. Constant cries for pain-killers were often ignored by those qualified to administer the drugs, leaving us to deal with the patients' shouts and curses. As an added complication, I was required to work the night shift, despite having two small children who needed me. The personal convenience of workers was of no concern to the authorities. Everyone must make sacrifices for the Motherland. Exhaustion blurred days into weeks.

I dreaded being identified as a German at the hospital, automatically blamed for every pain and injury that had befallen the Russian people as a whole, and these patients in particular. It made little difference that I was there to help them, in fact, was ordered to be there. Was there any way to combat this growing sense of alienation in my own country?

The interrogations continued, now on a weekly basis. The KGB showed no sign of relenting in their determination to obtain information. My answers never varied.

In March, 1942, amidst escalating warfare, eighteen-month-old Alla contracted measles from other children in the nursery. The doctor assured me that it was a mild form, however she needed a blood transfusion. It was a two-kilometre walk to the clinic and I heard gunfire echoing in the distance. When I arrived, they examined her but did not take my blood for a transfusion as I had expected. Avoiding direct eye contact with me, they wrapped her up again, murmuring vague instructions about her diet.

I was nearly home before I realized that something was seriously wrong. My baby gazed up into my face, gave a little sigh and died in my arms.

"No! *No!*" My screams brought a neighbour running to my side. *"No!"* With one look at my baby she knew. My feet were rooted to the ground, unable to move of their own accord. Leaning heavily on her, I stumbled over the last short distance to my house.

My mind blanked, refusing to accept what had happened. *They* said it was a mild case of measles. *They* said she would be fine. But *they* must have known she was dying. The tiny glucose bottles were taped to her skin without feeding into her veins. *They* had not wanted to tell me, and now my beautiful baby girl, wearing her prettiest dress, was dead. I willed this to be a bad dream from which I would waken to find her laughing at me. Or playing with her favorite spoon. Or just sleeping. But nothing changed. My baby was gone. I was dimly aware of the women who sat in solemn vigil around the little table where she lay, undisturbed by their songs and prayers.

The factory where I worked provided a tiny coffin. I watched in numb silence as others fitted it with straw cushioning and baby-size pillows trimmed with lace. Finally it was ready to receive her. She looked so peaceful lying there. In a way I envied her. The booming guns would never waken her to fear and trembling. She would never know the pain of losing someone she loved. I had once believed in a place called heaven. Where was that assurance now when I really needed it? Instead, I felt as cold and lifeless as the little fingers that would never again respond to my touch.

"Our Father who art in heaven.........." The words came unbidden from deep inside, piercing the fog. It had been a long time since I'd even thought of praying. *"Hallowed be thy name...."* Papa had often told me to keep the words in my heart. But did God, if he existed, even listen to someone who only prayed when disaster struck?

Because of the constant shooting, we waited for five days instead of the customary three to bury her. The shelling slowed at night and a small group of neighbours and friends accompanied Yuri and me to the cemetery. Religious services, or even symbols, were banned from funerals so Alla was laid to rest with little ceremony. The caretaker traced a tiny cross on the mound of dirt covering her coffin. It was done.

"Who will bathe her? Who will dress her? She can't stay there with nothing to eat!" Yuri was frantic, unable to understand what had happened to his little sister. I tried to explain that she was in heaven and didn't need food or clothing any more. "But I want to play with her!" he wailed. I cried too, for my baby and also for Mama and Papa, who would know much better than me how to answer the endless questions, Yuri's *and* mine.

Grunya came home again, grief-stricken over Alla's death and blaming herself. If she had stayed, my baby would not have been exposed to all the contagious diseases rampant among children whose parents dare not miss work to stay at home with them. I silently agreed, but refrained from voicing any accusations. I needed her support more than ever.

The war and its incessant demands allowed no time for grief. Neither did the KGB. The weekly routine became a familiar interruption in my life, now more irritating than threatening. One morning, pre-occupied with other thoughts, I failed to notice that the customary exit pass was not handed to me as I left the interview.

"*Propusk!*" The security guard held out his hand.

"Oh, I forgot." I turned to go back for the missing paper but he beckoned me to follow him down the stairs and through a dark corridor. I thought he was showing me a different way out when he opened a door and stood back for me to enter. In the dim light, it took a few seconds for me to realize that I was standing in a cell. As I turned to question the guard, the door slammed shut behind me.

"What are you doing! You can't lock me in here! I have to go back to work!" The bolt crunched into place and the guard calmly returned to his post. He must have known all along that the KGB would never *forget* to issue the pass. No doubt he had his orders but how could one little piece of paper make the difference between fresh air and this......hole! A rickety cot occupied one corner and I shuddered at the thought of lying on it, certain that it harbored a miscellaneous assortment of ticks and fleas. I avoided looking at the bucket in the other corner. What could this mean? Why had they waited until I was leaving the building before placing me under arrest? Would they advise Grunya of my whereabouts? I knew she would panic when I failed to return home after work. *Why was I here? What could I possibly say that would finally satisfy them? What would get me out of here?*

For four weeks I lived in monotonous isolation. I knew that other cells around me were also occupied, but was denied contact with anyone except my interrogators. Other than the time of day, my sessions continued as before. Now I met with them at night, usually after 11:00 p.m. The questions were the same, only with more emphasis on subversive activities by a supposed underground resistance movement. As before, I knew nothing.

Their schedule for me ensured that I never saw daylight and I lost all track of time. I slept fitfully whenever I was tired, my dreams a jumble of past and present where various members of my family appeared and disappeared at random. A few books and magazines were offered to me, none of them interesting. Constantly alone with my thoughts and memories, I wondered if I could actually lose my mind in this place.

The routine one night in early May, 1942, was the same as countless others preceding it. I endured their tedious questions for an hour, wondering again how long this stalemate could continue. The KGB did not quietly back down from a position or admit to error. How far would they go to obtain information they were so certain I possessed?

I had an unconscious habit of trailing my hand over the cold smooth surface of a marble table standing at the head of the stairs as I passed by on my way back to the cell. Tonight my hand brushed against a slip of paper which I picked up, idly rolling it between my fingers as I started slowly down the stairs, extending my limited freedom as long as possible.

I was always skeptical of anyone claiming to hear voices when there were none, and yet this is the only way I can describe the sudden inner command to stop and look at what I was holding. I unrolled the little scrap and my knees turned to jelly. *A propusk!* This insignificant little square of paper was my ticket to freedom, complete with the current date stamp and time. Could this really be happening?

But what if I showed it and the guard asked me for my identification papers? I had nothing with me and if he checked further and found me trying to escape, my fate would surely be worse than if I just quietly returned to my cell. By this time I had reached the door which led outside. Beside it stretched the corridor that returned me to captivity. My hand seemed to operate independently of my mind as I handed the pass to the guard.

"*Dosvedanya!*" He wished me a good evening and opened the door, locking it firmly behind me after I was outside.

What now? My legs wobbled and I had forgotten how to breathe. I leaned against the building, certain that at any moment my captors would discover the error and come looking for me. That thought gave new strength to my limbs and I started moving through the darkness, staying close to the building's shadow. I had successfully passed by one guard, but knew that others were posted at various locations around the property. Curfew violators, with or without papers, provided target practice for bored sentries. No one would concern themselves with the death of an undentified vagrant and, even without a mirror, I knew that four weeks in a basement cell had taken a toll on my appearance.

The nearby market, usually bustling with activity, was eerily silent. I avoided open areas, slipping unobtrusively from one building to another. Neighbourhood dogs noisily announced my presence and I clenched my teeth, certain that someone would check on the commotion. No one did.

Where could I go? Home was out of the question, partly because I had to stay on main streets to get there. Besides, this was the first place they would look for me, knowing that I was desperate to see my son again.

Paulina! She lived a short distance away across from the railway station and I was sure she would help me, even though our paths had rarely crossed after my marriage. Since our friendship was not common knowledge, I felt momentarily safe. I regretted that other friends would likely be questioned under suspicion of hiding me, but the only way I could spare them was to turn myself in and I was unwilling to give up my unexpected freedom. I could only hope for the best.

The most direct route lay under the railway bridge, a security-sensitive area well populated with guards. Then I must somehow navigate my way through the freight station with its stacks of lumber and finally scale a high fence. Deciding to avoid the bridge itself, I scrambled up its embankment and walked along the tracks, hoping to go unnoticed.

Shouts from the guards below told me otherwise but I kept walking. Perhaps the sport of hunting me in the darkness was not worth interrupting whatever they were doing to amuse themselves during the night watch. From their coarse language, I realized that they thought I was a 'lady of the streets' and therefore harmless. Tonight I felt no need to set the record straight.

I soon left their raucous jesting behind, concentrating on staying in the centre of the tracks. A sudden sprain would seriously jeopardize the next stage of my dash for freedom. Childhood play had trained me well for climbing and I easily topped the first perimeter fence, leaping from one pile of lumber to another until I was on the other side of the freight compound. I could see the house! Hurtling myself over one last fence, I landed unceremoniously in a row of bushes similar to poison ivy. But this was no time to worry about itch and I disentangled myself from the prickly nest, sprinting across the road to safety.

I knocked on the door, certain that I was creating fear on the other side; visitors after midnight were rarely bearers of good news. Paulina's elderly mother opened the door and when she saw me standing there, she dropped in a dead faint. Then Paulina came into the room and threw her hands in the air with a little shriek.

"Where did you come from?" She stared at me as though she had seen a ghost, completely overlooking her mother, now slowly reviving on the floor. Events in my life had taken such a dramatic turn that I had given no thought to the effect my sudden appearance might have on others.

Once past the initial shock, they brought me into their home, questions falling over each other more quickly than I could answer them. I learned that Grunya had desperately tried to find me, unsuccessfully asking the police and various officials of my whereabouts. Knowing of my dates with the KGB, she feared the worst. We all agreed that it would be better if I remained "lost" for a while until we could make concrete plans. Of course the authorities would look for me, contacting my friends and acquaintances, but recent developments gave me new hope. The German army was on its way, in which case the threat to me was almost over.

There was an unexpected complication. Paulina lived with Nikolai Petrovich, a communist officer sent to Pyatigorsk from Ukraine to manage the vast stockpiles of food which the government kept for military use. She pointed to the bathroom and when the sound of running water ceased, she nervously put her finger to her lips. She quickly decided that I would call her "Mom," temporarily becoming her daughter Emily, who worked in another city and had come to Pyatigorsk for a surprise visit. Nikolai had not yet met her so Paulina felt safe with this impromptu fiction, particularly since the train schedule made my late arrival plausible.

I was most uneasy with this arrangement. *Had I been miraculously freed only to find refuge under a roof shared by my enemy? Would he not question my lack of even basic luggage? And how would I explain my rumpled appearance that could hardly be explained merely by the rigors of a long train trip?*

I was spared meeting him that night. The next day Paulina, ever resourceful, took my key to Grunya's house and filled a bag with clothing and other necessities, secure in the knowledge that my mother-in-law was again looking after her nephew's children in another town, this time taking Yuri with her. If questioned, Paulina was ready with an innocent story about needing my clothes to make a pattern for herself. I desperately wanted to see my son again but she restrained me from even attempted contact with him. A little boy, happy to see his mother, would gladly share that secret with everyone!

I avoided Nikolai as much as possible, fearful that in an unguarded moment I would say something that would raise unnecessary questions about my "daughterhood." Just when I began to relax in my new role, he came home unexpectedly one afternoon when I was alone.

"I know who you are," he said sternly, his eyes holding mine as though daring me to deny it. "You're not Emily. You're Lydia Mueller." He handed me a sheet of paper covered with photographs. My face stared back at me along with ten others, all with German names, all of us hunted. My heart stopped.

"Don't worry," he continued, his voice softening. "I'm not going to report you." He went on to tell me how the day after my "release," the KGB had called an emergency meeting to discuss my escape — and who was to blame. It was a total mystery to everyone how I could have given the guard a *propusk* with the correct date and time stamp when no one had given *me* one. I told Nikolai how I had found the small piece of paper and about the voice that told me to look at it — about how my hand had reached out to the guard despite my fears of being caught without the necessary documents. Perhaps it was an angel!

Nikolai shook his head, at a loss to explain what had happened. But an *angel?* Well versed in communist ideology, he was on shaky ground here. It was safer to return to more practical matters.

"As long as I have a piece of bread in my home, I will share it with you." I tried to hide the tears that sprang to my eyes with this assurance of his protection, reluctant to let Nikolai see me as anything but the strong and confident woman who had escaped the KGB.

"But," he added with a twinkle in his eye, "don't tell your 'mother.' Let her think that nothing has changed."

I agreed, though a bit reluctantly. It didn't seem right to deceive the person who had sheltered me, regardless of possible consequences if she should be discovered. And yet I could appreciate that the need for secrecy be kept uppermost in everyone's mind. If continuing our charade lessened the danger to all of us, I would co-operate fully.

I lived there four weeks, virtually a prisoner again although this time by choice — and necessity. During the day while Paulina and Nikolai were at work, I spent time with her mother and son, also named Nikolai. If someone came to the door, I retreated to the pantry.

In June, 1942, a bulletin from Moscow crackled from the speakers, stopping people in the streets to listen. The Germans were coming and the Russian army had orders to retreat to Stalingrad.

They did not leave emptyhanded. Looting was rampant, the soldiers now more intent on taking property than in gloriously defending the Motherland.

Nikolai received orders from his government superiors to dynamite the massive supply warehouse which covered two city blocks. With German occupation an impending certainty, the wealth of food must be destroyed rather than risk its usefulness to enemy armies. A chauffeur waited to drive him to the airport where a plane for Moscow was ready to whisk him safely away when the job was done.

"Go on ahead, and if I'm not at the airport when the plane is ready to leave, don't wait for me." Nikolai's instructions to his driver met with a puzzled stare. "Go on," he urged impatiently. "I'll find my own way." The driver looked doubtful but did as he was told. It was getting harder and harder to know whose orders to follow. Nikolai watched until he was out of sight, wondering how long it would be before Moscow's wrath fell on him — and what form it might take.

Nikolai had reached a decision. He was a man of integrity, whose basic principles of decency survived communist indoctrination with its unquestioning submission to authority. Surrounded by people whose lives were controlled by a growing struggle against food shortages, *he* would not be responsible for lighting a fuse that would blow up a feast for thousands.

When the German army entered the city, Nikolai stood in front of the warehouse gate to prevent anyone from entering. The entire area had been mined previously as a deterrent to thieves and he wished to prevent needless injury before the devices could be safely removed. Officers on motorcycles rode up to him and tried to brush past him onto the property. They spoke no Russian and Nikolai spoke no German.

"*Mina! Mina!*" He hoped the German word for "mines" was similar and that they would understand what he was trying to communicate. They didn't, becoming increasingly aggressive, finally slapping him across the face in frustration. Paulina's son saw what was happening and raced back to the house.

"Mama! They're hitting Nikolai Petrovich!"

Paulina was frightened but helpless to intervene. She didn't ask me to help but I owed a debt of gratitude to her and this man who had risked so much for me. I wasn't sure what I could do for him. Would they even understand me? Perhaps I spoke a different German dialect than the soldiers now confronting him. But I had to try.

Swallowing my fear, I left the house for the first time since my midnight arrival four weeks earlier. Nearing the cluster of military uniforms, I saw one of them look at me and say in German, "She looks like she crawled out of a grave." I didn't really care whether they meant that I was pale with fear or from lack of sunshine; I understood what they were saying! With growing confidence born of anger that they would attack Nikolai, I approached them.

"*Guten Morgen!*" I wanted them to know immediately that language barriers were no longer an excuse for their behavior.

"*Ah, sprechen sie Deutsch?*"

I affirmed that I spoke German and without further small talk, addressed the main issue.

"Why are you hitting this man?" I hadn't seen it for myself, but believed Paulina's son. Nikolai explained that he had been guarding the gate due to the mines planted throughout the yard. "If I let them in, we'll all go sky high!"

Just then another motorcycle, this one with a sidecar, roared up to the curb. The little group of soldiers snapped to attention with a chorus of "Heil Hitler!" The new arrivals were evidently of some importance.

"What's going on here?" The belligerence in the soldiers' voices changed to deference tinged with fear as they explained the situation.

Still enraged by their treatment of Nikolai, I chimed in with my own report of the assault on my friend.

When the offender was identified, the officer who seemed to be a commander of the troops ordered him into the sidecar and told the driver to take him back to headquarters. Turning back to Nikolai he asked, "Can it be *un*mined?" I translated the question into Russian.

"Certainly," Nikolai responded, "however I need to work with the same people that planted them in the first place." He had been in charge of the operation but did not have the exact locations of all the devices. Removing the mines was not part of official plans.

I could hardly believe how quickly everything had changed. A few minutes ago, Nikolai had been struck by a German soldier. Now I was translating an offer of a car, driver and whatever assistance he needed to recruit the people who had originally installed the mines.

The operation was successful, although one explosive was accidentally detonated, destroying the motor operating the cooling system. Huge quantities of perishable food — meat, fish, ice cream, butter and eggs — would quickly spoil.

"Tell all your friends to come and help themselves!" I rushed back to Paulina's house, and then to my mother-in-law's, telling everyone I met along the way about the windfall. Starving people ask few questions and they took the warehouse by storm, arriving with carts, wagons, bags and anything else that might help them carry the bounty home.

Their gratitude to me was embarrassing. With the arrival of the German army, I was instantly free from KGB harassment, once again able to walk the streets as before. Everywhere I went, people seemed to know who I was, greeting me with hugs and kisses, thanking me for what I had done. They brushed aside my objections to all this notoriety, ignoring my assertions that I hadn't done anything. The food, after all, was not mine to give. I was only a messenger to a few people and rapid word-of-mouth had taken care of the rest.

I feared for Nikolai's safety. By communist standards he was a traitor and I shuddered to think what might happen to him. Not only had he violated an order, but in doing so, collaborated with the Germans.

"But I *didn't* do it for the Germans. I did it for these people."

I urged him to leave Pyatigorsk and to change his identity, growing more and more frustrated when he refused. It was easy to forget how often I had responded in the same way when Grunya urged me to disguise my German background with another name. My own stubbornness had finally met its match!

I wanted to shake him. Did he actually believe that selfless motives would shield him from KGB bullets? His decision was firm. Whatever the consequences, he would remain Nikolai Petrovich. And he would remain here.

10

The shabby treatment of Russian citizens by their own army convinced many of them that the Germans were their liberators and they welcomed the invading army with the traditional offering of bread and salt. Despite Papa's repeated reminders that every country is made up of both good and bad citizens, I still believed that they were a nation of villains and determined to keep myself at a safe distance.

The Russian army, now under orders to retreat, mustered a last show of force, trading fire with the Germans across the city. Their favorite weapon was the *kadusha*, which spit hundreds of pieces of deadly shrapnel in a single volley, causing severe injury to anyone trapped in the line of fire.

To ensure that the victorious Germans would have little to celebrate, they now bombed Pyatigorsk. The injuries mounted along with massive property damage, both from the explosions and the resulting fires. Eventually the hospital's supply of bandages ran out and all of us contributed our own sheets to the cause, tearing them into narrow strips.

Despite the ongoing firepower, a festive mood filled the streets as we rejoiced in our new freedom. Churches reopened and people flocked to the services, waiting in long lines to have marriage ceremonies performed and children baptized. I stayed away, uninterested in resuming my once active belief in God. While disillusioned about everything that communism represented, with my family life in ruins I saw little reason to believe that Papa's God cared what happened to me. Yuri and I were alone and it was useless to pretend that anyone besides me would look after us.

Shortly after their arrival, the Germans posted big signs requesting that all German citizens remaining in the area register with army officials. Despite the Russians' determination to rid the area of all "subversive" Germans, those of us married to Russians, particularly if we had children, had been allowed to stay, or as in my case, *forced*. I was curious about what was to happen now and decided that Yuri and I would go for a Sunday stroll to see for ourselves.

A large gathering of uniforms near one of the bridges caught my eye and I ventured closer. For such a large group, they seemed rather quiet and then I heard one voice stand out. He was preaching! Yuri pulled at my sleeve, impatient to move on, but I was irresistibly drawn closer. The words wakened an echo from deep inside. Once again I was a little girl with shiny shoes fidgeting beside Papa in the little Lutheran church in Nikolevka.

This time the words from the pulpit flowed into the darkest corners of my heart like springs in a parched desert. *"God loves you. Nothing can separate you from him!"* I closed my eyes, aware of nothing but a warm sense of well-being flowing through my body, melting all resistance in its path. Suddenly they started to sing. The melody was as majestic now as I remembered from long ago and my lips moved along with the words that I had easily memorized as a child. *"A Mighty Fortress is our God...."*

I could almost feel Mama and Papa standing with me, singing along. But even more powerful was the sense that *God* was right here! *Was it possible that he used the dreaded German army to let me know that I was not alone? That with everything that had happened to me, he still loved me? Cared about me? Even though I had abandoned my childhood faith as 'old fashioned?'* My cheeks were wet and Yuri was anxiously staring up at me, at a loss to understand how soldiers singing on a street could make me cry. He'd seen more than enough of my tears lately and I squeezed his hand, allowing him to pull me away from the group.

"Guten Morgen!" Soldiers approached me on the bridge. At first I ignored them, unwilling to let them know that I was German. They persisted, wondering why I was crying. The compassion in their voices was all the encouragement I needed and suddenly I began telling them about losing my family and the memories of my childhood that came flooding back through the music. I even told them that my uncle had been a Lutheran minister in Germany. They listened intently to my story, genuinely interested and (could it be?) caring. To my amazement, all fear was gone. Papa was right. There were good people in *all* peoples.

This newly discovered sense of God's presence always stayed with me after that day. I also recognized how he had guided and protected me in the past, even when I had discarded my beliefs as a school girl. I resolved to teach Yuri to pray the *Our Father* although I didn't know the words in Russian. It would be good for him to learn some German.

After years of displacement at the hands of Russian authorities, we were pleasantly surprised to learn that the Germans seemed determined to help with food, housing and jobs.

"Can you speak, read and write German *and* Russian?" The official's question caught me off guard when Yuri and I came to register. They were in desperate need of interpreters to cope with the flood of applicants, and to help them transact business with the Russian population. I started work immediately, Yuri at my side.

Despite curfews, the streets after dark were unsafe and rather than risk the lives of innocent people going to and from work, the Germans provided housing for us across the road from the office. Grunya once again cared for Yuri at home, coming to get him each day while I worked.

My newfound confidence in the invading army was shaken when a former classmate confided a disturbing rumor to me: German soldiers were ordered to shoot Jews. I knew that Jewish students had been removed from most universities and relocated but had difficulty believing that the atrocities she described could actually happen by government order. Since I now felt more secure after the Germans' arrival than under Russian rule, it was a good question for my diary. The opportunity to satisfy my curiosity came sooner than expected when Herbert, a German police officer who worked with me, stopped by one day for a surprise visit. We had become friends and although I never asked him about it, I was fascinated with the unusual strip of white hair on the left side of his otherwise dark head.

My diary lay open on the little desk in the room where he waited for me, my question the most recent entry. When I entered the room, he hardly greeted me before pointing to it. "I didn't try to read your book, but a blind man could hardly miss something like that!" His voice was harsh. "Don't you know that if an SS officer read that, he would shoot you?"

I was stunned. Of what possible interest was my little diary to the mighty Secret Service? "Why should they shoot me? I haven't done anything." I resented anyone taking that tone with me, especially in *my* home.

"Doesn't matter. If they don't like you, they shoot!" I saw genuine fear on his face and felt my bravado slide a notch. Maybe I should pay attention. Perhaps I'd been too easily swayed from previous fears by the nice people I'd recently met among German troops. I resolved to be more guarded in trusting strangers.

"Well, do they? Shoot Jews, I mean?" I still wanted to know.

"They used to, but not anymore. Now Jews are used for forced labor." I knew that. Approximately eleven thousand medical students, many of them Jewish, were brought to Pyatigorsk from Leningrad to replace workers who had been conscripted into the army. Or sent into exile like my family.

"Do you see this stripe?" His forefinger pointed to the shock of white. I nodded. How could I miss it? I often saw people's eyes drawn upward to the crown of his head, especially when meeting him for the first time. He continued. "One day we were ordered to shoot thousands of Jews into trenches which they had dug. The first group was in line at the edge of the trench and we stood behind them with loaded guns aimed and waiting for the command to shoot when a little boy turned around and said, 'What did I do to you that you are shooting me?' My arms went weak and the gun dropped to the ground. I couldn't shoot but I couldn't save his life either because other soldiers took over for me. That little boy showed me that these were *people* we were killing. We were always taught to think of them as disgusting animals, not the same as us. I was so shaken that a strip of my hair turned white."

I was shaken too. How could being Jewish, or *any* nationality lead to such mass slaughter? When I was growing up, differences just made life more interesting. How could one race be so threatening to another that masses of its people must be destroyed? And what kind of barbarism forced condemned people to dig their own graves?

My earlier fears rekindled, but now focused on the SS or death squads as they were known, with the lightning symbol on their uniforms and death head on the caps. Due to the secrecy of military operations and the subtle ways of gathering information, these symbols were often hidden. Herbert cautioned me about voicing some of my thoughts publicly; my audience might not always be who or what I expected!

The German occupation was brief. Unprepared for the short but unusually harsh winter, they were no match for the rejuvenated Russian army now on its way back from Stalingrad to reclaim lost territory. I was certain that the KGB would remember the humiliation of my escape from their clutches and their subsequent failure to find me. If they had concerns before about my involvement with underground activities, several months of German occupation, during which I had worked directly with the army, would remove all doubt.

When the Germans retreated from Pyatigorsk, I knew that I must go with them. My marriage to a Russian soldier, even though raising his child, no longer protected me and I was certain that the communist authorities would redouble their efforts to purge the area of all German influences. Besides, I was tired of war and, although reluctant to leave the Caucasus, for now I felt ready to relocate anywhere away from armies with their guns and bombs.

I had little time to prepare. The two suitcases lying open on my bed seemed to grow smaller by the minute as I alternately chose, then discarded things to take with me. Grunya urged me to take warm clothing, advice that I largely ignored. After all, I intended to return by spring and this unusually severe winter would soon be over. We packed and repacked many times before the lid finally closed on an assortment of belongings for both Yuri and me. Whatever else I must leave behind, the jewellery box stayed in the suitcase. As Papa said, we would carry each other in our hearts forever, but the box was a tangible comfort and I preferred to sacrifice clothing space in order to keep it with me.

Rummaging through my dresser drawers, I found a pair of Mama's delicately crafted underpants. I could see her painstakingly sewing on the lacy inserts, remembering my own despair of ever learning to make fine lingerie. I tossed them into a second suitcase which, besides some daily necessities and clothing, contained a random selection of tablecloths, a linen sheet, and, of course, my diary.

Grunya feared for me. As we sorted through my belongings she tried to express her concern with advice, trying not to scare me, yet convinced that I failed to appreciate the gravity of my situation. "You must always think ahead about how to take care of yourself. Don't depend on others to know what to do. Keep your head straight. *Think* but don't panic." She was trying to be helpful, but I couldn't help remembering that she had deserted me at a time when I needed her most. Missing from Grunya's advice was any reference to God, and ever since that wet Sunday morning service where he met me so powerfully amid a sea of German uniforms, I knew that my destiny was fully in his hands.

January 3, 1943. The temperature dipped to minus twenty-eight degrees with no sign of a reprieve. For now I welcomed the warmth of my fur coat, although in a day or two when the weather must surely improve, I would need some place to store it. Our bus was ready and besides soldiers, many of them too ill to join active troops, seven women and three men from our office waited to board. Most of the suitcases were loaded into one of the trucks in our entourage and the rest were packed into the trunks of vehicles carrying various German officials and leaders.

Grunya came to see us off, carrying my warm winter boots which I had left behind as unnecessary baggage. My feet, despite heavy woolen stockings, were already numb from the unaccustomed cold and although I still protested loudly rather than admit to being wrong about anything, I was secretly relieved that she had brought them. When she tied an expensive new cashmere shawl around my neck, I had a sudden lump in my throat. While she would never replace Mama in my heart, her care for me was that of a mother for her daughter. I felt a stab of guilt that I had not always treated her with the appreciation she deserved and resolved to change that when I returned.

She also had a suggestion, one that I was reluctant to consider. Why not leave Yuri with her? In the previous days of packing, every time I mentioned coming home by spring she had been strangely quiet. Now she looked me straight in the eye. "This is wartime, Lydia. You don't know where you are going. You don't know when you can come back. These decisions may not be yours to make." I wondered if she had really meant *if* I came back at all.

She was right; my destination *was* uncertain. Was this the best choice for Yuri? Did I really want to risk him freezing to death? These cruel temperatures were dangerous for adults, and subjecting a child to such cold was sheer folly. Neither of us mentioned the threat of an enemy attack on the road, although we both knew it was a distinct possibility. On the other hand, there were changing conditions here in Pyatigorsk as well. Was he safer with or without me? Yuri was my only remaining family. Could I risk never seeing him again? Wasn't it better that we stay together through whatever lay ahead?

I vacillated for an hour before relinquishing him to her. For now, his safety with her was more certain than with me. Besides, the war would soon be over and I would surely return in spring with a plan that would make us a family again. An all too familiar pain wrenched my heart as I held him close for the last time.

"I love you very, very much. Always remember that." His dark eyes stared solemnly back into mine, once again brimming with tears. "Listen to Grandma. Be a good boy." *Who cared if he was a good boy for Grandma? I wanted him to be with me, good or otherwise.* "I'll be back soon." I tried to sound convincing but my voice faded to a choked whisper. And with that assurance, I had to let him go. He looked so small standing beside Grunya, bravely waving goodbye. I pressed my face to the window until they were hidden from view, my tears freezing in icy drops against the glass. *Would the goodbyes never end for me?*

An hour after my departure, Russian soldiers invaded Grunya's house, looking for "Lydia Mueller, the fascist." Failing in that quest, they confiscated and burned all personal belongings, including mine, accusing her of hiding me. I had arranged that everything I owned should be used for Yuri's upbringing if something should happen to me, but nothing was spared, from pictures on the walls to valuables buried outside. Aside from pushing and shoving, no physical harm came to either of them, but Grunya knew that if they had found me, I would now be dead.

11

My company, SD-12, was the last group of Germans to evacuate Pyatigorsk. Our bus eased onto the main highway now choked with military vehicles, all part of Germany's army or *Wehrmacht*. Tanks, trucks, jeeps and buses all vied for space in a rush to outdistance the pursuing army which was determined to rout the former victors from Russian soil.

Surely this could not be happening to me. I was leaving my home. My country. *My son.* Alone. Each familiar detail of the passing landscape imprinted itself on my mind as though to ensure that regardless where this journey took me, I must always remember the familiar streets of home.

Grunya was right. I didn't know where I was going. None of us did. And I was terrified. The orders that directed our journey were radioed from afar and our only duty was to follow obediently wherever they might take us. My need to be in control had suffered numerous setbacks in recent years, yet I had never felt so helpless in my entire life. I was just a tiny insignificant speck in this massive exercise called war, and suddenly my confident predictions of returning in spring seemed highly unlikely.

We huddled together under blankets, as much to comfort each other as for warmth. I turned away from the window, unable to absorb the disturbing sight of bodies lying motionless beside the road. Had they frozen to death? Were they killed by bullets? Was someone at home vainly waiting to hear their footsteps at the door? Warming a meal that would never be eaten? I shivered, determined to keep my mind focused on my own situation, the tragedy surrounding me more than I could comprehend. Our breath soon frosted the windows, mercifully shielding us from the view.

We quickly learned that there is no guaranteed safety in retreat, and bursts of gunfire were a constant reminder that the battle raged only slightly behind us. Tanks at the rear of our convoy kept a steady barrage of firepower aimed backward at the Russians. The *Eisenbahngeschutz*, a special cannon-like machine operating from the railway track, had long-range capability which kept the enemy temporarily at bay. I still had difficulty thinking of the Russian army as the enemy, wondering if some of my former classmates might be among our pursuers.

The soldiers travelling with us, although unfit for battle duty, tried valiantly to keep a lighthearted atmosphere in the bus, entertaining us with jokes, songs, and stories. They were partially successful, but eventually we all withdrew to the futile questions of our own struggles and fears. *Was there any escape from our pursuers? Where could we go? Would we ever be permitted to return? Or might we soon be one of the nameless corpses littering the landscape?*

We drove continuously, stopping occasionally to refuel from the big truck accompanying us and, of course, for comfort stops which were anything *but* comfortable. Though we all tried to postpone the inevitable as long as possible, eventually the bus halted on the highway and after a frantic whispered survey, all of us needing to relieve ourselves took turns holding up privacy blankets for each other beside the road. These failed to shield us from the view of soldiers perched high above in tanks, but we soon resigned ourselves to the routine, hoping that their attention would be diverted with more pressing matters.

An already embarrassing necessity was further hampered by layers of heavy clothing, and icy blasts of fresh air penetrated every nook and cranny when they were removed. The men enjoyed an obvious advantage in this area and we tried to ignore their grins at our discomfiture. When Papa had talked to me about the losses resulting from war, he failed to mention dignity!

Periodically the bus stopped without explanation while leaders of the various components of the *Wehrmacht* conferred by two-way radio. These discussions were highly secretive, often resulting in a change of direction depending on new information about developments at the front. We could only hope that any decisions included our safety as a consideration. At least we had sufficient food supplies, both in the bus and in a separate vehicle. In other circumstances I would have enjoyed the picnics of bread, wine, cheese and *Dauerwurst,* a spoilage-resistant sausage especially prepared for military campaigns. Now I ate to preserve warmth and strength, tasting nothing.

We tried to sleep, as much to block our fears and worries as from weariness, but the rigid seats discouraged actual rest. Occasionally we dropped into a fitful doze, only to be jolted awake by a burst of gunfire nearby which set our hearts racing madly as we crouched down below window level, wondering if our bus had become a target.

There was ample time to think. *How was Yuri?* I missed him desperately, but comforted myself with the assurance that he was safe at home with his grandmother. Would Alexander ever return? I wondered again how a soldier could disappear so completely from company records. I still believed that the army knew more than they were prepared to tell us, but there was nothing I could do. And Mama and Papa. *Someday I will try again to find them.* It was a promise that I hoped to keep — soon.

Besides the pursuing armies on the ground, we were constantly alert to the threat of aircraft flying overhead. The solid phalanx of German vehicles stretching as far ahead as we could see must surely present an irresistible target to Russian bombers. My breath caught in my throat each time one of the planes passed above us but the dreaded explosion never came. Bridges were especially vulnerable, frequent bombing targets for either side. Whenever possible, the German army destroyed a bridge after crossing to ensure even a brief delay for their pursuers.

For three weeks we criss-crossed the countryside in a stop-and-go attempt to evade the battlefront. Washing hands and faces with snow was the extent of our personal hygiene. We finally arrived in Kropotkina, a city approximately four hundred kilometres from Pyatigorsk, still wearing the same clothes as when we had left home. Army officials knocked on the door of a house, advising its occupants that for the next five days we would be their guests while the supply of gasoline and food for our fleet was replenished. The front had, for the moment, moved in another direction and we were safe from attack.

Our hosts gave us their best. Everything was a treat, from a bathtub with hot water where I scrubbed away three weeks' accumulation of travel grime, to a home-cooked meal, and finally the luxury of a real bed. I stretched my cramped muscles, wiggling my toes against the clean sheets. Each of these simple pleasures used to be so commonplace and I could never have guessed when I left home that in three short weeks I would gladly have traded Mama's jewels for a hot bath.

During the second night of our stay in Kropotkina, we abruptly wakened and ordered to leave immediately. The Russian army was a scant kilometre away and there was no time to lose! Reluctant to leave our warmth and comfort of our beds, we nonetheless scrambled to board the bus, the cannons booming ominously behind us. Once again we roamed the countryside like homeless gypsies, narrowly evading the Russians' relentless pursuit.

A week later we reached the Donau River, together with hundreds of other military vehicles waiting to cross to the city of Rostov. To minimize loss of life in the event that the Russians bombed the bridge, vehicles were ordered to keep a space of approximately twenty-five yards between each other, further slowing the crossing. Our driver, anticipating a long wait, allowed the women to warm up in a shed where a blazing fire was kept stoked for the bridge guards. Record-breaking temperatures still held the country in an icy grip and we welcomed the brief stop. When we returned to the queue of vehicles our bus was gone. We stared at each other in dismay. What now?

Dietrich, an officer in our company, had accompanied us to the shed and he immediately approached officials in other vehicles to see if we might be able to ride with them. Each query elicited the same response: no. Every unit had its own orders, often subject to immediate change, and even if there had been room, the confusion of mixing military personnel and operations was more than anyone would authorize. With Russian artillery crashing behind us, walking was our only choice.

Civilians were forbidden to cross the bridge without military escort and we were thankful that Dietrich had chosen to join us instead of remaining with the bus. It was noon when we set out on foot, the warmth of the shed quickly replaced by the piercing chill sweeping off the river. I tried to keep my thoughts away from the very real possibility of an explosion under my feet which could hurl us to the frigid waters below. At least Yuri was safe and warm at home and with each slippery step, I thanked God for guiding my decision to leave him behind.

We reached the other side of the river intact along with hundreds of other military pedestrians, whose only immediate goal was surviving both the bitter weather and the Russian advance. Unlike the remnants of the exhausted German infantry plodding through the snow, we were suitably dressed for the extreme conditions. When I saw the rags wound around their tattered boots, I understood how an entire army, unprepared for the harsh winter elements, could be defeated regardless of brilliant battlefield strategy. Under my warm fur coat and hat I shivered on their behalf, wondering how long they could withstand the wind's penetrating chill with only thin overcoats to protect them. I silently thanked Grunya for insisting that my warm boots come with me.

I hardly recognized the bombed ruins of Rostov as the beautiful, bustling city where I had attended university. It had become the object of a Russian-German tug-of-war, each side alternately winning, then losing control, each battle raining bombs and bullets on a terrified population. All streets and boulevards were deserted, a noisy flock of gulls the only visible occupants. A biting wind whistled eerily through the rubble, now cloaked by a snowy shroud. I knew that the broken walls of these silent houses and apartments still sheltered survivors, no doubt many of them injured, and wondered how the damage could ever be repaired. And yet, the outer wreckage must be minor compared to the devastating wounds hidden in the hearts of the people whose homes and loved ones had vanished in one explosive second. Now they were forced to scavenge amongst the abandoned ruins to sustain what remained of their battered lives. Rage welled up inside as I thought of the anonymous pilots on either side who had returned safely to their bases, proud of a job well done.

My active lifestyle had prepared me well for this journey. Irena, one of the other interpreters in the group, was more fragile, suffering (we learned later) from tuberculosis. She withheld that information in order to spare us the obligation to look after her. Even so, we made frequent stops so that she could catch her breath before continuing.

Unable to hold up the flow of vehicles in order to wait for us, our division leaders had placed crude signs along the way, arrows indicating the direction that Unit SD-12 was travelling to ensure that we could eventually find them. We hoped that each corner or curve would reveal the familiar blue and gray bus waiting on the road, but each disappointment met with "maybe next time." Every few kilometres, we joined clusters of soldiers warming themselves around firebarrels fuelled by wood from bombed houses. Sometimes the crumbling walls themselves offered a short reprieve from the driving gusts of snow that stung our faces, temporarily blinding us. A special camaraderie developed among us as we held stiff fingers toward the heat. Without even a crust of bread in our pockets, we gratefully accepted any offerings of food from strangers. Faced with hunger, distinctions of rank and title were irrelevant. Each morsel contained its own storehouse of energy for one more painful step, one more tedious kilometre. I wrapped Grunya's shawl firmly around my head, allowing only eyespace between it and my hat.

Conversation was sparse, each of us conserving breath and energy for walking. When we spoke, it usually began with "what if....?" There were endless possibilities, each one more frightening than the last. Dietrich tried to keep our spirits up, assuring us that we *would* find the bus and the rest of our company; that we *would* soon be out of immediate danger; that we would *not* be among the frozen corpses that others pitied from the safety of their vehicles. Fear of being among that grisly number lent strength to my legs and I forced myself to go on, and on .... and on. I tried to think about God but even that was difficult.

God must be punishing the Germans for coming here! I remembered my neighbour's explanation for the extraordinarily cold winter; perhaps the temperatures that stubbornly hovered around minus thirty degrees carried a message to all of us. God could hardly be pleased with what was happening in the world, and it seemed quite reasonable that he might use dramatic ways of getting our attention.

Night fell. Street lights were banned due to wartime blackout conditions and Dietrich's army-issue flashlight was our only means of examining the signs for our company's location. Now we appreciated the snow which brightened our way sufficiently to keep us from tripping over the debris littering the road.

Fourteen hours and thirty-two icy kilometres after we set out, we finally stumbled, exhausted and numb with cold, into the bombed ruins of a windowless house, recognizing our bus parked in front. Other than a firebarrel with its welcoming heat, the place was bare of furnishings, and people from our company propped themselves against walls deemed solid enough to support even minor pressure. After days of cat-napping in a bus, which continuously bounced and swayed from one rut to another, everyone was ready for uninterrupted rest. Snores from various corners of the room told me that some were finding it.

12

Our journey, destination still unknown, resumed the next evening. After only a short distance the bus started to swing out of control on a steep and very icy hill.

"Get out! *Get out!*" Somehow all of us leaped to safety before the bus began its wild descent, flipping onto its side and rolling over and over until it crashed into a stand of trees at the bottom. Shaken by our narrow escape we stared at each other. What were we to do now? Even in the dim light, we could see that this bus had come to the end of its road, thankfully without us on board. There were things, including our food supply, that could be salvaged, but in the darkness it would be foolish to attempt the steep slope.

For the second time in as many days we found ourselves stranded in bitter temperatures. This time, however, there were cars available to drive us the eight kilometres back to Rostov. It was nearly midnight when we arrived at the house we had occupied earlier but it was now taken over by soldiers.

Another partially demolished house caught our attention, this one with a flickering kerosene lantern in the window. A woman answered our knock, fear widening her eyes when she saw the uniforms. Her voice quivered as she explained that she didn't have room or food for seven extra people. We assured her that all we wanted was a place to stay warm until the next day, even offering to share our supply of sausage, bread and cheese with her after we collected our supplies the next day. She motioned us inside, still wary but hopeful that the risk would be fruitful.

We had only been there about an hour when a bomb exploded beside the house. Amidst the screams and confusion, someone noticed the cupboard tilting precariously and shouted for help. By bracing ourselves against it, we prevented the weakened wall from caving in on the crowded little room, at least for now. Our hostess had dived under the bed, her bottom protruding from under the frame the only visible sign of her whereabouts. We dared not look at each other for fear of offending her with untimely laughter, but even an inner giggle helped ease a bit of the tension.

The next morning we learned that due to a shortage of gasoline we must travel by train. It was now my turn to board a freight car. Leaders of our division, still travelling by car, told us that they would meet us in Dnepropetrovsk, a city in Ukraine. All I cared about was finally leaving Russia's misery behind. Many trains waited at the station with hundreds of cars already loaded. To my amazement, many of the passengers were German people I knew from the Caucasus area, also evacuating. All around me I heard stories of Russian atrocities against their own people as the army descended once again from Leningrad to repossess their territory from the hated fascists. Fear squeezed my heart. *Was Yuri safe?*

Still smarting from our frosty hike two days earlier, I had a question for our company commandant. If trains had been available in Pyatigorsk, why were *we* required to take the bus? He gave me a don't-ask-me-I-just-follow-orders shrug. Government officials, both Russian and German, were masters at deferring responsibility for any action to a higher authority. The army needed us to work and we must all stay together.

The freight car was unheated but well supplied with bundles of straw. We burrowed into the prickly padding and managed to stay warm despite the ongoing chill outside. I appreciated being able to change positions occasionally, the most favorable trade-off for the dimness in the car with its tiny windows.

"Watch out for the mice!" It was a caution repeated regularly in the days to come due to the spread of a deadly infection attributed to the rodent. As if guns and bombs were not sufficient cause for worry!

Until officials were certain that any imminent threat of bomb attacks had passed, the trains remained at the station. At four o'clock in the afternoon they permitted us to leave. Six days later, after many long waits and interruptions to our journey, we finally arrived in the city of Dnepropetrovsk. As planned, we reunited with our company leaders who had already set up a makeshift office and awaited our services as interpreters. Reinforcements to the German *Wehrmacht* had held off the Russian offensive and we were presumed safe, at least for now. With little warning, local homes were once again recruited to house an invasion of military guests. Regardless of convenience, our hosts always graciously offered us their best.

Three weeks later, all the women in our company were released from duty without explanation. We were once again ordinary citizens, free to go wherever we chose. Three friends and I decided that Zaparozje, located in western Ukraine, was a good choice. *West* surely meant peace, a concept we scarcely remembered and sorely craved.

As we waited on the station platform to board yet another dimly lit, straw-lined boxcar, sudden shouts and commands sent everyone scurrying for cover. Soldiers travelling on the same train raced en masse away from the station, machine guns poised for action.

Curiosity momentarily overcame my fear and I edged my way down the platform for an uninterrupted view of the commotion. I stared in horror. Approximately one kilometre away and advancing through an open field toward the station was a solid wall of Russian soldiers! How could our hastily summoned troops running haphazardly through the field ward off what appeared to be an organized attack by a well-equipped battalion?

There was no doubt in my mind that a bloodbath out in the field was imminent, followed by another one on the train if the Russians continued forward as planned. Defenseless fleeing German refugees, hiding like rats in a boxcar, were simple target practice, easily dispatched in a hail of bullets.

I ran back to join the others, gasping my news. Some began to sob hysterically. I shared their terror but, determined to stay calm, decided to pray instead. Since God's recent reminder to me of his continued care I had prayed often, but never more fervently than now. Gunfire erupted, the crashing volleys sending us diving for cover under the straw. We huddled together, alternately crying, praying and assuring each other that everything would be fine.

After an hour, the gunfire ceased as suddenly as it had begun. We held our breaths in the quiet, wanting to believe that our prayers were answered. Our fertile imaginations invented fearful scenes in which bloodthirsty Russian soldiers sneaked up to the station, terrorizing the waiting passengers in a surprise ambush before killing everyone on board the train. There was, however, nothing furtive about the heavy boots mounting the platform. And the voices were speaking German! We had defeated the Russians!

After the past hour's tension, we were giddy with relief when the train finally pulled out of the station. Our high spirits made us impatient with the train's slow progress and frequent stops. Surely we could reach our destination more quickly by a direct walk than by remaining on a train that frequently altered its course. The temperature had, by now, gradually eased upwards into a normal springtime range and I was anxious to trade the dusty staleness in the boxcar for fresh outdoor breezes. My companions agreed, and we jumped off at the next opportunity.

Refugees clogged the roads. Young couples, children, and grandparents all moved in a westerly direction to find peace and safety, some on foot, some fortunate enough to have a horse and wagon. All carried with them their most prized earthly possessions, forced to leave many things behind which by now would surely be confiscated by communist predators. I thought of my own agonizing decisions about what to take, what to leave. At least my most valuable treasures were in the safe custody of my company leaders. For now, we carried a minimum of clothing and food in bags over our shoulders.

I watched the children trudging somberly beside their parents, many of them Yuri's age, and fought sudden tears. I missed him so much! Even so, my longing was tempered with relief that he did not have to endure these conditions just to satisfy my need to have him with me. I had been the same age as many of these when I had openly declared a hope for war. The little faces around me reflected the pain of what I once thought of as adventure, already knowing more of life's harsh realities than many adults.

The search for religious freedom in the West, now only a distant memory in Russia, brought many of our fellow travellers on this journey. Without any reason to hope for change in the foreseeable future, people of all faiths — Lutherans, Baptists, Mennonites, and Orthodox — abandoned their homes for a new life, although few of them knew exactly where they wanted to go. They adopted us as their own, willingly sharing food and fellowship as I knew Mama and Papa would have done. And, like my parents, they always turned the conversation naturally back to God and how he had led and taken care of them. Their faith was so strong, so uncomplicated, despite the inescapable agony of war's death and destruction.

I never grew accustomed to hearing about the callous acts of brutality that seemed so unnecessary, even in a state of war. We came to a German village apparently populated only by women and children. When we asked why there were no men, one tearful woman spoke for all of them, telling us how Russian officers had entered their town, ostensibly recruiting men for military service. This raised an immediate red flag in my mind: Germans were *never* enlisted for Russian army duty.

The rest of her story confirmed my suspicion. She told of trying to overtake her husband's "regiment" in order to bring him a warm coat which he had forgotten at home. After only a short distance she met a man on a bicycle who told her that the regiment was no longer where she expected to find them, that she should turn around and go home. Determined that her husband should be as warm as possible, she pressed on. What she found at the designated site was a layer of freshly dug soil concealing the bodies of German men, slaughtered by a few bursts of machine gunfire. There must be no traitors left to join the hated German conquerors. Her husband no longer needed his jacket.

When we decided to leave the train, we failed to realize that privileges granted to army personnel, such as overnight accommodation in private homes, did not extend to mere civilians. Our new freedom entitled us to sleep outdoors or in whatever shelter we could find on our own. Other travellers took pity, inviting us to share their wagon beds which, although hard, kept us off the wet ground. During the day, the air was warm and the road sloppy with spring thaw but at night I was thankful for my trusty fur coat, my only shield against the piercing chill of darkness. My boots, now caked with mud, were barely recognizable as the new pair that had rested on the floor under the coat hooks back in Pyatigorsk.

One night, desperate for a normal place to sleep and perhaps to wash ourselves, we knocked on a door to see if there might be an available corner where we could rest. My relief as the people invited us into their home was short-lived when I realized that pigs and chickens enjoyed free reign in this household. A picture of Nadia's father sprawled across a bed wearing barnyard boots flashed into my mind. That scene at its pungent worst was pristine compared to what I found here, but I tried to appear grateful.

I was awake all night, unable to ignore the pig snuffling in its sleep a few feet away. And why was I so itchy? By morning I knew. The walls crawled with lice. *We* crawled with lice. I remembered how disdainfully I had treated other children years ago if they failed to meet my standards of cleanliness. If they could only see me now! At the first opportunity, we washed ourselves and our clothes in kerosene, fumes radiating from us in a potent aura.

The trek to Zaparozje lasted a week. We found a place to stay through our new friends, relieved to have survived this gruelling part of our westward journey. The war was far behind us and it was time to do some serious planning. Without any orders from some shadowy, distant authority, we were free to do whatever and go wherever we pleased.

No one shared my optimism about returning to Pyatigorsk. The Russians, once again firmly in control, zealously committed themselves to ridding the area of all remaining German citizens. It was best to keep a safe distance. Reluctantly I gave up the idea, wondering if Yuri would be disappointed when I failed to come home. What if there was word from Mama and Papa and no one knew where to reach me? Perhaps when, or if, I ever had a home again, I could resume efforts to locate them. For now, there was little choice but to go forward. My survival, for the past few months, had been linked to the German army and perhaps the 'Fatherland' I had been serving would provide refuge.

Our freedom was cut short by a visit from the leader of our company, who had somehow managed to locate us amongst the migrating throngs. New orders required us to return to our posts as interpreters — back in Dnepropetrovsk. After a week of slogging through mud, sleeping in the cold, and harboring fleas, this man was *ordering* me to go back there? He was and I did, although none too graciously. Did the army think they owned us, jerking us here and there like puppets on a string without logic or explanation? The answer was simple: yes. And when the army called, every loyal citizen hastened to obey. Except, of course, that I was not even a citizen of Germany. I didn't belong anywhere for that matter.

For all my resistance, a secret part of me welcomed the delay to full independence. If I could not return home, Germany was my next choice and as long as I was with the army, I felt less vulnerable than on my own. This time we travelled by car. The roads still streamed with sad-eyed refugees and from the comfort of the vehicle, I identified with them; I too had walked in their shoes.

By the end of March, the German army was once again forced to retreat in their endless military see-sawing with the Russians. We travelled by car to Digenhagen, a German colony in Ukraine, where the residents welcomed us like long-lost family, offering us their best beds and food. We stayed there for a week and only here did I learn what to me was the most shattering news since leaving home. *My suitcase, containing the jewellery box, had been burned back in Kropotkina!* Lacking the time to restock adequate supplies of gasoline before our hasty departure, our commanders had ordered that all vehicles in our convoy must be torched rather than leave anything of value for the Russians to use against us later. I felt the color drain out of my face as the leader tried to explain how there had been no time to remove personal belongings. While sympathetic, his tone implied that we must all be willing to make sacrifices for ultimate victory. Besides, we were still alive and that was the most important thing.

He was right, although at the moment, I felt as though life had suddenly been sucked out of my very soul. Everything was gone! *All* of it! If only the jewels were lost to me, I could have handled it, but the letters... My last messages from my family were reduced to ashes and lost forever to the four winds. I turned away, determined not to cry in front of people who deplored soggy displays of sentiment when national honor was at stake.

The tears waited until bedtime, when I pulled blankets over my head to muffle the sobs that tore out of my chest until I could hardly breathe. Painful wounds of relinquishing my family at the train station ripped open with new savagery as I lost them yet again. Unconsciously, I had cherished the future moment when we might land somewhere long enough for me to be reunited with my belongings, when I could once again read the letters, my only tangible reminder of the life we had shared. And the pictures! The pain stabbed ever deeper. Would I never see their faces again?

One question nagged from the edge of the torrent: *Where was God?* I believed he *was* with me — had never left me — but why was he so determined to wipe everyone and everything that I held dear out of my life? Why should I, who had always basked in the closeness of friends and family, be so totally cut off, so alone? *"Our Father, who art in heaven....."* The words formed in my mind, if not my lips, gradually quieting the turmoil inside. I knew that Papa, who had impressed this prayer on my heart, often repeated it himself. I drew comfort from knowing that even as I prayed, God could see me *and* my parents and brothers — which meant that we actually had a link far more powerful than any paper message. It was all rather mysterious, but calming, and I eventually fell asleep.

Then, a small miracle. In the frenzy of packing and repacking before leaving home, I had included a few stray pictures in the suitcase which had travelled separately from the truck. Papa in his army uniform. Mama as a bride at her first wedding. Small pictures of Yuri and Alla. I hugged these to my heart, thankful to have a tiny record of my past life restored.

13

We stayed in Digenhagen for most of April, working at routine paperwork in the hastily assembled office. As it was a German colony, the interpreting requirements were minimal and to occupy our time we helped our hosts with housework and gardens.

In early May, a new set of orders arrived, this time directing our company to Poland. This was a move in the right direction, bringing me closer to my ultimate goal of Germany.

Our route took us through White Russia, otherwise known as Byelorussia. Our relief at leaving the Russian army far behind was short-lived when we learned of a new threat infecting the country. Here partisans, rather than the actual war, were responsible for much of the property damage and loss of life. Ostensibly aiding the Russian cause, they were feared more than the army and operated independently of laws or official structure. They were, however, well organized under their own leadership, surprise being a key weapon in their success. Whereas the Russian front was an identifiable location, the partisans struck randomly throughout the country, their attacks on terrified citizens followed by looting and destruction.

Our company leaders took these reports seriously, again zigzagging across the country in an effort to avoid an encounter. A favorite partisan strategy was to fire down on unsuspecting convoys from leafy treetop hideouts. We encountered several such ambushes, our soldiers returning fire with fire. The rest of us rolled under the trucks to escape the ricocheting bullets, huddled with arms covering our heads in pathetic defense against a stray missile. I tried to still the terrifying hammering in my ears with words of prayer on my lips, now a reflex response to fear and danger. I was more fortunate than many, receiving a direct but superficial hit to a portion of my anatomy that made sitting very painful!

Partisans targeted other means of transportation as well. During the day, along with other ordinary laborers, they repaired railway lines; at night they planted mines under these same tracks. Locomotive engineers, wary from past experiences, pushed gravel cars ahead of them which triggered the explosive devices before they could endanger the train and its cargo.

They used brutal recruitment tactics, sweeping into farming villages and demanding that people join their cause. Anyone refusing to co-operate was shot, like the young woman we saw lying dead in the street, her nine-month-old baby vainly attempting to snuggle against her still body. When time permitted, villagers fled to the forest with their livestock, leaving as little as possible behind for the pillaging bands.

After two nerve-jangling weeks on the road, we arrived at the Polish border. Before granting us permission to enter the country, the authorities required us to take delousing showers followed with a liberal sprinkling of medicated white powder. While I welcomed the assurance that I was bug-free, I longed for the simple pleasure of a hot bath and subsequent feeling of cleanliness without a chalky residue on my skin and clothes.

In June, 1943, I finally arrived in Lodz, Poland. There was still a long road ahead to Germany, but for the first time in months I felt able to think about the future instead of merely surviving the present. Considered to be part of the German army, we lived in a camp with other workers. It was clean and there was plenty of food, but I looked forward to the day when I could leave for Germany, where I would immediately find a house or even an apartment. After months of close and usually uncomfortable quarters, all I wanted was a private space to call my own.

We worked as interpreters in a busy office where people obtained German citizenship papers. Once again, I was thankful for my typing lessons. In fact, all my office experience was proving to be invaluable. As long as my translation and clerical talents remained in high demand, I could continue to travel under the army's protection and to enjoy its privileges.

We were painfully conscious of our drab, travel-weary clothing, sadly contrasting with the stylish dresses and suits worn by local women who eyed us disdainfully on the street. The weekly pay envelopes helped restore our battered vanities. Just visiting a dress shop boosted sagging morales! We discovered the delights of black market shopping, which, although very expensive, offered a wide selection of merchandise otherwise unavailable. At night we attended theatre productions or restaurants, largely frequented by German soldiers, and danced to live band music. Other than the family-shaped hole in my heart, life almost felt normal again.

Partisans remained a constant threat. Committed to ridding Poland of its German plague, they terrorized their fellow citizens, particularly those who refused to join their ranks. Our superiors strictly cautioned us against venturing beyond a particular boundary, even to a beauty salon, for fear of a fate worse than a bad haircut. We learned which shops and businesses had partisan affiliation, where Germans customers entered at their peril.

As a wife and mother, preoccupied in my own little world with work and children, I had paid scant attention to news reports back in 1939 describing Germany's invasion of Poland. Snippets of Papa's worried comments now came to mind as I heard conversations around me discussing the changes to the country in recent years. Agriculture suffered as Polish farmers were driven off their land, displaced by Germans brought in to take over the prosperous operations. Even with my new but limited grasp of the Polish language, I understood that beneath an outer mask of acceptance, resentment smouldered. Retaliation was often swift and deadly.

I now saw for myself that Jews were marked for special treatment, but still failed to understand Herr Hitler's obsession with them. When Herbert had seen my diary and lashed out at my carelessness in leaving it out in plain view, he also confided his own views about the German leader, whose impassioned speeches littered radio airwaves. Hitler, he said, was a fanatic and a danger to the entire world, which he was determined to control one corner at a time. Jews stood in the way and must be eliminated. While I knew they had been culled from schools and universities in Russia, I was unaware of any actual movement to destroy them as an entire race.

During my first ride to work on a city bus, I saw for the first time what it meant to be a Jew in Hitler's Reich. Our route lay through a Jewish ghetto, a fenced enclosure separating its residents from the rest of the city. When the bus arrived at the gate, a black-coated Jewish man wearing the traditional earlocks and black hat replaced our driver, the yellow Star of David prominently displayed over his breast. He drove to the other side of the ghetto, where a Polish driver resumed the remainder of the trip. The scene remained the same day after day, people sitting in their doorways, blankly staring, while the rest of the world went about its business. Most of them had lost their skilled jobs, leaving them with only an endless supply of bricks trucked into the ghetto from bombed ruins to chisel clean of mortar. Many of the women wore red lipstick, the only brightness in this pathetic little island of gray.

In June, two men in smart Nazi uniforms arrived in our camp, recruiting volunteers who might be interested in an official training program for interpreters — in Germany! What could be a simpler way of reaching my destination? Fluent in both Russian and German, I was assured of acceptance. My friend Theresa wanted to come too, and we packed all our new clothes and other belongings in readiness for the train trip to Dresden. The course was ten weeks long but we intended to find a way to stay there when it was over.

As I expected, the training was easy and both Theresa and I excelled in each of the weekly tests of skill and knowledge. Knowing both languages gave us a definite advantage over some of our classmates, who struggled with the unfamiliar words and alphabet.

In the fourth week of the course the instructors introduced Morse Code and showed us how to operate a transmitting apparatus which fit snugly around the waist. Finally there was something new to learn! I was ready for a real challenge — or so I thought.

Sitting on our balcony one evening, I overheard a conversation that changed everything. One floor down two German officers relaxed over *schnapps* and cigars as they discussed this especially bright student crop, unaware that one of them was shamelessly eavesdropping overhead. At first, I felt a glow of pride. Then I heard their plans. The best and brightest trainees were to be parachuted behind the Russian front to report, via Morse Code, all activities which could impact German military success. We were unwittingly being trained as spies!

I motioned for Theresa to come and listen, a shushing finger at my lips lest a careless word reveal our presence. We stared at each other, stunned by this little insight into German strategy unfolding below. Our newly adopted country which, as yet, had not even given us refuge, was already prepared to sacrifice us. We had assumed that we were being trained for safe office jobs translating documents. Having come this far, neither of us was willing to be launched out of a helicopter onto Russian soil once more! I whispered a quiet *thank you* for yet another demonstration of God's protection. But what now?

We felt guilty about hiding our new information from other students. It was hard to watch them intently studying, unaware that they were being groomed for a deadly mission. At the same time, we knew that in a group this size there were probably informers ready to gain the confidence of unsuspecting recruits and we decided to trust no one.

We gradually removed ourselves from the list of top achievers, trying to be subtle about our sudden lack of ability. Even so, one of the instructors noticed and asked if there was a problem. By this time, politics dominated the course material and our failure to understand enough to translate it correctly was almost true. I was totally disillusioned with Russian politics and its harsh treatment of innocent people. There was now little reason to expect more from the German version.

Three weeks after overhearing our intended fate, Theresa and I were sent back to Poland, our once-exemplary grades now "shamefully" unsatisfactory. We tried to show appropriate remorse when given the news, hardly daring to exchange glances for fear of betraying our relief. Our request to remain in Germany was denied, and for now we happily returned to Poland, wanting to put as much distance as possible between ourselves and the school.

The camp housed a diverse collection of people, all of us German but coming from various corners of Europe. I was disappointed to learn that even within a common language background, we remained in our various national groups and were judged accordingly. Russian Germans were generally scorned and placed near the bottom of camp hierarchy. I still failed to understand why minor differences of race or nationality should divide people. We were all equally homeless with uncertain futures. I chose to make friends across all these artificial barriers, deliberately defying petty social rules.

Through communism's mandate to wipe out religion in Russia, I had lost both interest and opportunity to attend church. The lofty domes and spires of Lodz cathedrals now rekindled my desire to be in a place of worship, although I knew that God could be found anywhere, even on a street full of German soldiers. Since leaving Russia, he had often heard from me in unlikely places but suddenly it was important to visit his house.

Uncertain what awaited us in a Roman Catholic church, Theresa and I slipped into the back, hoping to escape notice. I hardly knew where to look first. My spirit, starved for beauty, drank in every ornately crafted detail: sunlight streaming through the stained glass portrait of Mary and the baby Jesus; the apostles gazing down at us from recessed alcoves; the crucifix above the altar. I watched worshipers arrive, kneeling and making the sign of the cross before entering a pew. When the pipe organ's majestic tones signalled the start of a processional, I felt as though I could soar to the arches high above with their melody. There was a sudden lump in my throat as the music reminded me of Papa.

This service was special, marking the First Communion for children in the congregation. I supposed this to be comparable to the Lutheran Confirmation at age sixteen, which I had missed due to the forced closure of our church. These children were much younger, probably six or seven. There was a large group of them, each little girl dressed in white and the little boys in suits — looking much less comfortable than the girls in their fancy attire. The large number of boys fascinated me. At home, only the elderly, most of them women, attended the single Orthodox church permitted to remain open. Young people, especially boys, were conspicuously absent.

The Mass was conducted in both Polish and Latin. I understood little that was said; just being there was enough for me. They worshipped the same Jesus that I knew. Labels were unimportant.

14

German citizenship papers were our first priority, an idea shared by thousands of other displaced Germans from all over Europe, some of whom had been waiting for years. Again the army connection proved useful, and within twenty-four hours mine were completed. I felt a pang deep inside as I handed my Russian documents to the official sitting under a stern portrait of *Der Fuhrer*. *Would I be able to return someday? Would I see Mama and Papa again? And Yuri? Could Germany ever really be "home" without those who defined what that actually meant? Did the man across the desk understand that part of me was dying inside?*

The only thing on his mind was my health and whether I harbored subversive communist views against the Reich. There were two main rules of citizenship which he read to me in a voice bored from frequent repetition: I must not marry outside my nationality, and I must never give my new German papers to anyone under any circumstances. With a brisk "*Heil Hitler!*" and the regulation salute, it was official.

We were impatient to live in the land of our new citizenship, but instead were assigned to work in the same office where we had received our passports. As good soldiers of the Reich, we must be ready to work wherever needed, and for us that meant staying right where we were. Once again I found myself handling payroll duties.

Herr Meyer, my supervisor, questioned my determination to go to Germany. I wondered why he looked at me so strangely when I talked about the normal life I would finally live there, free from fear of enemy armies with their guns and bombs. I distrusted his motives when he told me that there was more bombing in Germany than anywhere else in Europe. Impossible! He just needed me here to work!

I understood little about the Nazi movement sweeping Germany. I didn't even know that our war involved the foreign nations of America, Great Britain, France and Canada. As far as I was concerned, right now any place outside of Russia was a haven, especially Germany.

He tried another tactic. Appealing to my love of shopping, Herr Meyer described for me the restrictive German system of ration cards, issued monthly and necessary to buy food, clothing, or heating fuel, all of which existed in short supply. It didn't matter how I spent them. I could use the entire allotment in the first week and have nothing for the remaining three, or I could spread out my purchases little by little. When the card was used up, I was on my own. By contrast, I could buy anything I wanted here in Poland, as long as I was willing to pay outrageous prices. I wished he would stop trying to scare me. Despite stories of bombs and rationed food in Germany, my determination to go there never faltered.

Weeks later, Herr Meyer casually asked me one morning if I still wanted to go to Germany. What a question! I had been chafing at the delay ever since the ink was dry on my citizenship papers, my temper operating on an ever-shorter fuse. He smiled at my eagerness, acknowledging defeat. I had his permission to be on a train leaving that afternoon. He wished me well.

My suitcase was quickly packed, but how would I ever complete the complicated de-registration process in time? Onerous red tape, rather than speed, was the trademark of the Reich and each of three separate departments involved a staggering amount of paperwork to be processed and stamped before I could leave. Herr Meyer pushed me gently out the door. He had made the arrangements earlier and everything was ready and waiting for me.

The morning passed in a blur as I rushed from one office to another, but I finally arrived at the train station, only to learn that my train was leaving from a different one across the city. There was no time to lose and a man passing by with a horse and buggy agreed to drive me there for one hundred German marks. We arrived on the platform with only moments to spare.

Herr Meyer was surely mistaken about Germany. As the train sped through the lush green countryside, I watched for signs of war but all I saw were farmers peacefully at work in their fields. Storybook houses, with white lace curtains at the windows and red geraniums spilling out of flower boxes reminded me of Mama. How I wished she could enjoy this with me! In a way, I already felt at home.

My contentment evaporated the moment I stepped off the train in Zwickau. Uniformed guards immediately shuffled us into a fenced enclosure, separated from the outside world as though we were prisoners. Ignoring our protests, an official using a megaphone announced that we would soon be leaving for our destination. Those with children could ride on a transport truck. All others would walk. A new acquaintance with two children hastily attached one of them to me so that we could both ride.

To my dismay, we eventually arrived at a camp. Built big enough to accommodate large groups of people, it consisted of a huge dining hall and barracks housing forty people to a room. Even to ravenous new arrivals, supper was barely edible, a glutinous mess ladled into soup bowls. After the meal we were each assigned a mattress with a thin blanket that left us shivering in the room's chill, momentarily distracting us from the rumbling in our unsatisfied stomachs.

In the morning we learned that we would be working in the factory next door to the camp. There had to be a mistake! We were German citizens with valid papers, issued under Herr Hitler's portrait! Why did they treat us as forced laborers? Did Herr Meyer know this might happen? Was this why he had tried to convince me to stay in Poland? Why was I so quick to believe only what I wished to be true? I thought of my narrow escape from a career in espionage behind the Russian front. How could I know whom to trust?

When we first reported to the factory, they gave us a lengthy set of papers to complete, listing our education and work experience. Many others in the group were professionals: doctors, nurses, teachers, and engineers. So far, the flow of information was completely one-sided and no one would tell us what the factory produced or what we would be doing there. I was certain of one thing: under no circumstances would I become a manual laborer. There seemed to be a mistake anyway, and as soon as it was rectified, I would leave the camp *and* the factory. Until then, I would work only in an office.

Determined to shed my naiveté, I refused to sign the forms, unwilling to put my name on anything which I did not understand. The administrator grew impatient, repeatedly assuring me that it was only an agreement with workers to keep factory operations confidential. When I continued to shake my head, eventually he gave up in frustration. I felt a glow of satisfaction at this small victory. There were no apparent ill effects since I was, as requested, assigned to the office, handling twenty-one thousand files pertaining to parts for *Der Fuhrer's* war machinery.

A few weeks later, without explanation, they released all of us new arrivals from the camp and gave us our own suites, either in private homes or, in the case of families, in a hotel a short distance away which had been converted to living quarters.

Though my job at the factory continued, I was relieved to have another place to call home at the end of the day. Frau Leissner, my elderly landlady, took a motherly interest in me, easing some of the aching loneliness that lurked continually at the edge of my thoughts, smothering me with a vengeance at night when I tried to rest. At least in the privacy of my own room I could cry without the added worry of someone hearing me and wanting an explanation.

I often lay awake at night, questions that I managed to suppress during daytime busyness returning to haunt me in the quiet hours. *Why was I here? Why had God taken me away from my little boy? Let my baby die? And why, when my parents were such devout believers, had he allowed them to be sent away by people who dismissed him as a fantasy? They* seemed to be winning this contest! I tried to imagine what Papa would say if he could hear my thoughts. He would certainly disagree, that is, if he was still alive, but at least he and Mama and the boys were together.

My office career ended abruptly when I was chosen to manage some barracks occupied by the workers brought from the east, or *Ostarbeiter* as they were known. This meant four weeks of classroom training, again in Dresden, followed by practical application in Leipsig. I preferred my first job, but for once did as I was told with only silent objections. Until I knew whether to believe the rumors about concentration camps awaiting those who rebelled, I felt it best to co-operate. I resolved to remain watchful, listening carefully to everything I heard without passing on information myself, or becoming involved in the noisy debates that waged constantly around me.

I had expected that nationality-based discrimination would disappear once I was a bona fide German citizen, but I soon learned otherwise. Two co-workers at the factory were particularly hostile, labelling me a 'Dumb Russian,' and therefore totally responsible for any losses inflicted on the German people. It rankled them that I, as one of the lower class Germans, served in a leadership role. They were not alone. One man, whose arm was severed in battle, bitterly hated all things Russian, especially me. I reminded him and everyone else that I was German by birth, and had struggled to maintain my heritage in the only country I had ever known. They, on the other hand, knew nothing of what it could cost to be German.

In the orientation tour with my supervisor, Fraulein Hansel, I quickly realized that my newly completed training was at odds with actual procedure here. The women had strung makeshift clotheslines across their cots, hanging rain-damp articles to dry while their owners went to work. She tore them down one by one, deliberately stomping on the clothes now strewn on the floor. Then she methodically checked under each mattress, removing any hidden food items or anything else of interest. "They have no right to these things," was her only explanation when I demanded to know why she was doing this.

On Sundays visitors came from other barracks, often bringing fabric or yarn remnants from the parachute or woolen factories where they worked. At the camp gate, Fraulein Hansel checked every bag and parcel, confiscating anything brought as a gift. I suspected that she kept anything of value for herself.

I was assigned three hundred young women, forty per room in the barracks. Every morning I wakened them in time for their shifts and ensured that they all appeared in the dining room for breakfast. If they were sick, I sent for the doctor. If they missed work for any reason, I was responsible to provide an explanation. Every sneeze and wheeze must be duly noted for office records.

I preferred to follow the principles of leadership that I'd learned during my Dresden training than from Fraulein Hansel's dubious example. It seemed logical that if workers had leisure activities to enjoy, they would be more productive at work. Camps were fertile ground for loneliness and boredom. And trouble. Lacking a *good* reason for getting up in the morning, discontented women easily created their own diversions. Wondering how long it would take Fraulein Hansel to report me for insubordination, I began building friendships with those under my supervision. Long conditioned to view anyone in authority with hostility, at first the women were suspicious and withdrawn, gradually warming to me when I repeatedly demonstrated my interest in them as individuals.

I knew I had won their confidence if they shared their stories with me, many of them evoking painfully familiar memories of my own past. Under tough outer disguises all of them grieved losses of family, friends, and vocations, with little hope of picking up the broken threads to build a future, even after the war ended. It was difficult to think beyond the bleak present and, although I tried to be encouraging, it was hard to tell them what I sometimes had difficulty believing myself.

One day the mail held a surprise for me — a letter from my favorite cousin, Amelia! My spirits soared at this unexpected contact with family. But how had she found me? Her family had also been forced out of Nikolevka, however by then she had already left the area to work elsewhere. Like me, she had married a Russian who had been conscripted into the army at the same time as she learned that she was pregnant. Unlike me, she knew her husband's fate. He died in Danzig, Poland.

Her letter explained that when it had become too dangerous to remain in Russia, she too attached herself to the German army as an interpreter, eventually arriving in Lodz, Poland. One day she had checked personnel files to see if she recognized any names from home, and had been thrilled to see me listed there, complete with forwarding address in Germany. She wrote to me immediately, sending a photograph of herself so that I would know that it was really her.

I immediately set official wheels in motion to bring her to Zwickau. After resigning myself to the loss of *any* family connections, this discovery became an urgent mission. I wanted her near me as soon as possible.

Our reunion was mixed with laughter and tears, both of us talking at once as questions tumbled over each other in both directions, interspersed with frequent hugs. Joy mingled with sadness as we talked about our families and the possibility that we might never see them again. About her husband. My dead baby girl and the little boy I'd left behind. Her baby would never know its father or grandparents. Our journeys, though differing in detail, were ultimately the same.

Much of her travelling had been on horseback, while the German officers' girlfriends rode comfortably in cars. Her voice hardened. Gritting her teeth, she had determined that whatever it took, she and her unborn child would survive. And here they were!

Amelia's arrival was a powerful reminder of life as it used to be, intensifying my loneliness for my parents and brothers. Her talk about the expected baby brought back all my own memories of new motherhood. How I missed Yuri! I longed to hug him, to read him stories, to teach him funny poems. I craved the smell of the woods around Pyatigorsk and wished that I could take him for a walk — perhaps up the mountain with all the raspberry bushes at the top. *How long would he remember me? What did his grandmother say about me?* I knew how easy it was to portray someone in my position as a bad person who caused trouble and was best forgotten. Though I wrote letters to them everytime there was an opportunity for someone to take it into Russia, I received no reply.

I never understood the automatic suspicion directed at all members of a race or nationality in the name of politics or war, becoming unconsciously defensive every time my Russian origins were mentioned. When a woman prominent in local government invited me to speak to various ladies' groups about life in my homeland, I was amazed to realize that their interest was genuine. I enjoyed these occasions immensely, telling them about my home and mountains in pleasant detail, momentarily without the pain that usually surfaced with these memories.

At the factory, however, the 'Dumb Russian' treatment continued unabated and eventually I decided to risk the Reich's displeasure by insisting on a different job. The manager shrugged. If I could find someone to replace myself within fourteen days, I was free to go. His tone dismissed this as highly unlikely.

Before I had a chance to make other arrangements, the camp administrators decided to reorganize the barracks into larger units, making one supervisor responsible for each section. Apparently my work was more satisfactory than they openly credited me for because they asked me to consider staying as a leader under these new terms. I agreed, though not surprised when I was assigned to a unit notorious for its problems. What better opportunity for them to prove that I really was to blame for everything that went wrong?

The women in my division were clever and well-educated. Robbed of the opportunity for a career, they refused to be intimidated by power-hungry leaders such as Fraulein Hansel, openly contemptuous of all authority. A major dormitory cleanup was due — an ideal opportunity for a showdown.

Every March the straw ticking in the mattresses needed to be replaced, walls and floors washed, and everything sprayed for bedbugs. When I met with them to review the project, I told them that as a 'little person' in the overall scheme of things I had no authority on my own, that my choices were directly related to theirs. In other words, if they co-operated, we would get along fine. If not, I must report them.

To everyone's amazement, especially mine, they worked hard, completing the job in record time, and with a minimum of complaining. They seemed to recognize that although I held a position of leadership, my life in the camp was difficult too. It was easy to encourage their after-work hobbies, especially their talents on mandolins and balalaikas. Music had been scarce in my life since Mama and Papa were sent away and sometimes the plaintive melodies filled me with a bitter-sweet nostalgia for happier times. Sometimes I stayed there longer than necessary, enjoying their company along with the music. Only a few of them were openly interested in the war's outcome. They sometimes tried to involve me in their discussions, which quickly escalated into heated arguments. I withheld expressing opinions as much as possible. As far as I was concerned, the tragedy of war had no winners.

Despite my success as leader of a difficult unit, critical tongues still wagged behind my back. I realized that I could not take it personally, that anyone disadvantaged, especially if a foreigner or *Auslander*, became a target for ridicule. At the same time I was fiercely protective of a Russian gentleman, formerly a mathematics professor, who worked as an interpreter in the factory. In his sixties, he carried himself with a quiet air of nobility, noticeably lacking in the crude behaviors among many of the other workers. His mannerisms and even the shape of his hands spoke eloquently of dignity and bearing. The camp leaders saw only his shabby clothes and poverty, scorning him with word and gesture. My cutting replies in his defense further antagonized some of my colleagues and we conducted our own private war within *the* war.

After all the dirt and danger of my journey thus far, it was hard to accept that Germany was not the peaceful refuge of my fantasies. As Herr Meyer had warned me, Germany received her share of bombs too. Allied planes with their deadly cargo passed regularly overhead en route to other cities, and at first Zwickau escaped enemy notice. Nonetheless, there were strict blackout rules and every evening we carefully lowered blinds and drew curtains, careful that no sliver of light from our windows should bring a patrol to our door.

A year after I arrived it was our turn. When the siren's ominous wail rose in the darkness, we scurried to the nearest underground shelter, each clutching a suitcase previously packed with items necessary for flight and survival. The narrow stairwells choked with people pushing and jostling their way to safety. Sleepy children, dragged from their beds, cried in terror at the crush which threatened to separate them from a parent's grip. Family members, desperate for reassurance that each loved one was safe, called to one another as the tide swept them downward. In the blackness of those moments, I longed to hear *my* name called — to know someone cared that I was safe. To know that I was not alone.

At first I joined other panic-stricken residents of my building in the basement, but decided that I would rather risk bombs above ground than burst pipes and suffocation from gas fumes below. Violating one of the strictest rules of air raid procedures, I slipped away from the stream of evacuees, flattening myself against walls to escape notice. I tried not to think of how quickly rock-solid buildings such as this one disintegrated into crumbling rubble with the blast of enemy explosives. My body trembled uncontrollably and I drew slow, deep breaths to steady the pounding in my chest. *Would the next shower of missiles whistling to the ground find their deadly target on my street?* The thought had barely formed when a massive *BOOM* rocked the earth under my feet. Dirt and debris hurtled through the air and I threw myself to the ground face-first, arms covering my head in a frail protective shield.

After an eternity of terrified waiting for a brick avalanche to bury me alive, I heard the all-clear signal. I lifted my head to a choking cloud of dust and smoke that seared my eyes and lungs, joining thousands of others emerging cautiously from shelters to examine what remained of their world, now forever changed.

In my blacker moments, I almost wished that a bomb *would* find me, ending my unhappiness once and for all. Then the idea of dying in the streets filled me with panic. No one here would know, or care. No one would wonder if someone should be notified; I was just a 'Dumb Russian.'

As I had just proven, the other alternative was to survive. Since God had brought me this far safely, perhaps he had a purpose for keeping me alive, even if I didn't understand what that might be. If this was true, the least I could do was co-operate. My parents were right; war was *not* the adventure that my foolish childhood imagination had craved. I hoped that some day I could tell them so.

One day Hans, another camp leader, failed to report for work. His colleagues clustered in furtive little groups and I often overheard whispered references to *Gestapo*, Germany's version of the KGB. It was an open secret that he regularly listened to the BBC, an activity strictly *verboten* by the Reich. Citizens who distrusted the official Nazi version of the news tuned in anyway, at great risk of being sent to a concentration camp if discovered.

The incident troubled me for days and I was again reminded of my discussion with Herbert after he read the entry in my diary. Ever since Mama gave it to me, I faithfully recorded life's events, good and bad. It was one of my suitcase 'essentials' and now weighed heavily on my mind. *What if my room was searched? What if someone less sympathetic than Herbert read it?* I could carry it with me, but if my handbag was stolen or searched the result would be the same. Was I unnecessarily jeopardizing my safety, perhaps my life, by its contents? I kept hearing his voice — *"If they don't like you, they shoot!"* The diary must be destroyed.

I looked at the stove in my room, a fire crackling cheerily in its rounded belly. The usually comforting sound now filled me with dread. With a heavy heart, I began to tear out the pages, wanting to imprint each of them on my already overloaded memory before feeding them to the hungry flames. Tears stung my eyes as I paused over the tear-smudged paragraphs describing the agony of parting from my family, hearing again the crossbar crashing into place, separating me from them forever. Now I was severing the final physical link between us, uncertain if it was even necessary.

My back-to-front ripping stopped when the handwriting changed from mine to Mama's. The book took on a new significance for me in that moment, perhaps because I too was a mother. She had given me the gift of life, but I was also a gift to her. And she wanted to share every part of that gift with me — every event that I might someday wish to recall, even if she had no way of knowing exactly how precious each memory would someday be. My hand caressed the pages, drawing comfort from touching something that her hands had also touched. My needlework lessons. My trip up the mountain. My illness and their fear of losing me. Even early references to my stubbornness. Tears rained onto the pages as I tore and tore until the book was empty, its cherished contents lying crumpled at my feet. Steeling myself against the pain, I stuffed them into the stove, watching the edges brown and curl as the embers burst into a lively dance, then quickly died into nothingness. There it was, the story of my life, reduced to a pile of smoldering cinders.

In a way it was symbolic. Now *I* was all that remained of my life — my hopes, dreams, and possessions. *But why? For what purpose?* I had an absurd need to ask my family's forgiveness, as though I had willfully purged their memory from my life. I knew they would never want me to compromise my safety for the sake of a book, even one that kept them alive in my heart, but the heaviness remained.

"Our Father Who Art in Heaven......" This tie was untouchable by weapon or flame, and I clung to it more tightly than ever.

15

If the sirens sounded during working hours, we fled to nearby mountains, hiding in bunkers until we heard the all-clear signal. Once we encountered German soldiers guarding a group of Allied prisoners and, fearing that they might shoot anyone seen running, we chose to stay in an open field while bombers strafed the city. Anti-aircraft guns responded and a plane came crashing down in a nearby cemetery, crushing the stone markers into powdery oblivion. We crouched together low to the ground, too terrified to move, yet afraid to stay as easy enemy targets. Just when we thought it might be safe to return, a bomb exploded beside us, sending deadly shrapnel flying in all directions.

A searing pain shot through my leg as a stray fragment imbedded itself in my flesh. I was bleeding heavily, unable to walk. By locking their arms together into a human chair, some of the other workers carried me back, first to the factory and from there to a hospital.

Later, while sitting with my bandaged leg propped on a chair in front of me, I received a visitor. Frau Seggelken frequently came to the hospital to visit the wounded, but I had met her for the first time only last week when she came to my home and invited me to come live in her house. The invitation puzzled me, but she explained that she was interested in cross-cultural experiences, and wanted to learn from a foreigner what it meant to be transplanted into German culture. Actually, I felt more like a German who didn't belong *anywhere* and while I appreciated her kind gesture, I declined the invitation. My personal effects still fit easily into a suitcase, making me quite portable, but I shrank from disturbing whatever fragile roots had taken hold. After my recent uncertain months on the road, without home or destination, I was content with a comfortable room and friendly landlady.

My injury changed everything. According to hospital staff, I must not even think about trying to climb three flights of stairs in my condition. Upon hearing this, my new friend returned to my home and packed my few belongings, only telling me when it was *fait accompli* that I was now her boarder. I was furious. How dare they treat me like a child! I was injured but I was also strong, and certainly capable of deciding such details for myself. Only when I realized that the elderly Frau Leissner was also concerned about my ability to negotiate the stairs, particularly since she could not help me if I fell, did I bow to practicality and accept my new lodgings with better grace.

Frau Seggelken treated me royally, waiting on me hand and foot as though I was a true invalid. She planted me in her rocking chair where I did nothing more strenuous than read stories to her children. When I assured her that I was capable of being useful in other ways, she brought me a basket of socks with holes as well as a supply of yarn, laughing at my blank stare. How could a woman reach my age without learning the art of darning from her mother? I smiled to myself. She couldn't begin to know just how many even more important lessons Mama had neglected to share with me! Compared to those, darning was a minor oversight. Frau Seggelken graciously offered to teach me yet another needle skill, and though I was less than enthusiastic, it would have been ungrateful to refuse since she had adopted me as one of her own family.

As part of this family, I also shared their table. War was quickly depleting the nation's food supply and I was pleased when she invited me to eat with them. Their meals had much more variety (and quantity) than I could manage alone. It had been years since I'd been offered second servings and I savored each morsel, especially meat. In return, I gave her my ration cards, in a small way helping to supplement the supply of staples. She and her husband, a geologist, owned a farm near Berlin and the harvest of fresh vegetables was a delicious change from the meager selection at local markets.

The wound in my leg healed and I reluctantly returned to work. The peaceful acceptance in my new home sharpened the contrast of the factory environment where I was still the 'Dumb Russian.' I longed to be away from there permanently. The opportunity came sooner than I expected.

Besides the air raid siren, there was also an enemy alarm which indicated that we might be surrounded, but did not mean an automatic evacuation. On one such occasion, I missed hearing a general order that all the employees must leave the camp, however no one came to tell me. Engrossed in my work, by the time I noticed that I was alone, all the others were returning. While their failure to notify me may have been an honest (and dangerous!) mistake, intuitively I felt it was deliberate.

"You're not going back there!" Frau Seggelken's assessment of the incident was the same as mine. We had received new orders to stay away from the factory for three days and she encouraged me to extend my leave — forever! Despite official reports of glorious victories, there were increasing rumors that Germany's defeat was imminent. If this was true, American armies would be arriving at any time, in which case the factory was obsolete. The war machine was *kaput*.

Herr and Frau Seggelken, fearing a spree of rape and murder at the hands of victorious American soldiers, left Zwickau for the comparative safety of their farm. They invited me to join them, but I preferred to remain in the city where it seemed easier to plan for the future. One of my friends, also named Lydia, stayed with me and although my landlords were reluctant at first to leave us on our own, they were also relieved that the house would not sit empty during the uncertain days ahead. They gave me a massive collection of keys for every cupboard and desk in the entire house, advising me that in the event of robbery, they preferred that I open all the locks rather than risk serious damage through forced entry.

May 8, 1945. The war was over, Germany defeated. More important than who won or lost was the almost deafening silence of guns and cannons. Allied planes now dropped only pamphlets on conquered cities, requesting orderly surrender. Nazi swastikas and uniforms disappeared from Zwickau streets, replaced by a convoy of jeeps carrying hundreds of American troops — and all of them were black! Lydia and I watched in amazement from the second-storey window as the unfamiliar uniforms passed by below. *Were there only black people in the American army?* My question was answered a short time later as another convoy of jeeps passed by, this one with only white soldiers.

Needing space to house the troops, one of their first acts of liberation was to empty the camps, freeing all the *Ostarbeiter,* some of whom immediately made arrangements to return home. I was horrified by stories of how others gained access to machine guns, using them to terrorize local citizens by forcing them out of their homes and then stealing everything they could carry. We heard reports that the Americans actually gave them permission to loot and pillage at will for seven days. From my second-storey window I watched as Russian girls, some of whom I recognized, carried bags and boxes of merchandise stolen from stores, laughing and giggling as they compared booty.

I was thankful that in the entire time I had worked in the camp, I had not divulged my address to the women, despite their curious attempts to find out where I lived. Frau Seggleken had cautioned me to stay indoors in order to avoid a possible meeting with anyone who knew me from the factory. They all knew of my Russian background, but she feared that some in my group might find this a perfect opportunity for vengeance against anyone representing German authority. I reluctantly agreed. It was difficult to decide which side of the German-Russian fence was most dangerous to me at any given time.

Though the threat of bomb attacks was over, Germany was far from peaceful. The defeated government had not yet been replaced and anarchy ruled the streets. People feared for their safety, particularly with no controls placed on rampaging workers with their newfound liberties. The situation came to a head when *Ostarbeiter,* looting a train for coveted American uniforms, were shot and killed. After the state of chaos which they had encouraged, the American soldiers themselves resorted to violence in order to restore a semblance of order.

The Seggelkens had built their home with tight security. Surrounded by a high concrete fence and railing, its fortress-like appearance instantly attracted the attention of American officials seeking a base. Lydia and I rarely left our posts by the window, noticing with some apprehension that our house was undergoing close scrutiny. When the gate buzzer sounded, I ignored it, hoping they would go away. Well accustomed to barriers in the battlefields, soldiers in top physical form easily cleared the fence, all carrying machine guns. Now they pounded on the door.

My heart echoed each thump and taking a deep breath I opened the door, hoping that my face showed a proper disdain.

The soldiers pleasantly informed me that this house was now the headquarters of the American army in Zwickau as long as it was needed. My friend and I would remain in residence and keep house for them. It was an order. From now on, the house was off limits to visitors and, for security reasons, we were forbidden to leave the premises.

I now felt like a prisoner in the house where I had always come and gone in total freedom. At the same time, I appreciated the sense of security that came from seeing armed guards patrolling the front gate. Spring breezes and budding flowers beckoned me outside but the streets were still unsafe for ordinary citizens. For now, I had to be content with looking out the window. Meanwhile, my 'captors' provided an interesting diversion.

The commander wrote daily letters to someone in America named Frances, always coating his mouth liberally with lipstick before sealing the envelope with a greasy pink kiss. The cook planned to be a millionaire by the time he arrived home, constantly in search of golden opportunities for profit. He dried used coffee grounds and mixed them with a small measure of new coffee, for sale at exorbitant prices on Germany's thriving black market. Cigarettes sent from home found willing buyers at eight times their original price.

One day when I showed signs of rebellion at my captivity, they gave me reluctant permission to visit Amelia, who lived nearby with her new baby boy. When she saw me at her door her eyes widened with fear.

"You must be very careful," she cautioned, pulling me quickly inside. "The house next door is full of people from the same camp where you worked, and they have already killed one leader!" I knew that my cloistered existence in the American base shielded me from most of what was happening in the rest of the world, but surely this could not be true! She nodded vigorously, lowering her voice to a whisper as she described how they had cut him in pieces and thrown him in the river. Several other leaders had been severely beaten and robbed by their former subordinates.

I wanted to believe that my efforts to befriend the women would protect me now. At the same time, I represented years of hated German authority, and there was no reason to think that I might escape similar treatment. The principle of *do unto others as you would have them do unto you* seemed out of place in war and its aftermath. I regretted my foolish determination to make this visit, already dreading the short walk home.

The sun was low in the sky when I set out. I had nearly reached the house when I saw a girl standing on the street corner whom I recognized from the camp. She was argumentative and rebellious and I could easily imagine her thirst for vengeance. I shivered, wondering how I could avoid this meeting but she had already seen me coming.

"*Heil Hitler!*" Her voice was heavy with sarcasm as she stiff-armed the Nazi salute, no doubt practiced regularly in jest with her friends. She calmly informed me that now she was free to hit me if she felt like it.

"Why would you do that?" I forced my voice to remain casual, hoping that my face would not betray the fear hammering in my chest. "What have I done to you?"

There was nothing, of course, except the giddy sense of power that came with knowing the 'Master Race' was defeated, together with the pleasure of humiliating any of its members. In dormitory discussions, she always tried to force others to bet on the ultimate winner of the war, Stalin or Hitler. I had steered clear of making predictions and now reminded her what I'd said during their heated debates; none of us, whether Russian or German, could determine the war's outcome. Our role would be to cope with the results.

She lost some of her aggressiveness, but still tried to impress me with her bold new freedom. I asked her why she was still here instead of returning home with the trainloads of other displaced Russians who were anxious to shake German soil from their tattered soles. They were taken to Chemnitz, a point where prisoner exchanges were made between the nations representing East and West.

"Oh I've already been to Chemnitz," she replied airily. "I saw them separating men, women and children into different trains, I think," her voice lowered, "to send them to Siberia. I like it better here so I came back." She proudly went on to tell me that she and her friends had a car which they had commandeered from its owners, along with their house. I was sickened to know that those who only last week had been oppressed, now found such joy in being the oppressors.

While I disagreed with their tactics, I could understand the motivation behind them. Of all the foreigners brought to Germany to labor in camps and factories, workers from the east, primarily from Russia, Ukraine, and Poland, were treated the worst. Even though performing the same tasks as the French, Italians and Czechs, they received poorer quality food, often inedible, and in disciplinary matters, much harsher treatment. Any opportunity to lash out in revenge, however brief, was welcomed without scruple.

We parted without incident but her news about Chemnitz was alarming. The threat of deportation to Siberia was very real, should I decide to try to return home as originally planned. My immediate concern, however, was for some friends and their children who had recently made that journey. They had entered Germany with me and were also now officially German citizens. I feared that their fate upon entering Russia would be even worse than Siberian exile.

My fears increased when I learned that the American soldiers had transported all the families living in the former hotel to Chemnitz. These housing arrangements were made at the same time as I found my first home, and all these people, like me, were legal German citizens.

"We have papers! We have ration cards just like everyone else!" Their desperate cries went unheeded as disinterested soldiers, acting on orders to return all Russians to Russia, rounded them up in trucks. Ignoring all protests, the convoy sped off with yet another delivery in an endless collection of displaced people. A well-timed walk in the park with their children was all that saved two of my friends from this evacuation. When they returned from the outing, the place was completely deserted.

Many felt compelled to return to Russia despite the risks. I knew that I could never safely go back, but perhaps I could reach my son through others. With every opportunity, I sent letters to Yuri, to my mother-in-law, and even to Alexander's cousins. I had no way of knowing if the letters, or those entrusted to deliver them, ever reached their destination, but I felt better making the effort.

16

The war was over but life remained complicated. Negotiations were underway for new national borders and to my dismay, I learned that Zwickau's corner of Germany would soon be under Russian control! *What now?* A group of us gathered to discuss our limited options. Our citizenship papers allowed us to move only inside a six-kilometre radius of Zwickau, well within soon-to-be Russian territory. All of us were anxious to move on, but how? And where?

The Russians, already authorized to take anything they wanted from the area, focused on the silent and deserted factories. They dismantled everything, loading the pieces onto railway cars for transport to Russia. The new owners were unfamiliar with their new equipment and reluctant German machine operators were "invited" to accompany the load. We knew it was just a matter of time before official interest turned from machinery to people. Whatever we planned to do must happen quickly.

"Lydia!" Hearing my name called loudly set my heart racing. Some control was now restored to the streets after the initial chaos, but I was still wary about visiting the shops. Two women from the camp, with whom I'd developed as close a friendship as circumstances permitted, raced to catch up with me. I was delighted to see them. In our brief chat they made several references to me as their leader but I stopped them immediately. That role belonged to another time when we all had different orders to follow.

"Do you want to stay here, or would you rather leave?" What a question! I explained that my friends and I had discussed it at length, but were limited by the six-kilometre rule.

"We're all going west to Turingen with the Americans. Why don't you come too?"

"My status is different than yours," I explained. "I am now a German citizen, whereas you were foreign workers. They won't let me go with you."

"No, no, you can come too! Do you have forty marks? We can get you a Red Cross card and you can come with us!" Their excitement was contagious and I felt a flicker of hope. Of course I had the money, but could it really be so simple? And what about my rather large company of friends?

No problem! Forty *Deutschmarks* per person guaranteed passage out of the Russian danger zone for each of us.

Everything happened quickly. The cards were delivered as promised, together with notice that the train would leave in three days. Once again I packed a bag with my few worldly possessions, thinking of how my definition of *essential* had changed in the past few years. I wondered if I would ever again know what it meant to surround myself with comfort and pretty things.

My excitement at finding a way out was dampened by Amelia's refusal to join our group. I understood her reluctance to begin yet another uncertain journey, especially with a new baby, but at the same time I feared what could happen to both of them under Russian rule. She placed more confidence in her new citizenship papers than I did, and remained firm in her decision to stay. Perhaps after everything settled down and her baby was a bit older she would rejoin me. Meanwhile, we would stay in contact by letter. My heart was heavy as I hugged her good-bye. Present opportunities rarely waited for future convenience.

The departure time was suddenly moved up by two days and we scrambled to meet the new schedule. We arrived at the station, stacking our belongings together on the platform amidst a swirl of activity. *"Have you seen......? I told him to meet us near the...... Did you bring the.......?"* Voices were fraught with panic as anxious passengers scanned the bustling throngs for *that* person who must not stay behind. Hundreds of empty cars awaited and I dreaded the order to board for fear of being trampled. This station totally lacked personnel and, apart from the engineers operating the trains, no one seemed to be in charge.

With much pushing and shoving we eventually all found places for ourselves and our baggage, settling in as comfortably as the hard floors and walls allowed. As the train slowly pulled out of the station, I had second thoughts about what we were doing. How did we really know that we were going to the west? I knew that the train's route took us through Chemnitz but what if it didn't veer off to the west as expected? What if it stopped there and allowed officials to inspect the passengers? I knew that on one pretext or another, all of us could be detained, and from here, returned to whatever Russian fate was deemed suitable for German 'collaborators'. I kept my thoughts to myself but withdrew from the exuberant conversation and laughter around me.

Yuri was never far from my thoughts, and every time I faced relocation or a new situation, I wondered if this decision increased or reduced any chances of seeing him again. Now that the war was over and stability was slowly being restored, I promised myself that I would double my efforts to find out if there was any way that we could be together again. Perhaps I could locate Mama and Papa too!

Engrossed with thoughts of my family, I hardly noticed that the Chemnitz station was speeding by, with no sign that the train might be slowing down. On the platform, uniformed guards with machine guns slung over their shoulders shouted,

"Welcome home! Welcome to your country! Comrade Stalin welcomes you!"

The car fell silent. Freedom was close, but not yet a reality. If the train stopped, the warm words of welcome would quickly become menacing orders.

But the train continued on its way, curving gradually to the west. *Thank you, Lord.* With that involuntary little prayer, the tension in my stomach eased. When the last car cleared the station, pandemonium erupted. Free at last of Russian threat, my fellow travellers alternately cheered their futures and cursed the villains of their pasts, still within view.

A short time later the train stopped in the middle of some fields where American soldiers waited. They boarded the cars and with the help of interpreters, checked our papers, including the Red Cross cards. *Where were we from? Where did we wish to go?* Our immediate goal was to be as far removed from Russian control as possible, and beyond that, who could say what we might do? Life unfolded one day at a time, and it was better to expect surprises than to risk the disappointment of thwarted plans.

The train, now under American control, continued to its final destination of Eisenach where transport trucks waited to take us to some former army barracks already overflowing with countless other refugees. We held back, unwilling to be absorbed into a human holding tank while authorities decided our fate. Just processing the inevitable mountain of paper for all these displaced people could take months or even years.

We approached some railway employees, hoping that they might know of other accommodation. They directed us to other still-empty barracks and we moved in, happy to escape the crush of people all looking for a stray corner to call their own.

Our stay was limited to four days. Non-residents of towns and cities must keep moving due to a housing shortage. Many buildings in which people sought shelter were extremely unstable, often collapsing on those inside, and local authorities were ill-equipped to cope with both rescue attempts plus the daily influx of new arrivals. But where should we go? How would we get there?

One of my friends knew someone living in Wurtzburg, designated a Red Cross city and exempt from bombing raids. This surely meant solid houses, and therefore no restrictions placed on non-residents. Once again we approached the railway employees for assistance. Trains usually stopped at this station only to replenish water and coal supplies, but for a small fee, they agreed to arrange our passage.

We were ready and waiting on the platform, loading our belongings into the open freight car as quickly as we could. Not quickly enough, however. A woman and her two children, who guarded the pile of baggage while we loaded, were left behind when the train suddenly pulled out of the station. We couldn't get off and she couldn't get on. At every subsequent stop we quickly posted signs directing her to Hanau, a main station, where she could hopefully soon rejoin our group.

We waited at the station for two days watching a steady stream of freight trains pass by, many of them carrying Russian passengers on their way back home. I wondered if any of them would actually get there. We took turns guarding our belongings, leaving others free to explore the town and to buy food.

One evening I overheard several young Russian men, who stood in the open doorway of a waiting freight car, making bold plans to steal our things when their train was ready to depart. "That's what you think!" I said to myself, giving no sign that I understood every word. When the others returned, I ordered them to move everything onto one big pile, covering it all with blankets and sitting on it. Their plot foiled, our would-be thieves cursed us from a distance, redirecting their attention to more careless victims.

While we had travelled beyond the current Russian zone, the threat of being returned was not yet behind us. Aware that many of their former citizens now carried valid German papers, Russian soldiers considered it sport to locate them, forcibly returning them to Russian soil. Germany, in its ongoing state of chaos, would offer no reprisals. A favorite ploy was to approach a 'suspect' and to ask a simple question in Russian, hoping for a reflex Russian response in an unguarded moment.

My friend Lydia, warned repeatedly about indiscreet responses which placed all of us at risk, was nearly dragged away after telling two strangers the time — in Russian. She was rescued by American Military Police, who demanded that the Russians release her as they had no authority in this region.

After waiting four long days, our patience was rewarded. Sitting under some tanks on an incoming freight train was my friend and her two children, as well as the rest of the baggage left in her care. What a relief! We had been reluctant to leave without them, yet realized that we could no longer postpone our departure.

Now that we were ready to move on, all the trains seemed to be going back in the direction from which we'd come. "Trains to Wurtzburg leave from over there."

A man motioned toward tracks far removed from where we waited. But how to get there? Directly crossing the tracks was out of the question. Trains were always in motion and even if one was stopped, it could start moving without warning with unspeakable consequences for anyone attempting to cross underneath. We had no transportation which could take us and our belongings miles around to the other side by road.

Hungry German soldiers came to our aid. Also waiting to return to their homes and lacking their previous authority to force others to help them, some had not eaten for days. We had extra supplies and negotiated a deal with them. If they would help us get to the right platform for Wurtzburg, we would share our food. Without hesitation, each took one or two items of baggage, crawling under the stationary boxcars until they reached the right tracks. We took courage from their example, eventually arriving at the specified platform with all body parts intact.

Now all we needed was a train with room for passengers to take us the rest of the way. Train after heavily loaded train passed by without stopping. Those that did stop were already overcrowded. Just when we were ready to give up, American soldiers rescued us. Rearranging a freight car full of gasoline canisters, they made a cozy little corner for our group and helped us on board, waving good-bye as we pulled out of the station.

17

We stood on the platform in Wurtzburg, staring in disbelief at the bombed ruins of houses and factories. *How could this be?* Wurtzburg was a Red Cross city, supposedly safe from attack! All public clocks were stopped at 9:30. We learned later that the city had refused an Allied order to surrender despite repeated warnings and ultimatums. The results were devastating.

Only moments ago we had been so confident this would be our new home that alternate plans seemed unnecessary. Uncertainty about what to do or where to go was, by now, an all-too-familiar predicament and at times I regretted embarking on this futile journey. I noticed the entrance to an underground tunnel used by pedestrians for crossing the tracks and, lacking a better idea, followed a stream of people down there. It offered temporary shelter from the driving rain now falling outside while we reassessed our plans.

For five long days we camped in the tunnel, watching the people coming and going. Most of them ignored us or deliberately looked in another direction, as though acknowledging our presence might somehow commit them to our rescue. By now we looked sorely in need of rescuing. After nearly a week of restless sleep, propped against a pile of baggage, we mirrored each other's grime and dishevelment.

One lady, always dressed in black, stood out in the constant stream of passersby. I wondered if she was mourning a husband or son lost in the war. Few families emerged from years of battle untouched by the death of loved ones. To my surprise, she stopped beside us one day.

"Why are you sitting here?" Her curiosity was greater than her fear of involvement.

I shrugged. "We don't know where to go. At least it's dry here." Somewhere along the way, I had become the unofficial leader of our ragged little band and wished that just once someone else would come up with an idea.

She told us about a school which had been converted into a shelter for homeless wanderers and gave us directions to get there. "Like everything else around here, it's been damaged by the bombs, but inside it's okay. They provide meals and give you a place to stay while you decide what to do next." With those words, our Good Samaritan continued on her way.

We located the school without difficulty. As she said, this building too had been ravaged by enemy bombs, but, compared to the tunnel, it felt like a luxury hotel. With an immediate soap and water treatment, we finally emerged from under a week's accumulation of dust and mud. There was even a hair salon nearby open for business, as long as we brought our own hot water. We found some bricks to make a little firepit, and in no time we had enough steaming water for shampoos.

I was the last in our group to go and as I walked down the street, a car drove slowly past me, then stopped. As I drew close the passenger window slid down. "*Zdrastviche*!" I kept walking, as though I hadn't understood the Russian greeting. *How could they be this far west? They had no jurisdiction here! Was this a trap? Were they hoping to surprise me into identifying myself as a Russian?* They tried again, this time asking in German for directions to the school. Panic tightened my chest and I felt my hands grow clammy. Why were Russians interested in the place where we were staying? I tried to act and sound indifferent as I pointed in the general direction.

I forgot about my shampoo, anxious only to warn my friends about the Russians' impending visit. When the car was out of sight I raced back to the school, taking a back route rather than the main street. "We have to leave — quickly!" I herded them out the back door and into a neighbouring yard where we hid among tall weeds, just as the car pulled to a stop outside the building. The men emerged, casting furtive glances over the property as though sensing watchful eyes, before entering the front door. I wondered about the caretaker. What would he tell these intruders? He seemed friendly enough, but appearances could be deceptive. *Did he know what could happen to us if these men knew we were from Russia?*

We hardly breathed until the men returned to their car and drove away without a backward glance. I was almost giddy with relief to learn that the caretaker had not betrayed us. At the same time, I felt it would be wise to let him know that we *were* from Russia, but that we all had German citizenship papers issued in Poland. He was happy to join our conspiracy. As far as he was concerned, there were *no* Russians living in his little camp.

The next day the men returned, still suspicious after their first visit. "I don't have Russians here." The caretaker was firm, his voice showing genuine irritation. "They're all from Poland!" Encouraged by his boldness, we offered our papers for examination. There it was for all to see — German citizenship, issued in Lodz, Poland. The men stared intently at each of us as though to intimidate us into a confession. Reluctantly they left without their anticipated quarry.

We stayed at the school for the entire summer, looking for work and a more permanent place to live. An ad in the local newspaper caught our attention. The owner of a bombed chemical factory wanted to rebuild and needed workers to help him. He planned to build barracks for us to live in and, if anyone asked, would declare that we were citizens of Wurtzburg. Our task was to chisel sooty debris from the bricks of his demolished factory, a filthy job which blackened our fingernails and hands despite vigorous brushings with soap and water. He paid us each an hourly wage of one *Deutschmark*.

At the end of September, twenty-five thousand people, including longterm residents as well as refugees, were ordered to leave Wurtzburg. Every day unstable walls crashed down on occupants of bombed dwellings, trapping them without hope of rescue. At the same time, we learned that our employer had no permission to build either the factory or the barracks. Availability of cheap labor had presented an opportunity to advance his unapproved plans at bargain prices, hopeful that in Germany's present disorganization no one would notice until it was too late.

Once again we awaited transports to take us to another unknown destination. By this time, we considered ourselves to be family, not caring where we went, as long as we could all stay together. At the end of a long day of waiting and travelling, they deposited us in a picturesque little farming village which had miraculously escaped the notice of Allied bombers. One house stood empty, ready to become our home. There was one serious drawback; once again the newly created Russian border nibbled at our heels.

The villagers were highly suspicious of city people and avoided us as much as possible. Their duty fulfilled in providing us with ration cards and housing, the authorities abandoned us to idle boredom. There was nothing to do and despite our determination to stay together, tempers flared at the slightest hint of conflict.

When we heard that area farmers needed help harvesting potato crops, we rushed to inquire if we might be hired, uneasily aware that Russian soldiers patrolled nearby. The woman in charge was more interested in our clothing than our ability to work. "You can't pick potatoes wearing that!" Her scorn for

Mama's first marriage, 1908

Papa in German army uniform
(below)

Aunt Charlotte and children (left)

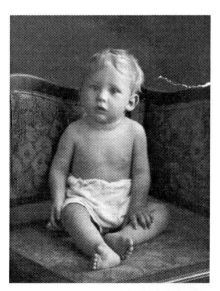

Lydia, age 24 (top left)
Yuri at 7 months (top right)
Alla at 4 months (center)
Tony, Lydia and Lilia under a chestnut tree
(bottom left)
We're going to Canada! 1950 (bottom right)

Tony and sugar beet harvest helpers (above)

A Saturday outing in Calgary (below)

Big sister Lilia, and Stanley

Tony and Stanley, age 2

Yuri, son Sergey,
Heinrich,
Alexander in
Pyatigorsk, 1967

Mama and Papa, 1963

Airport reunion with Yuri,
1977

Catching up on 35 years

They don't make hats like this
in Russia.

Our new brother!

Stanley and Monti - true
HOGs!

Stanley and Carol

Christmas, 1984

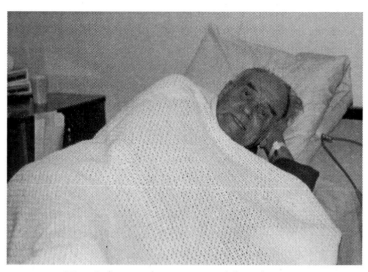

Tony's hospital stay, 1985 (above)
Lydia and Tony, 1985 (below)

Visiting Tony's grave with Luke

Stanley, Lydia and Lilia, 1993

Victor's here! 1994

Touring Drumheller Badlands.   Stanley's memorial, Pigeon Mountain

Lydia with grandchildren, left to right (back), Monti, Jeanette, Jason, Debbie, Jim, Danny, (front), Raelyn, Danielle

Lydia with great-grandchildren, left to right, Shay Ann,
Christie, Adam, Luke, Sam and Tony

Lydia with Ed and Lilia

80 years young!

ignorant city folks was evident as she eyed our dresses and shoes. These were hardly fashionable even by wartime standards, but elegant beside the rough, serviceable garments worn by workers in dusty fields. I suggested that perhaps she could decide on our suitability *after* seeing us at work, rather than judging us by our clothing. Our transient lifestyle demanded that we travel lightly, and we always took with us the best of what we had, leaving the rest behind. I wondered what Mama would think of my 'Sunday Best' dress soaking up dirt in a German potato patch.

"All right, you can start tomorrow." The woman still sounded doubtful but at least we were employed.

The next day we trudged behind a horse-drawn contraption resembling a rake which pulled the plants out of the ground, leaving potatoes scattered along the rows. We picked them up, filling basket after basket. Amazingly, our baskets were filled and emptied more quickly than those of veteran farmers.

And the food! The last time any of us had feasted so royally, both for lunch and supper, was a distant memory. Even when our shrunken stomachs cried "enough!" there was still more food. These people enjoyed resources far beyond the provision of ration cards. At the end of the day, the woman handed us a basket laden with bread, cheese, potatoes, apples and cream of wheat.

"You are good workers. Come again tomorrow." Her tone now held grudging respect and we were happy to accept the invitation. For two weeks we picked potatoes and every night a basket of treats went home with us. We wanted to do something to thank her and finally came up with an idea. She had a nine-year-old daughter and we decided to make a patchwork dress for her. Each of us contributed an item of clothing that we no longer wanted or used and the result was a delightful

169

combination of colors and textures that we were sure she would enjoy wearing.

"I'm sorry, I can't keep this dress. It's much too fancy for my daughter to wear." We begged her to let the girl try it on but she was adamant. The dress was unsuitable for life in the country and fancy ideas in a child would only lead to trouble later.

After the harvest I found another job, this time helping a woman operate a guesthouse. Her husband had been arrested by the Americans after someone reported a Nazi flag in his attic, leaving his wife to tend both their farm and the business. At first she doubted that I could be of much use and I wondered what it was about me that sent out a signal of incompetence. Mama's early protectiveness about chores had long since given way to my own homemaking responsibilities. It had taken time, but I had learned to manage a household. When I once again demonstrated my domestic talents, she welcomed my help.

A few members of the group, including the other Lydia, decided to venture out on their own. It was more practical for me to move into the guesthouse rather than make the long walk twice daily to and from the house where we had lived together. I enjoyed having a real home again with real furniture and best of all, a good collection of books. Time slipped away unnoticed as I immersed myself in one story after another after the day's work was finished. So great was my hunger for reading that I sometimes forgot to sleep. The knock on my door at two o'clock one morning took me by surprise, especially when I opened it to an American MP.

"Why is your light on?" he demanded. I stared at him, seeing no reason why my light was his concern now that the need for blackout was past.

"I'm reading." I held up the book, my tone discouraging further interference.

"It's past two o'clock and you're still reading?" What audacity! He actually seemed to think I needed his permission.

"What business is it of yours? Are you telling me that I can't read?" By now I was angry, particularly as his eyes never stopped roaming around my room, finally lighting on some little bars of soap lying on top of the dresser. The Americans occupying my landlady's house in Zwickau had given them to me, and I liked the bright flowery paper in which they were wrapped.

"Ah, you have American soap." Ignoring my outrage he pushed past me into the room. "You have an American boyfriend too?" The soaps disappeared into his pocket and he turned his attention to the closet, riffling through its contents as though he had a right to inspect them. "You have too many clothes," he announced, taking a few of my dresses off their hangers. Then he discovered a suitcase that I was storing for one of my friends and inspected its contents as well, taking out several items. "You have too much," he said again, his voice faintly accusing as though I had violated some law of ownership. "My girlfriend has nothing and can use these." With that he draped his choices over his arm and sauntered out of the room, leaving me open-mouthed with astonishment and rage. *How dare he!* But what could I do? And all because I chose to read rather than sleep!

I was quickly learning that a uniform, regardless of which country it represented, was a license to dominate. But of all the uniformed officers I'd encountered, Americans puzzled me the most. How could soldiers, hailed as liberators throughout much of Europe, be capable of the behavior I'd witnessed in Zwickau, and now again in the supposed safety of my own bedroom? Their help in arranging our transit out of the Russian zone was invaluable, and yet I never fully trusted them.

171

18

I stayed at the guesthouse for another month when Lydia came back for a visit, bursting to tell me about a young man she had met on a train with whom she was now madly in love. She had decided to settle in Fulda, a distant town, to be near him and urged me to join her. I hesitated, unwilling to leave what remained of our group that was both family and friends to me. She assured me that there were plenty of jobs available for all of us and after a brief discussion, we packed and moved yet again. When we arrived at the address she had given me, the lady who answered the door told us that she didn't live there anymore, that she was married and living in a camp.

A camp! We looked at each other in dismay. The word revived unpleasant memories of experiences that none of us was anxious to repeat, despite this woman's glowing descriptions of the food and living conditions enjoyed by those who lived there. Lydia knew of my aversion to camps and I was angry with her for misleading me. As we set off to find her, I mentally rehearsed a few heartfelt sentiments that expressed my outrage at being lured here under a false pretext.

A security guard gave us directions to her home and she was delighted to find us waiting on her doorstep. Unrepentant, she laughed when I confronted her about the slight 'error' in her address. "You wouldn't have come if I'd told you I live in a camp. I know you by now!" She was absolutely right about that!

I reluctantly conceded that she had at least been right about employment opportunities. I worked at a variety of jobs such as sorting vegetables in a grocery store and cutting fabric for uniforms. Despite a shortage of housing, I found a place to live on my own and with work to occupy my time and a roof over my head, I was content. I wondered what Papa and Mama would think if they could see me now. How I missed them! When they were sent away, I still had very definite ideas of what I would or would not do. I could hardly believe I was the same woman who felt the world was unfair because she was not allowed to teach. Now I was happy to pick potatoes and to cull rotten carrots from market bins.

Lydia and Martin, her new husband, often visited me in my top-floor room. One night they brought a young Polish man with them. Tony Oushal was charming, handsome, intelligent and fun-loving. My friends' intentions were obvious, but when he asked if I would allow him to visit me by himself, I was indifferent. "Come if you want to — the road is open." Undaunted by my cool welcome, Tony became a frequent guest.

Romance was the farthest thought from my mind. My youthful vow to remain single if something happened to Alexander belonged to a time when all we envisioned was a future of happy togetherness. But even with more mature insights of how quickly a secure situation can change, I felt it betrayed my husband to succumb to the first man who paid attention to me. Besides, love and close relationships were an automatic formula for the worst kind of pain. Why would I even consider setting myself up for more?

To be honest, I rarely thought of Alexander as part of the family I had left behind and with whom I longed to be reunited. He belonged to my childhood. Apart from his role in my becoming a mother, our relationship was more the love of special friends than that of a married couple. Given a chance, things might have changed, however the army's letter effectively closed this chapter of my life.

Tony often talked about marriage but I kept him at a safe distance. Even without considering whether or not we loved each other, who knew what tomorrow would bring? Without a shred of hope for stability in our lives, marriage was an unnecessary complication. Anyway, there was really no decision to make. As a German citizen, regardless of when this citizenship had been adopted, the law forbade me to marry a foreigner. Not easily discouraged by rules and red tape, Tony used every strategy known to lovelorn man to change my mind. When he, together with Lydia and Martin, appeared on my doorstep with bags of food, I knew something was amiss.

"Why are you giving me these things? I *do* have ration cards and I'm not starving!" If he thought for one moment that after coming this far I suddenly needed someone to look after me, he was sadly mistaken.

"Actually it *is* yours." He momentarily avoided direct eye contact with me and I suspected that there was more to this story than sudden concern for my welfare.

Unknown to me, Tony, assisted by Lydia and Martin, had registered me as a resident of the camp. As a German, I was ineligible to live there even if I had wanted to, but what could be simpler than one more displaced *Polish* woman in a camp of thousands? "Lydia Brusintshewska" was added to the official rosters and the logistical nightmare of keeping accurate paper records of displaced persons ensured that it would be months (if ever) before my fictional residency was even questioned. Meanwhile, I held bags of food belonging to Lydia Brusintshewska. *Me.*

Who was this man so determined to link my future to his own? Like most of my acquaintances, Tony's story had shades of similarity to my own involving loss of family, flight and displacement. In one of his rare serious moments when we were alone, he shared some of his painful past.

He was born into a Polish family in White Russia. His father, a devout Catholic who served as organist in the church as long as he could remember, was sent to Siberia by the communist regime along with others known to have religious affiliations. Tony was the second youngest of four boys and also a devout Catholic. He completed his university education as a teacher, assisted financially by his older brother, a carpenter.

As more and more people were sent to Siberia, Tony felt that it was only a matter of time before he would join those numbers. If Siberia was inevitable, perhaps it was better to make that move voluntarily while he had some choice in location. Leaving his wife and two children for what he hoped would be a temporary absence, he moved to Siberia on his own, hoping to escape official notice.

It worked for a while. He found a teaching position and made friends, always careful to avoid any mention of his father that might provoke questions or curiosity. His own risk would increase dramatically if it became known that his father was in exile. A subtle remark one day by one of his colleagues led Tony to believe that his secret was known. If he was no longer safe, there was little reason to stay and he decided to return home to his family.

By this time the country was officially at war and as he travelled west to Leningrad, he met crowds of refugees moving east to get away from German bombs raining down on their city. He arrived home, successfully avoiding involuntary recruitment into the Russian army.

Amidst all the chaos, he still managed to find a job. Returning home from work one day, he found his mother dead on the floor in a pool of blood, shot in the back. There were varying reports, some saying that she was killed by German soldiers, others by partisans who wanted her cow. Tony's voice choked with tears as he relived the horror of this discovery. I at least carried with me a hope of someday finding my parents again. His hope died with her.

A short time later, Tony and his wife, children and in-laws, were sent to Germany where they worked on a farm. After the war, his wife left him for another man, taking their children with her to Poland. They had no further contact.

Until Tony appeared on the scene, I accepted my take-charge role without question. People assumed that I always knew the best thing to do in a difficult situation and that I would do anything in my power to help, no doubt Papa's legacy to me. But independence and responsibility was a very solitary road, and I slowly realized how comforting it was to know that someone cared for me again. With a steady job and a place to call home, my life once again had stability and routine, yet I still felt like an outsider. I wanted desperately to belong somewhere — and to someone. Now that daily survival was assured, my emotional needs cried for attention.

I enjoyed Tony's company. We spent more and more time together, sometimes with other friends, often on our own. Usually the centre of attention, he coaxed lilting tunes out of the most decrepit accordion or balalaika. He taught me high-stepping dance patterns to lively Russian music that left me flushed and breathless. I rediscovered my sense of humor, laughing at his endless repertoire of stories until my sides ached. When he arrived at my door, an inner spark, long squelched by tears and sadness, fanned into life. Tony was fun. Tony was joy. I wanted both.

I finally agreed to marry him, even without love as I understood it. Nor was this a practical arrangement. Tony wanted to leave Germany and, according to official emigration policies, must live in a camp to be eligible. As a German citizen,

I was not allowed camp residency, which meant that we must live separately, that is, if I was first willing to break the rule about marrying someone of another nationality. I wanted to stay in Germany, confident that in the time it took to process emigration applications, he would change his mind. My decision to remarry rose from the need to end the pain of separation and loneliness — *to belong*. And there were terms.

First of all, I refused to take the Polish name under which he had registered me. Secondly, under no conditions would I move to the camp, even if there was a way of circumventing the rules. We could visit each other any time we pleased, but I would stay in my own home. Any camp occupied by displaced *Ostarbeiter* was dangerous. German authorities happily assisted the Russians in repatriating former citizens if it meant easing the strain that foreigners placed on their resources. And thirdly, I refused to become a Roman Catholic.

Tony eagerly agreed to all my conditions and we were married by a justice of the peace. My concern about the law prohibiting inter-marriage was unfounded. We learned that hundreds of British soldiers had secretly married German girls, and after the war, boatloads of brides immediately set sail for new homes in England.

A year after our marriage, the camp at Fulda relocated to Gutensburg. I still resisted moving to the camp, although to my surprise, I was growing very fond of my new husband, and wanted us to live together. To my dismay, he remained determined to emigrate and refused to move into my place.

Now it was my turn to be persuasive. Life was gradually improving in Germany. I had a good job and lots of new friends. Now earning a salary, I was a regular customer in dress shops again. For the first time in years I enjoyed a normal life which I was reluctant to interrupt.

"I can help you *here!*" I pleaded. He could read and write German. Why did he need to move across the ocean where he didn't know anyone or anything, including the language? In the camp he taught school as he had done in Russia. He loved to teach. In a short time he could take classes and become certified here. I knew people who could help make it happen.

Tony remained firmly committed to leaving. There was nothing for him in Germany and no reason to stay. With a heavy heart, I resigned my job and joined him in Gutensburg. I was still barred from living in a camp, but since I had taken his name when we married, my German citizenship almost escaped notice. One of the camp leaders recognized me from my days at the factory in Zwickau, but since he was also German, we had an unspoken pact of secrecy.

Our living quarters were adequate but barren. I thought longingly of the Persian carpets which used to hang in my home and longed for even one to relieve the cold austerity of the room. I inherited Mama's need for beauty around me and her ability to transform a hovel into a home with a few simple touches. Digging through my boxes I realized that I had more than Mama's decorative touch. I had her underpants! Holding up the garment, I tried to visualize alternate uses for the fine batiste cotton with its delicately crocheted lace insets. By evening, Mama's lingerie graced our wall, elegantly out of place against peeling paint, and bearing no resemblance to its original shape and function. I could almost hear her laughter each time someone complimented me on the intricate needlework. *If only I could show it to her.*

We lived there for eight months before the camp was again evacuated, this time next to the city of Kassel. This was actually a collection of camps containing hundreds of thousands of displaced people, and I despaired of ever escaping refugee status.

I was now several months pregnant, and the dream of having my own home was becoming an obsession.

Americans supervising the camp operations offered a ray of hope. If we had an address for relatives in the United States, the officials would attempt to locate them on our behalf. Any overseas link to family was an advantage in the emigration process. I knew Mama's only remaining sister, my Aunt Mena, lived in the States. Although I did not have her address, I found a picture of her cousin with *Winnipeg* written on the back. I took the photograph to the Americans' headquarters nearby, presenting it to the official in charge of completing the necessary paperwork.

"Winnipeg is in Canada, not the United States." he laughed at my ignorance.

"Canada — the States — what's the difference?" I replied crossly. "It's all *North* America isn't it?" All I wanted was a permanent escape from life in a camp. If crossing the ocean was the only way it could happen, so be it. If we had to leave at all, I preferred sooner to later.

The man took what little information I had, promising to forward it to the Red Cross who would, in turn, attempt to locate my relatives. Within two months, I received a letter from Mama's cousin and he provided me with my aunt's address in New York. I wrote to her immediately, hardly knowing where to start telling her about my family and everything that had happened to us.

Amelia and I had exchanged letters regularly since I left her behind in Zwickau. I always notified her immediately of each change in address, not wanting to move again before I knew that she had received it. Suddenly her letters stopped and my most recent letter was returned to me by the post office. Worried, I wrote to her landlady whose reply filled me with sadness. The authorities had learned from informants that Amelia originally came from Russia. Her German citizenship meant nothing to them and they arrested her, leaving her baby with the landlady. A week later, they came for him too. All the woman could tell me was that Amelia had been sent away. I never heard from her again.

I felt newly determined to locate Yuri and my parents and started another letter campaign to Pyatigorsk, encouraged by reports that mail was once again moving in and out of Russia. If only I could re-establish contact before we left the country.

In the midst of our preoccupation with leaving Germany, my pregnancy developed unexpected complications. Excess fluid accumulating in my womb needed to be drained, requiring a weekly visit to the clinic. While the baby was not in imminent danger, doctors told me that this would be my last child.

July 26, 1947. To my disappointment, we still lived in the camp when Lilia Marie was born. In my delight at having a new baby to care for, other problems were, for a time, pushed aside. Our living conditions were basic but comfortable and we had enough to eat, so for now I relaxed and just enjoyed being a mother again. As I rocked her in my arms, I told her about her big brother Yuri, who was far away. And about her grandma and grandpa and uncles. I knew she didn't understand, but hearing the words myself helped ease the ache that time showed no signs of erasing. Would she ever meet them herself?

Tony regularly attended a local Mass. I accepted the church's requirement that we raise our child as a Catholic and was willing to comply with anything that Tony requested in this regard, as long as he did not insist that I myself embrace Catholicism. I occasionally attended Mass with him and while I enjoyed the Latin liturgy, my position remained firm. As I explained to the priest, I had been raised in a strict Lutheran tradition and believed that if I changed my religion, I would not meet my parents again in heaven. No earthly pledge must jeopardize that reunion! If God permitted me to meet them again in this life and they gave their blessing, I would join my husband and daughter in the Catholic faith. Without it, I was prepared to die a Lutheran.

By 1947 people from the camps, including many of our friends, were emigrating in a steady stream to a variety of foreign shores. Tony regularly completed the required application forms, stating 'teacher' as his occupation and they just as regularly returned with a bold *NOT NEEDED* stamp. Australia, Paraguay, Venezuela, Morocco, England — the verdict was unanimous: No country needed a teacher who could not speak the language of the people. Tony's dream was destined for a bleak future and he became moody and irritable.

One day visas from my aunt arrived in the mail, allowing us to emigrate to the United States. Anticipating quick validation of the documents, we took them to Frankfurt, only to be told that we needed a number which would be issued in a month.

A month later we went again, but the anticipated number had not been issued. The next month the answer was the same And the next. Two days later, an irate letter from my aunt explained everything. "I arrange your visas and you send someone else?" Our visas had been sold to another applicant, who had the audacity to appear on my aunt's doorstep in our place!

Confronted by two very angry would-be emigrants and an incriminating letter, the officials, who had previously seemed indifferent to our application, now fell over one another in efforts to compensate for their 'clerical error'. They assured us that the situation would be rectified, guaranteeing our imminent departure. Cynical about official promises, we resigned ourselves to yet more waiting.

Tony's Aunt Vera, also living in the camp with her sixteen-year-old son, shared her excitement about news that the Canadian government was recruiting able-bodied laborers for sugar beet crops. She intended to apply and suggested that this might be a solution for Tony as well. I appreciated her concern but happily for me, all our documents, including our passports, were at the American headquarters in the last stages of preparation for our entry into the United States of America. If I had to leave Germany, this was where I wanted to go.

I wasn't sure if Tony was genuinely interested in becoming a sugar beet farmer, or if he was just tired of fighting the language barrier in his determination to leave Germany. Even without the required documents, he forged ahead with yet another application, this one to Canada. Again, there were endless forms for all of us to complete. As far as I was concerned, it merely provided Tony with something to do while we waited for mountains of paper to be processed through official channels.

To my surprise, the Canadian Immigration Office invited us to an interview. Countless questions later, the verdict was in: "Tony Oushal, Lydia Oushal, Lilia Oushal, you are going to Canada. Vera Zawaroska will *not* go to Canada. Your son must be healthy first." We stared at each other in disbelief — but for very different reasons.

I had humored Tony through this process, not for one moment thinking that our application would be approved. After all, regulations stated that application for entrance into one country precluded similar applications elsewhere. If thoughts of going to Canada temporarily eased the growing discouragement that I saw in my husband, I saw no harm in co-operating. Surely the Americans would be notifying us at any time of our departure date and all this commotion about going to Canada would end.

Now *we* were going and Tony's aunt, who had started all this, would stay in Germany because her son had a sniffle. Aunt Vera, looking as though she might cry, wanted an explanation. The man shrugged. "Canada is a cold country," was all he offered.

Tony was elated. I was upset. "What are we going to do in Canada?" I stormed. "At least in the States my aunt could help us!"

"No problem!" Tony's enthusiasm would not be dampened by my temper. "I will find you a housekeeper when we get to Canada. Everything will be *fine!*" Nothing, including total ignorance of farming in general and sugar beets in particular, dulled his optimism. I wondered how anyone could so consistently see everything as 'roses from heaven.' All *I* saw was black.

19

May 23, 1950. For seven days following our departure from London, the ship heaved and tossed on the stormy Atlantic. Inside our tiny cabin, I did the same, the inside of a bucket my limited view of the entire crossing. We were in more danger than any of us realized, learning later that other ships in the area had been placed on alert in case a rescue operation became necessary. Tony, untroubled by sea-sicknesss, took charge of Lilia, leaving me to retch in peace.

The flurry of preparations to leave Germany had increased my opposition to this move. *What were we doing? And why?* Compared to our destination, which I could only picture as bleak, even a camp sounded cozy. In one of his letters, Mama's cousin had written, "not everything that glistens is gold," and though I was uncertain of his exact meaning, the phrase implied a warning. There was some consolation in knowing that we already had friends and acquaintances living there and I looked forward to seeing them again. But Canada, in my imagination, was comparable to Siberia and given the choice, I would gladly have chosen the latter. At least I would have the comfort of sharing my parents' life, if indeed they *were* still alive, whereas every minute on this ship placed more ocean between me and those I loved.

Yuri was never far from my thoughts. In the past, I had no choice in moves that took me ever farther away from him. Now that the war was over, surely the likelihood of seeing him again was greater if we were at least on the same continent. Yet here I was, voluntarily placing more and more distance between us, if unwilling submission to my husband's choice could be termed 'voluntary.' By now my son was twelve years old, that is, if he had managed to survive the stigma of his semi-German heritage. I refused to dwell on the alternative.

Just when I thought the voyage would never end, Tony burst into our cabin to tell me that the flat, misty horizon now showed a city skyline. Halifax. By this time even a foreign shore was a welcome sight, and I slowly dragged myself to the deck where passengers gathered at the railing to catch a first glimpse of our adoptive homeland.

Finally we docked and passengers thronged to the gate, impatient to feel firm ground underfoot once again. My stomach, sensitive from hours of turning itself inside out, recoiled from an overpowering fishy smell. Struggling to maintain my feeble grip on our bags, I wobbled onto the pier, frustrated at the weakness in my arms. Tony kept a firm hold on Lilia, who for once was too distracted to squirm out of his arms, watching all the bustle and commotion with wide-eyed wonder. Various orders of priests and nuns waited to welcome us; European ships always included an abundance of Roman Catholics. They presented each of us with a rosary, and Lilia with a new doll.

Canadian immigration processing was amazingly quick. Once our documents were verified and our baggage checked, we boarded a train for the final leg of our journey. According to the map hanging on the station wall, it promised to be a long one. Exactly how far, I had no idea, since the scale was written in miles rather than kilometres.

As the train wound its way westward toward Winnipeg, I grudgingly admitted that Canada was a beautiful country. Compared to the centuries of history in Russia and Europe, I felt an untamed newness in this land, which sped past my window in a kaleidoscope of color and form. Tony gazed as though transfixed, analyzing every lake and rock formation with data from his geographical storehouse of knowledge. He happily shared it with me, even if my responses did not always reflect his own enthusiasm. It was difficult to describe; everything was so *extreme*, whether forest, rocks or water. As we approached Winnipeg several days later, I added *flat* to the list. And *wet*. Very, very *wet*.

As we emerged from the Canadian Shield onto the Manitoba prairies, it was obvious that farming activity on the flooded fields would be delayed indefinitely. Train personnel reported that conditions were the same in the city.

Organizers changed our destination, advising that we would continue westward to Lethbridge, Alberta, where there was no danger of high water. Desperate to leave the train, my earlier despair returned, increasing with each mile after empty mile of prairie farmland, with only an occasional tree to relieve the flatness. Sometimes I dozed, vainly hopeful that I might waken to bushes, mountains, or *anything* of scenic interest. It was a silly thought, but sometimes I wondered if the train was actually moving. How could so much time produce so little variation in the landscape?

We arrived in Lethbridge at midnight, June 1, 1950. Our new employer, a taciturn Polish farmer, met us at the station and I was so relieved to know that we spoke a common language that I forgot to resent his apparent lack of interest in us. He drove us to his home in total silence — and the most intense darkness I had ever experienced. Why were there no lights? It reminded me of blackout conditions during the war, but of course there was no threat of bombs here.

We eventually turned into a driveway, pulling to a stop in front of a huge house. Even in the dark, I could tell that this was a prosperous operation. He unloaded our baggage, still without comment, motioning for us to follow him inside. The house still smelled of new wood and carpeting and I learned the next day that German prisoners-of-war had built it. He showed us where we were to sleep, promising to take us to our own home in the morning.

Exhausted, but unable to sleep for more than few hours, I climbed out of bed long before the rest of the household was awake, anxious to see our new world. In broad daylight I finally understood the darkness of night. Apart from this farm, there was no recognizable sign of human habitation as far as my eye could see. I should have been prepared for this during the endless train trip from Winnipeg, but how was I to know that when we actually reached civilization, we would be the sole occupants! My hands went to my head in an unconscious gesture of dismay. To which end of the earth had Tony brought us?

A comforting hand patted my shoulder, startling me out of my thoughts which were rapidly approaching panic-mode. "I know what you're thinking." Absorbed in my new surroundings, I failed to notice the man emerge from the barn. He addressed me in German, eyes twinkling his understanding of my plight. "I felt the same way when I came a year ago." His accent identified him as Ukrainian. He pointed to some trees in the distance and I could now barely make out the peak of a roof behind them. "That's where you will live." And then pointing in another direction, he indicated that the little town of Coaldale was seven miles down the road.

He showed me a second house on the same yard where another family lived who helped the owner farm his twenty-three hundred acres. I had assumed that the European system of farming villages would also be practiced in Canada. Who would have thought that people actually preferred to live on such isolated parcels of land?

A mile to the road and seven more miles to town. How would we get there? I could already list ten fingers' worth of difficulties in adjusting to life in this remote outpost. First of all, I had to convert eight unfamiliar miles to kilometres before deciding if legs or wheels would take me shopping. As though he really could read my thoughts, the man assured me that under the terms of the farmer's contract with the immigration authorities, he was obligated to take us into town once a week for groceries, and to provide milk for our baby. When he explained the math, I decided that thirteen kilometres one way was definitely too far for grocery bags and a toddler.

After breakfast, our employer took us to the house which his hired man had pointed out to me earlier. Despite many areas of common background, he still showed little interest in us, or what had brought us to his door. The house was plain but adequate, located close to the fields for which we would be responsible.

I quickly learned that my best efforts at housekeeping were no match for the constant southern Alberta wind. The old house acted like a sieve, allowing dirt and draft alike to penetrate every nook and cranny. Moments after sweeping the floor, a gritty residue scraped underfoot.

To my horror, our well's water supply came from an irrigation ditch inhabited by snakes, frogs and miscellaneous other creatures. Regardless of how long I boiled the water, I could never pour a glass without visualizing microscopic vermin back-stroking their way down my throat. Ironically, for weeks prior to boarding the ship, we were poked with needles and immunized with every known vaccine to ensure our health and welfare in Canada. Did any of these protect us from the simple act of quenching our thirst?

By June 5, the farmer expected us to be sufficiently rested and settled to begin our new career. Once again, my clothing was inappropriate. My only garment suited to hot weather was a sundress with straps that stylishly criss-crossed my back. It had plenty of wide open spaces, not unlike my new environment, I thought, annoyed at the farmer's disapproving stare. He brought us to a ten-acre field, a mile long and wide enough for ten rows of beets, tersely indicating that we were to hoe them. Then he left.

We discovered that at this stage in the growing season, *all* plants have a green tenderness about them, including weeds. "Do you know which are beets?" We asked each other the question simultaneously. Quackgrass, a universal plague, was easily identifiable unlike the other plantlife waiting at our feet. Fearing that any action by our hoes would be dangerous to the crop, we leaned on them instead, hoping that someone would come by to enlighten us.

"Why aren't you working?" He had driven up again and was leaning out of his window.

"We don't know which plants are beets and which are weeds. Will you show us?" I thought it was a reasonable request.

"If you don't know, I'll plow it over!" He was gone again.

Was he serious about plowing under the crop? Without proper instruction, we could accomplish the same thing, one plant at a time. We stood for a while longer, poking at the leaves in an attempt to identify something that was as foreign to us as the ground on which we stood. Eventually we noticed a woman coming toward us from a neighbouring field.

"Is something wrong?" she asked. "I saw you standing here before the boss arrived and you haven't moved." She listened to our dilemma, all the while eyeing my dress.

"Let me show you." Her capable manner was reassuring as she explained the differences between weeds and beets, then demonstrated the way they should be hoed and thinned for maximum growth. It looked easy when she did it, but by the end of the day, both Tony and I had discovered sets of new, untrained muscles as we sank into bed stiff, sore, and exhausted from our first day as beet farmers. Unprotected from both sun and wind, I had burned a brilliant red. A generous coating of salve and buttermilk did little to ease the soreness.

Other workers wore pants and long-sleeved shirts, neither of which I owned. Tony's clothes, while not a perfect fit, nonetheless protected me from the sun, although the woolen fabric on skin already scorched raw, left my legs even more sore and bleeding. On my first shopping trip I found some blue jeans, the standard local garb, and while wearing "men's clothes" violated some early rule of propriety for me, new times called for new measures. They were surprisingly comfortable even though the dye stained my sweaty limbs blue. Rubber boots completed my ensemble, replacing the sandals I'd worn with the sundress.

Shoes were my fashion weakness, and although we had been selective in the belongings which accompanied us from Germany, I managed to find room for twenty-one pairs of them, each of which belonged to a specific outfit. On her first milk-delivery visit to our home, the farmer's wife stared open-mouthed at the rack where our clothes hung. She had never owned a selection of dresses like mine, no doubt wondering how a new immigrant had accumulated such a wardrobe. How could she possibly understand that after years of living out of one small suitcase, my main interest when finances again permitted it, was to restock my closet with pretty clothes? Then I realized that the look on her face was more than curiosity. Could it be that this woman with her wealth of land, house, and cars actually *envied* my little hoard?

Two-and-a-half-year-old Lilia patiently endured two days of continuous dust and wind in the field. On the third morning she declared a mutiny, howling in protest as we prepared to go. I shared her sentiments but was reluctant to leave Tony carrying the load by himself. Neither did I want to leave her alone in the house. Fortunately we were working nearby so I arranged her blankets and toys close to the window. Most of the time she sat contentedly playing there, respecting my stern instructions to stay where I could see her.

Finally I suggested that Tony go back indoors to be with her. I seemed to have more stamina in this heat than he did and worked faster. The way sweat poured down his face frightened me. What if he died from over-exertion, leaving me here all by myself? Just the idea was enough to make me cry. *Why had the Lord allowed us to come here? If we were supposed to die, we could have done that in Germany!"* With each day's exhausting routine, Tony's cheerfulness faded a little more. He even admitted that he should have listened to me before we embarked on this adventure.

Our workday began at four o'clock a.m. and ended at sunset. An already short night was made even shorter every time I woke Tony, asking him to check noises which could surely only be made by someone breaking in. He quickly lost patience with me when we learned that our 'intruder' was only the constant swish of long grasses against the house.

Absorbed in the initial shock of adapting to life in a new land, it took some time for me to realize that for the first time since my early childhood, I was free — completely and totally free. Other than our disgruntled employer, no one seemed to know we were there. No one lived in fear of the police, and no one stopped me on the street demanding to see my passport. To my amazement, many people here didn't even own passports. No one demanded that we register at the town hall, and certainly no one questioned my right to read the night away — assuming that I had the energy to do so. Sometimes I just leaned on my hoe to savor the tranquillity. It was already difficult to remember a world where people milled about in camps, obeyed uniformed officials, and completed endless application forms.

In fact, when I recalled the complicated paperwork required to bring us here in the first place, it seemed very strange to be left so completely on our own. *Was no one interested in how we were doing or even if we had arrived?*

As though in answer to that thought, several men with suits and briefcases arrived at our house one day but lacking both a common language or interpreter, we were unable to speak to them. No sooner had they departed when the farmer, who had until now neglected the part of the contract requiring him to provide weekly transportation for shopping, suddenly appeared, laden with eggs, milk, chicken and fruit, anxious to know more about our visitors. I concluded, from his sudden, friendly generosity, that he wished to avoid any negative reports about his treatment of us.

The next day the men returned, this time accompanied by a translator. They confirmed that we were alive and surviving the life of beet farmers, without asking detailed questions about our accommodation or how we were being treated. They handed us a book with pictures and information about Canada and left, their duty done. With the freedom from interference also came the uneasy awareness that we were truly on our own here. Unless we failed to meet the terms of our contract, the immigration department had no further interest in our welfare.

Everything was strange in Canada, from food to tradition. I bought meat, expecting a certain flavor, only to find it inedible after the way I'd prepared it. Store-bought pastries were a big disappointment, their fancy packaging invariably promising more flavor than was ever delivered. And who would imagine that small-town Canadian hotels were more useful as drinking houses than for sleeping? My face still burned when I remembered the burst of laughter around me after I ordered buttermilk in the tavern where my boss was drinking with friends. I hadn't wanted to be there, but when he drove me to town for groceries, he expected me to wait patiently until he had finished socializing.

The Coaldale area had a large German-speaking population, many of them from a Russian Mennonite background. They were most welcoming, greeting me on the street like long-lost family and inviting us into their homes.

With so many fellow immigrants in our vicinity, I easily postponed any active interest in learning English. I thought I knew some words before coming to Canada but when I tried to use them, people always asked me to repeat, as though they hadn't heard right. I wished now that I had studied English in university, but at that time had given no thought to leaving Russia.

I wondered if I would ever grow accustomed to addressing others as *you* rather than the respectful German *Herr* or *Frau* followed by the person's surname. It seemed harsh and callous, offending me for reasons too difficult to explain even to myself.

Fortunately, most canned goods in the grocery store pictured their contents so I knew what I was buying. The proprietor saw me studying the labels and asked me what language I spoke. His face lit up when I told him. He was also a Russian-born German and could understand my new challenges.

"The best way to learn English is through the Bible. I will give you an English Bible and you compare each verse with the German Bible and this way you will learn the words." It sounded like a good idea but before long I realized that unless I could read a word-for-word translation, I still had no grasp of even a basic vocabulary.

Other people told me that comic books were a sure way to learn English. With words *and* pictures, how could I go wrong? That too seemed reasonable and I came home with bundles of comics. I looked at the captions without understanding them, instinctively doubting that this was a normal way to converse. Another immigrant who had lived in Canada for years, laughed when I asked him if people really talked like the cartoon bubbles.

"Throw those away," he said, "or you'll never speak properly."

Without our own transportation, regular church attendance was difficult. Besides, Sundays were just regular workdays to our employer, weather permitting. Our new Mennonite friends sometimes invited us to their church and I appreciated the simplicity of the occasional services that we could attend, reminded that God places less importance on specific affiliation and labels than we do.

One visiting Russian pastor spoke of life as it continued in my home country. Clergy and congregations alike were subjected to increasingly harsh restrictions; many were imprisoned and tortured, or sent to Siberia if they professed a faith in God. For the first time I recognized that the freedom in Canada, which still filled me with awe, was a gift — that against all odds, and the best efforts of the KGB, I had been virtually lifted out of the blackness swallowing Russia. *Why me? Why not Mama and Papa? And what about Yuri? Did my son not need his mother as he grew up?* I was slowly learning that flashes of insight often unleashed new questions. I might never fully understand why I was brought here, through no choice of my own.

With all the adjustments of moving to Canada and the long days tending sugar beets, at first I had little time or energy left for writing letters. Now that I felt a bit more settled, if not exactly happy, it was time to continue my search for Yuri, and to let him know that I was now on the other side of the ocean. I heard frequent reports from the Mennonite community in Coaldale of Russian families being reunited and wished that I too had a story to share.

Perhaps it was this longing that triggered a recurring dream that, once begun, disrupted many a night's sleep. It always began with me standing beside an underground bunker surrounded by mountains and trees. A wailing air raid siren brought crowds of people to seek shelter, including Mama and Papa. They disappeared through the door with everyone else and when the all-clear signal sounded, I always waited for them to come out again, but they never did. Each time, I wakened in a panic, my heart thumping in my chest. *Was this God's way of telling me that they were dead?*

By October the end of the sugar beet season was in sight, with only three acres remaining to be harvested. The farmer expected us to work every day with no time off until the job was done but I was feeling rebellious, particularly as it was Sunday, supposedly a day of rest.

"I don't care if the beets rot out there, I'm *not* going to the field today." My declaration suited Tony and we stayed at home, to the delight of our daughter who rarely saw us together anymore. Just then a big truck loaded with people drove into the yard and assuming they were lost, I called Tony since his command of English was stronger than mine. The sound of excited shouting brought me rushing to the door.

"Lydia, look who's here!" One after another, Tony's former students from the camps, together with some of their parents who had left Germany after us, jumped off the truck, hoes in hand. They had learned where we lived and decided to pay us a surprise visit. After much excited hugging, kissing and back-thumping they asked how much work we had left to do. Only three acres? Not a problem for young able-bodied students. Within hours it was finished.

We were more surprised than anyone when the yield from our ten-acre plot actually exceeded the farmer's requirement of ten tons per acre; we harvested nineteen tons, qualifying us for the dollar and twenty cents per ton bonus. This, together with the forty-two dollars per acre for the season's work of hoeing, harvesting, chopping and piling, was our total windfall.

After the harvest, we received another group of heartwarming visitors, this time from the surrounding area. When the cars first drove into the yard, we again assumed that they must be lost. We stared as trunks opened and boxes of food emerged: canned fruit, fresh vegetables, chicken, and meat. For some reason, they were giving it all to us! Seeing our absolute bewilderment, they explained.

Several months before, three men, all farm workers, had found themselves near our house at lunchtime. They were far away from a restaurant and had brought nothing with them to eat. When hunger pangs set in, they came knocking on our door. We were away, but familiar with the local practice of leaving houses unlocked, they tried the door. Their timing was perfect. I had just finished a generous cooking spree of cabbage rolls, perogies, and canned stuffed green peppers, all of which provided three hungry workers with a wonderful picnic!

196

They had cleaned up after themselves and when I returned, everything was immaculate. I would never have known they were there, although I had fleeting questions about the quantities of food that I *thought* I remembered cooking, which had suddenly shrunk in their refrigerator containers. But, I reasoned, perhaps I had over-estimated the amount, or maybe Tony had enjoyed a snack while I was outside. The green pepper jars, however, really did baffle me. I *knew* I had made four, yet now only two remained. I would surely remember having eaten those. They were a favorite for both of us, and two clean, but very empty jars on my cupboard defied easy explanation.

The hungry "thieves" had come to confess — and to repay us for our unknowing hospitality. They also wanted the recipe for the peppers.

In the weeks following the harvest, I detected a quiet wistfulness in Tony. He rarely expressed his deepest feelings in words but I suspected that seeing his students again reminded him that life as a farmer contrasted painfully to his former livelihood. I knew he missed the prestige enjoyed by teachers in Europe, and this high esteem was very evident in the way his students greeted him. He loved to stand in front of a classroom of lively young people; a crop of sugar beets, even though flourishing, was a poor substitute.

20

Tony and I were unanimous in wanting an end to our brief, albeit successful, farming careers. While we were under a two-year contract with Canadian Immigration there were other options available, either with the Canadian Pacific Railway (CPR), or the mining and logging industries. As long as we fulfilled the time requirement, we could transfer to another area.

After the harvest, Tony heard of a temporary opportunity to work with the CPR. While it meant that he worked away from home, the extra money would be useful, besides taking care of his moody boredom during the long winter months ahead.

I was overjoyed when Eva, a new friend, told me about a small house in Coaldale available for us to rent at six dollars a month. It was only one room, but more than we needed to hold our few possessions. She located a bed for another six dollars, although I was reluctant to buy it when I learned that the previous owner had died. I felt a little better after she assured me that this person had not been *in* the bed at the time. I learned to convert apple crates into storage cabinets and night tables. There was even a small cellar where I could store all my canned fruit, a new skill I'd learned since coming to Canada. A three dollar stove and plastic lace curtains completed the decor.

Now that we lived in Coaldale, with easy access to shopping and friends, Tony felt easier about leaving us for several weeks at a time. He was delighted when they offered him a permanent job the next spring as a section man, responsible for repairing and replacing railway ties. Although I was glad that farming was now only a memory, the new job meant that I must also leave Coaldale and the relationships I'd made there. Warm friendships more than compensated for cold winters and flat prairies, and I wished we could stay. I would have been even more reluctant to move if I had known how often this scenario would be repeated in the years to come.

Because Tony worked for the CPR, our train travel was free. The next place we lived, Tony assured me, would be furnished so it was simpler to leave our few household effects behind. Perhaps other newcomers could use them. Friends drove Lilia and me to the station, and with many tearful promises to keep in touch, we said goodbye to the first community in Canada which we could call *home*.

We arrived in Lacombe, a town in central Alberta, at about midnight, taking a taxi out of town to the place where Tony lived together with other CPR employees. This was my introduction to The Section House — a facility for workers assigned to maintain a particular portion of track. These were located at six-mile intervals, often remote from even small towns and boasting few conveniences. We would temporarily share the foreman's quarters.

This house lacked electricity, for which I was momentarily grateful. Even by a lantern's dim light, all I could see were cans, bottles, and dirty dishes and pots strewn haphazardly throughout the crowded space. The stove was a mess of burnt boil-overs, each day's contribution blanketing the last, with no discernible attempts made to chisel away the charred layers. I was already homesick for my cozy little house in Coaldale.

Daylight deepened my gloom. The rooms reserved for us were on the second floor, and according to the lady of the house, they were not quite ready. To me, this implied a quick dustmop treatment, an illusion quickly dispelled when we opened the door to the stairway. I reeled from the stench wafting down to meet us, hardly able to breathe. *Were we moving into a barn?* I remembered (almost fondly) the farm house where I'd found lice-infested shelter during the journey to Poland. At that time I could hardly imagine worse living conditions. Now I could.

The previous occupants were chicks — two hundred of them — needing a warm place in which to grow up. Everything remained as they had left it. Droppings and feathers were laminated to the floors and walls. All sunlight into the dismal room was blocked, the solitary window similarly encrusted. Even the ceilings wore a brown coating. *We were supposed to live here?* I burst into a quiet storm of tears.

Our hosts offered neither apology for the mess, nor help in cleaning it up. This was *my* project. Two months of shovelling, scraping, soaping and scrubbing eventually made it fit for human habitation, just in time for our next move.

New positions available within the CPR were filled through a bidding process, either for advancement or a change in location. When a job opened in Lacombe, Tony's boss encouraged him to bid for it. He was successful and we moved out of the section house into an upstairs suite. I was glad to be in a real town again, although this place lacked the German population I had enjoyed in Coaldale. It was time to make learning English a serious priority.

I made friends easily and was delighted when Sonya, a Polish neighbour, took me under her wing. She invited me to the local Catholic church and included me in all their activities. I had never heard of the Catholic Women's League but suddenly I was a member, even though I understood little that was said.

I met other immigrants and our conversation inevitably turned to the world we had all left behind in order to build a new life in Canada. A common thread of grief and suffering bound us together as we shared stories of family loss, flight, and heartbreak as well as a sense of wonderment that we, unlike millions less fortunate, had been plucked from destruction.

Martha, one of my new neighbours, told me that her husband was one of the Germans sent to displace Polish farmers at the outset of the war. An unwilling participant in this takeover, he pledged to the real owner that while this arrangement must appear to comply with German requirements, as soon as the present madness in Poland was over, he would gladly turn everything back to him. At the end of the war when the Polish farmers returned to reclaim their land, they had retaliated by shooting many of the Germans, Martha's husband among them. Her voice quavered as she shared the story and I cried with her. For all I knew, my family had suffered a similar fate but I still cherished the hope of finding them again. Her loss was final.

Sonya decided that it was time for me to learn an important survival skill. "Do you have a bank book?" she asked one day. Silly question. Of course I didn't have a bank book. You only owned one of those if you had lots of money. She disagreed. "You can open an account with a dollar. And when you have more, you can add to it."

I couldn't think of anything more humiliating than opening an account with one dollar. People would look at me and wonder why such 'wealth' needed a bank's protection. She dropped the subject, but the next time we went shopping she steered me into the bank. I looked in awe at the clerks who in one hour handled more money than I would see in a lifetime. Sonya had a brief conversation with the man behind the counter, then turned to me.

"Okay, you can open an account now. You just have to sign a form and give them some money." A warm flush rose to my cheeks, an irritating response to any situation where I felt out of control. I fumbled in my purse, thankful that it was Tony's payday, and that I was spared the indignity of having only one sad little dollar with which to launch my new fortune. I laid twenty-five dollars onto the counter, hoping that it was enough.

I couldn't read the form, but the man smiled encouragingly and showed me where to sign. After much initialling and stamping, he handed me my new bank book with its very official account number and first entry: twenty-five dollars! I hardly heard Sonya's further explanation about interest or service charges. I had a bank account! From then on, it was almost a game to see how much I could add every month after paying rent and groceries.

To my amazement, the account was easily transferred the next February when Tony successfully bid for a new job in Cochrane. Instead of closing it and leaving with my steadily increasing little stash of cash, the clerk handed me a slip of paper assuring me that my entire three hundred and seventy-two dollars would be waiting for me in a branch of the bank in Cochrane. Along with the balance in my book, my confidence in the system had grown during the past few months, but I still needed Sonya's reassurance that my money could safely travel to its new home without my help.

The bank book was my domain. Tony, pleased that I understood finances better than he did, signed over his paycheque to me every two weeks. I looked after paying rent, groceries and all household expenses, providing him with a twenty dollar allowance from each cheque.

I wondered if I was forever destined to live as a nomad, staying in one spot long enough to gain familiarity with the stores and to make a few friends, then packing up again when Tony's work took him to yet a different place. For now it was mostly a matter of inconvenience, but what would happen when Lilia started school? I always worried about our living arrangements, dreading the possibility of sharing space with other workers in the section houses, some of which rivaled anything I'd seen during my journeys with the German army for filth and chaos. Section foremen never lived in one place long enough to make buying a house a practical option but, to my relief, we managed to find a tiny house, complete with garden space to rent for fifteen dollars a month.

Temporary postings were considered standard with the CPR and I decided that it was up to me to bring *some* stability into our lives, starting with furniture. It was good to be close to a major city again and downtown Calgary boasted a variety of furniture stores. I checked them all, finally settling on one with good selection and reasonable prices. I purchased a bedroom suite, a chesterfield, and a table with four chairs for a total of two hundred sixty-one dollars. My nest egg suffered a major dent, but I was confident that I would soon build it up again.

Sonya's School of Finance had also introduced me to credit. Large purchases could be paid by installments which meant that my money would accumulate interest in the bank a while longer. I decided to test my newly acquired acumen. The salesman was very helpful and explained that if I paid something down, as long as my account was fully paid in ninety days, no interest would accrue. After that time, if there was a balance outstanding, I would owe an additional twenty-one dollars. I preferred interest coming in *my* direction.

There was no need to extend debt unnecessarily and I paid half right away. To my surprise, when I returned a month later to pay the rest, another employee informed me that the twenty-one dollar interest charge was also due. Whatever my limitations were with English, I knew that I had *not* misunderstood anything as important as twenty-one dollars and settled down in the store to wait for my salesman to return. When he did, he confirmed our earlier arrangement and to compensate for the trouble they had unwittingly caused, invited me to pick any light fixture in their inventory — free! My new tulip-shaped lamp with the elegant gold trim matched my furniture perfectly, a delightful reminder to me that bold initiative pays dividends.

21

I enjoyed Cochrane. After our Canadian orientation in the flat southern Alberta wilderness, I revelled in the rolling hills and thick stands of trees approaching the Rocky Mountains, a half hour's drive away. The snowy peaks reminded me of my home in the Caucasus, filling me with occasional bittersweet nostalgia. I loved taking Lilia into Calgary on the train; every trip was an adventure, even if groceries were our most exciting purchase.

The garden was my true delight. I anxiously waited for the snow to melt so that I could empty all my new packets of seed into the rich soil, which had no need of irrigation ditches for moisture. Every day Lilia and I checked for signs of new potato, bean, and cucumber plants, finally rewarded by rows of tender green shoots poking through toward the sunshine. Each stage of growth brought with it an agony of impatient waiting for the next one, and the final reward of fresh vegetables for dinner.

Unfortunately, someone else enjoyed most of my harvest. In June Tony bid for another position, this time in Yoho National Park, and we moved in early July. Since train travel was free, I came back a few times to pick vegetables, especially potatoes, but left the bulk of the crop to one of Tony's colleagues who lived nearby.

Our house in Yoho was a sad contrast to the one we reluctantly left behind. Again I felt as though I lived on a remote outpost, this time near the village of Field, British Columbia. The Cathedral Mountains towered high above our house and a scant hundred yards away the railway track emerged from a spiral tunnel. Lights from the train shone into our drapeless windows moments before it thundered by with bone-rattling vibrations that routinely wakened us several times each night.

Twenty feet beyond the track, the world dropped into a two hundred-fifty foot ravine. Our outdoor toilet perched on a set of railway ties perilously close to the edge, and I was always grateful to emerge safely.

A little grassy knoll was Lilia's only playground, but even there, I was always tense, fearing that she would fall over the embankment or decide to wander down the tracks if I failed to watch her every movement. In the house, I locked the doors to ensure that she stayed inside unless I went with her.

The radio, while a poor substitute for adult company, eased my isolation, even though I still understood little of what I heard. Hoping to increase my vocabulary, I wrote down every word that I could catch, brutally mutiliating the spelling in my attempts to apply German phonetics to English. I diligently repeated what I heard, trying to wrap my tongue around the unfamiliar sounds. Whenever possible I experimented with my growing inventory of new words, asking people to help me with both their meanings and pronunciation. I slowly graduated to simple sentences, gradually gaining confidence as I practiced on anyone who came near.

Lilia and I both enjoyed the outdoors and with little else to do, hiked the trails that criss-crossed our mountainous backyard. On his days off Tony sometimes joined us. Lilia loved to race ahead, exploring every thicket or rocky nook.

"Come look at this!" Each new wild flower or other forest treasure required our inspection. One afternoon when we were ready to go back she insisted that we look one more time.

"There's something warm coming from those rocks!" Reluctantly we let her drag us to view her latest discovery. She was right. A steady wisp of steam rose on the chilly air from behind an outcropping of rocks. Uneasy about her curiosity for a closer look, we pulled her away. A few days later a foreman cautioned us to stay away from that area — a favorite place for napping bears! .

One day, they visited me! The day was sunny but suddenly a moving shadow darkened the room. Passing by the window, I went weak-kneed with shock. Standing on his hind legs and staring at me, nose-to-nose from the other side of the glass, was the biggest bear I had ever seen! When I recovered I immediately checked the door, making sure it was securely bolted, fervently hoping that he was merely curious about his new neighbours. Evidently nothing he saw was worth the effort of getting inside and he finally dropped down on all fours, ambling across the tracks to a bush loaded with nearly ripened gooseberries. I had my own plans for those berries and my relief at his moving on to greener pastures was mixed with annoyance. His evident enjoyment of a leisurely feast on *my* fruit gave me every reason to think he knew I was watching. Lilia was concerned that the prickly bushes might hurt his mouth. I hoped so.

Common sense, combined with a little advice from people with years of mountain experience, gave me a healthy respect for wildlife, especially bears. After I returned from a shopping trip one day, Tony described how he and two co-workers had lured a bear *into my kitchen* with a sausage. I was horrified. What could they have been thinking? Once the bear was inside, they had panicked. What if he didn't go back out again? As the bear eyed them, sausage clamped firmly in his teeth, they grabbed anything in sight resembling a weapon — an axe, a poker, a shovel — uncertain whether aggression or quiet waiting would be most successful in ridding the house of their furry guest. Evidently realizing that he'd overstayed his welcome, the bear calmly backed through the door with his prize, disappearing into the forest.

I failed to comprehend the collective stupidity of three grown men. When I did everything in my power to fortify our house against marauders, how could Tony and his friends offer them *dinner!* Tony was as embarrassed about it as I was angry. He told me that the others had started it by holding out the sausage until the bear showed an interest in retrieving it and he didn't want to spoil their fun. By the time the animal was in the house and they all realized that his razor-sharp incisors could turn *them* into sausage, it was too late to shut the door. With great difficulty, I clamped my lips tightly shut. The scare had accomplished more than any nagging from me.

Our house was desperately short of storage space for pots and pans. Needing a project to occupy my time, I asked the foreman if I could borrow a hammer, saw, nails and some wood. He agreed, obviously curious. I just smiled and thanked him, saving my explanation until I knew that I could actually carry out my idea. Other than the machining I had done in the factory, my experience with woodworking was limited to birdhouses, but I had watched Papa make all kinds of things. Surely cupboards were well within my realm.

A pile of wooden boards used for building braces against the weight of ice and snow during the winter months lay outside the tunnel. A few of them could make a big difference in my house and I set about measuring, sawing, and hammering them into a new storage bench. One success led to another and soon we owned a new set of chairs, complete with an innovative carrying hole in the middle of the seats. The foreman, whose curiosity had brought him to our house for a quick peek through the window, was impressed!

22

I looked forward to weekends. On Saturdays we boarded the morning train for a day in Calgary and although ordering groceries and paying bills was a weekly routine, we always saved time for treats and a movie.

I was less than enthusiastic when some of Tony's co-workers, also taking advantage of free transportation, first invited him to join them for a little socializing in Calgary's many bars. At first he refused, but when they teased him about hiding behind my skirts, I told him that he was free to do as he wished, hoping nonetheless that he would spend the day with us as usual. But he went with them, leaving Lilia and me to watch the movie by ourselves. Later we all met at the station for the trip home. The men, including Tony, were in high spirits, laughing boisterously as the stories (and the language!) grew more colorful with each passing mile. I was thankful that Lilia had quickly fallen asleep.

He easily adapted to the new pattern. Disappointed that trips to Calgary no longer felt like family outings, I decided to stay home. Tony didn't seem to mind going without me, soon spending most of his weekends in hotel taverns. When I protested, he became defensive. Surely after a week of hard work, he was entitled to a bit of relaxation! I asked what our rights were as his family. He just glared at me and slammed out of the house.

Despite my determination not to worry, I grew increasingly anxious about these trips. Which of his unpredictable moods awaited me upon his return? Sometimes he was happy, telling me the day's newest jokes and playfully tickling me. More often he arrived angry and belligerent, shouting and cursing as he staggered into the house. Alcohol released a dark side of Tony's personality that I had never even suspected before.

At first I tried to remain optimistic. After all, it only happened on weekends, and I should be thankful that he never brought alcohol into our home. Then I made excuses. The work was too hard. They expected too much. His friends were a bad influence on him. Then I blamed myself. I was too impatient. I was stubborn. I should try harder. I shouldn't have..... I failed to...... If only....... The endless cycle of blame rested on everyone but Tony.

One night he hit me. I was carrying a lighted kerosene lamp when he slapped my face with his open palm. Somehow I managed to set it down without dropping it, fear of burning the house down momentarily stronger than my shock. No one had ever struck me before. I touched my stinging cheek and stared at him, even as he aimed again. This time I ducked the blow and his hand smashed into the wall.

I was awake all night, my churning mind trying in vain to make sense of what happened, my fingers gently massaging the burning spot on my cheek. *Tony had hit me!* I looked at him lying beside me, snoring peacefully. *What had I done to make him do that? Would he do it again? Would he hurt Lilia?* In the dark hours before dawn I promised myself that regardless of what he might do to me, if he so much as laid a finger on our child, he would be very, *very* sorry!

The next morning he *was* sorry — except that he remembered nothing. When I confronted him with the mark on my face, he had no explanation, only apologies. No, he didn't know why he'd done it. It would *never* happen again. I assured him that if it did, I was more than capable of hitting back. Even as said the words, I knew that I could never follow through with it. Time proved that his apologies and my threats were equally weighted — empty.

Each Monday morning, my *real* husband got up and went to work as though everything was normal. At night, we often went for a walk before Lilia's bedtime and I found myself watching him as he played with her like the devoted father I knew him to be. There was sheer happiness in his laughter and I reassured myself that whatever his problem had been, it must surely be over now. Perhaps next Saturday we could plan an entire day together.

As weeks and months passed, I could no longer pretend, even to myself, that this was just a temporary phase. Tony's weekend drinking escalated, as did the violence. The physical pain was, in a way, less than the shame I felt every time I gingerly examined the colorful collection of bruises on my body. *What was wrong with me, that I made him act this way?* I hardly recognized the face, puffy from weeping, looking back at me from the mirror. *Was Tony capable of killing me in one of his blind rages? Was Lilia safe?* He often shouted at her but so far he had not touched her. What would I do then? I always put her to bed long before he was due to come home, but I knew she heard him raging at me anyway. She was his pride and joy, and it hurt me to see her cringing in fear of him. How could he do this to her?

Every morning-after when Tony wakened, rubbing the sleep from bloodshot eyes, and saw the damage he had done to me, he apologized profusely, adding promise after promise to prove his sincerity. "I'm sorry, I'm *sorry*," he pleaded with me. "I *love* you! I will *never* do this again." But he did. Alcohol's tug proved stronger than all of his best intentions; I could only watch helplessly as his bottle-driven life spiraled downward, pulling us with it.

We had lived in Yoho for approximately a year when a position for *firstman* opened along another section of track, still in the mountains. Tony bid for it and I was relieved when he told me that we were moving. Lilia was ready to start school and unless we lived close to one, she would have to live away from home. A bus stopped conveniently right outside our house and took her to school in Banff.

When Lilia and I were by ourselves, we spoke German and when Tony was at home, Russian. My confidence in English was growing along with my lists of words, and when Lilia started school, I tried to help her as much as I could. She looked at me a bit doubtfully when I carefully pronounced every letter as I had been taught in German. The teacher had said it differently, but I assured her that my way was correct. The next day when her teacher corrected her, Lilia responded with "But my mom said....." Thus began our month-long linguistic tug-of-words.

Finally, the teacher invited me to come for an interview. She was very pleased with my daughter's progress. When I asked her what the gold star pasted to her daily worksheet meant, she told me that even though Lilia didn't understand much English, she only had to be told any set of instructions once, unlike some of her classmates who needed everything repeated over and over again. She did have a favor to ask of me — that I would no longer help Lilia with her reading. She explained that, unlike German, the English language has many words with silent or dead letters such as "e" at the end of a word which were not pronounced. This was a new concept. *What kind of language added useless letters?* I was welcome to read her lessons of course, and perhaps Lilia could even teach me!

I had difficulty adjusting to the idea of silent letters. How was I ever going to learn which ones to say and which ones were just decorative? Even those that *were* pronounced, such as "w" or "v", suddenly behaved differently in English, adopting a confusing new sound identity that I despaired of mastering. To my frustration, acquaintances often failed to tell me when I made a mistake. In fact, those who spoke Russian or German couldn't understand why I insisted that they speak to me in English when our birth languages were so much easier. If I had to stay in this country, I was determined to shed any "Dumb Russian" characteristics as quickly as possible, with or without their help. They laughed at my impatience, assuring me that it would come with time.

I found that to learn English, listening was as important as speaking. Each visit to shops or the train trip to Calgary was an opportunity to hear conversation flowing around me. Without the pressure of participating (when I had to be thinking about my next sentence) I could just enjoy hearing the words, adding new ones to my list for future practice. I was encouraged when I met women who had immigrated years before us, but whose vocabulary was even smaller than mine. Their lives centred around homes and families, and since their husbands looked after all business dealings, they had little incentive to learn a new language. I wondered how they would cope if they were suddenly left alone.

Tony's progress with English now lagged far behind mine. Most of his co-workers were also former Europeans and they usually found a common language in which to converse on the job. His social life required little vocabulary at all.

Soon after Lilia started school she began to ask why she did not have brothers and sisters or uncles, aunts and grandparents like other children in her class at school. Why was our family just *us*? I explained that she *did* have other relatives and that bad people had sent them to a place far away called Siberia. She vowed that when she grew up, she would go to Siberia with a horse and a gun and bring them back to live with us. I hugged her, praying that she would never experience the pain that still tore at my heart when I thought of my family. To lessen her loneliness, we bought her a cocker spaniel and a kitten and although she loved to play with them, I knew the longing continued.

"Who is that cute little boy?" Lilia was leafing through the photo album and stopped at the one surviving picture of Yuri, which I had hastily packed before leaving Pyatigorsk. I had often told her about the war and some of my experiences in fleeing Russia, but omitted telling her about him. It all seemed too complicated for a little girl to understand that her mama had been married before and that she, Lilia, *did* have a big brother. Part of me was afraid that if I told her that I had left him behind, she might worry about me leaving her too. Perhaps it was time she knew.

Her happiness at knowing that she had a brother was dimmed by learning that he had a different daddy. I hoped that in time she might understand that leaving Yuri was the hardest thing I had ever done in my life, that I would gladly make any sacrifice that could bring us together again.

With Lilia in school, I needed something to do and when a friend asked if I was interested in a job of my own, I accepted. A campground in Banff National Park needed restroom cleaners and I was soon equipped with a bucket, mop and cleaning solutions. Other than working the sugar beet fields, this was my first employment in Canada. I was ashamed of it.

"Why do you always hide outside the door when you see someone coming?" I hadn't noticed the American tourist approaching me. She belonged with the big trailer parked nearby. "I've watched you from my window and I don't understand why you do this."

How ironic that in trying not to draw attention to myself, I was drawing attention to myself! I decided to be honest with her.

"I went to university in Russia to be a teacher and here I am — cleaning toilets!" The bitterness in my voice surprised even me. I thought I was resigned to leaving all my ambitions behind, knowing that even an impressive degree in my homeland qualified me for only menial work here in Canada. Pockets of resentment still burned inside.

"There is no shame in cleaning toilets." Her voice was kind in its reproach. "You are earning an honest living and can hold your head high. *What* you do isn't as important as *how* you do it." I stared at her. I could almost hear Papa's voice through this total stranger reminding me that it doesn't matter what we do, how we look or how much money we have. I imagined him laughing gently at me now that I had become one of the people I'd previously scorned.

Even cleaning toilets had its rewards. With my first month's salary of one hundred twenty-seven dollars I went shopping to replace my tired old fur coat which had served me so faithfully in Russia. A new cloth coat, purse and matching shoes restored a spark of vanity to my closet. Our section house lifestyle offered rare opportunities to dress up, and my clothing in recent years was more serviceable than stylish.

Before long, Tony successfully bid on another position, this time near Canmore. I was glad to live in a town again, especially with a school close by so that Lilia could walk there herself. I hoped that if we were part of a real community again, Tony would see how families were supposed to live, and that maybe he would find interests outside of bars for his off-duty hours. Maybe he would again find time to spend with Lilia and me.

We found a third-storey suite to rent for twelve dollars a month — one of my less practical decisions. Everything had to be carried up three long flights of stairs, and four flights for our water supply which came from a pump in the basement. The second floor was vacant and sometimes used for dances or other community events. While the noise sometimes interfered with sleep, I preferred it to trains roaring by my window.

Tony worked out of town, living in a section house during the week and returning home on weekends. To my disappointment, even though he had been away from us all week, he still preferred the company in smoky taverns to ours. Shedding his dirty overalls, he always dressed as though for a night at the opera in suit, tie, and hat. Hours later he staggered home, slurring insults as soon as he opened the front door, his clothing stained and rumpled . By this time, I was a bundle of nerves, terrified of what awaited me. On a good evening, he attacked with shouts and curses. Other times, he slammed me into walls and furniture, or hit me until I was bruised and sore. I became agitated and jumpy, always trying to anticipate what he might do next, yet still unable to protect myself from it.

One night Tony noticed Lilia standing there in her nightie, tears pouring down her cheeks as she begged him to quit hitting me. I thought my heart would break when she invited him to hit her instead. Inexplicably, Tony actually seemed to hear her, his raised arm suspended in mid-swing. He sank onto the bed, tears of remorse trickling down his cheeks.

I was very protective of his job, fearing that he might arrive at work drunk. The company had a limit of three offenses before dismissing an employee, but I took no chances. If Tony was nursing a Monday-morning hangover, I forced him to stay home despite his protests and called his office to let them know he was unwell. I suspected that they knew the real problem, however he was a valued employee and as long as he did not report for work while intoxicated, they tolerated occasional absences. His paycheque kept a roof over our heads and food on the table. Nothing must jeopardize that.

Besides the continuous struggle to keep my home and family together, I experienced frequent attacks of nausea and vomiting, which I attributed to nerves and concern about Tony. I went to the doctor in Banff, who prescribed various medications for stomach disorders. Nothing helped. Puzzled by my lack of response to his treatments, he decided to give me a complete check-up. His nurse, a Ukrainian woman, translated our conversation since my vocabulary did not yet adequately describe the symptoms. They left me alone in the examination room for a while and when they returned, both of them wore broad smiles.

"Well, Mrs. Oushal," he announced, eyes sparkling, "you're pregnant!"

Pregnant? This word was not on my list. "What kind of sickness is this?" I wondered aloud. *And why were they laughing at me?*

"You have a girl already. Maybe you'll have a boy this time!"

A boy? I was going to have a baby? But they told me in Germany that I would never have more children. Now the symptoms made sense and I laughed with them. Another baby!

"But how can this be?" I asked, afraid to believe it in case they had made a mistake. I repeated what my doctor in Germany had said when Lilia was born.

"Sometimes things can change," was their only explanation. It was good enough for me. I was three-and-a-half months along, my due date approximately January 16, 1955.

Lilia was thrilled with my news, as I knew she would be. She wanted a sister and ignored all my attempts to explain that this detail was out of my control. Tony was happy too. I hoped that the added responsibility of a growing family would keep him out of the taverns. It didn't.

On January 15, 1955, two weeks into the new year, Tony arrived home, bringing with him a houseful of friends and enough bottles to raise their spirits for a week. Exhausted from the effort of every awkward movement, I was in no mood for coarse jokes and prayed that they would soon go. To my amazement, all of them left early and even Tony stopped short of his usual quota of Friday night cheer.

At three o'clock in the morning, I wakened with a pain in my side that could mean only one thing. I let Tony sleep as long as I dared, but by five o'clock I knew we should leave for the hospital in Banff. My next door neighbour had promised to come stay with Lilia at any time of the day or night and, although I had hoped not to inconvenience her like this, I was grateful for her help. For months I had worried that when the time came, Tony would be too drunk to take me to the hospital. *Thank you, Lord!*

The doctor's prediction was absolutely right. Stanislow Victor Jerry Oushal was born at nine o'clock that morning. Finally Lilia had a playmate! She thought otherwise. A baby brother was a big disappointment and she demanded that we exchange him for a girl. Only weeks later, when a visiting friend jokingly suggested that she was going to take Stanley home with her, Lilia's sisterly instincts took over. She told our friend that she should go to Banff, where babies were on sale for fifty dollars, and buy her own.

I saw the love and pride in Tony's eyes as he held our son for the first time, and just knew that things would be different from now on. I was wrong.

If anything, a baby in the house aggravated the situation. Stanley operated on his own schedule, loudly announcing each need to be fed, changed, or comforted through a bout of teething pain. His crying irritated Tony and if I failed to silence it immediately, he flew into a rage. I was relieved when his work took him out of town all week as it gave us a reprieve from the uncertainty of his moods. When I met my neighbours in the yard, their glances told me that our difficulties were no secret, but I held my head high, refusing to acknowledge their pity. Yes, we had a problem, but I was determined to deal with it on my own.

Tony's only friends were people he met in bars, usually in Calgary. Oblivious to time, he often missed the return train but some of his new bleary-eyed acquaintances always volunteered to deliver him home, regardless of their own conditions. One blustery winter night I found myself with several strangers needing food and a place to sleep, their car securely sucked into a massive snowbank. Forced to play hostess, I watched them devour a week's budget of groceries in one day. Confronted by my anger at this intrusion, Tony promised that it would not happen again.

A few weeks later, he again missed the train and returned home in a blizzard with strangers. Again I was housing and feeding people whom neither of us knew. I was thankful that Lilia was visiting friends; their foul language had no place in a child's ears. Unlike the soldiers with whom I had trekked across Europe, these men did not apologize for vulgarity in a woman's presence. They even lacked the common sense to carry winter clothing and equipment, taking my sugar beet boots to go check on the car and forgetting to return them.

Why did I stay with Tony? I grew to dread the question, a recurring theme from friends whose concern eventually overcame their reluctance to interfere. To be truthful, I never considered leaving him to be an option. I had married Tony for better or worse and even though *worse* was exactly how I could describe our marriage, did that give me the right to walk away? *Perhaps if I tried a little harder.....*

For me, this meant keeping our home immaculate, although Tony always found something to criticize. Several women visiting me for the first time seemed puzzled about something and asked me repeatedly if I lived there. Of course I lived there! Why did they even ask? They didn't really know how to explain, but with everything *always* in its place, apparently my home lacked a lived-in quality. It was my turn to be puzzled. Wasn't it normal in Canada to have a neat home? Mama had raised me to be tidy, but it raised a new question in my mind. *Were my children paying the price for my fear of Tony? Was it really so important that books and toys not cover the floor with happy clutter? Was I protecting myself at their expense?*

Making friends in a new place was easy; keeping them was not. Tony, on his best behavior, was still charming and funny but this could change in a heartbeat. Invariably, after a few drinks my husband's darker side emerged and new acquaintances quickly distanced themselves with polite excuses. He had no inhibitions about how he treated me in public. If he felt like shouting, calling me names or slapping me, the time or place was irrelevant. Even church offered no sanctuary from his blind rages..

Our friends gradually disappeared from our lives. I knew it was difficult for them as I heard first from one, then another, "You and your children are always welcome in our home. Our door is always open to you. But not to Tony." I knew they were concerned, and understood why they did it. At the same time, I felt that to continue relationships which excluded my husband was to betray the commitment I'd made in my marriage vows.

Ironically, my decision to marry him came from a need to belong, uncomplicated by emotion. Over time I had grown to love him dearly, yet now I felt more isolated than ever. If we as a whole family were unacceptable to our friends, I must withdraw as well. It hurt, but sometimes I crossed the street rather than meet someone on the sidewalk whose friendship now carried terms. I told myself that I was strong enough to handle things alone. My aching heart refused to listen.

23

When Tony announced his intention to bid for a foreman's position on the Morley Reserve my heart sank. What about school for Lilia? There were three others bidding for the same position and I prayed that one of them would be accepted. Tony received his wish and once again we packed our boxes, which were by this time showing signs of wear.

To my immense relief, Lilia was allowed to attend school on the reserve but I knew it was only a temporary postponement of the inevitable day when I must send her away. She loved school and told me how everyone wanted to carry her books and lunch box. People were all very friendly and I reluctantly admitted that I enjoyed Morley too.

I realized the true value of a supportive community when Stanley became ill with a fever, unresponsive to the medication prescribed by our family doctor. When the chief of the reserve stopped by our house with a vile-smelling herbal concoction, I appreciated his thoughtfulness but decided to stick to modern medicine. The fever continued unabated and in desperation I finally spooned some of the mixture into Stanley's unwilling mouth. He grimaced terribly and I felt guilty for adding to his misery — until an hour later when the fever broke and he slept peacefully.

Lilia constantly fretted at my elbow, wanting to know every few minutes if her little brother was going to get better and it was a relief to set her mind at rest. She had long since forgotten that she didn't want a baby brother and spent happy hours entertaining him. His eyes lit up in anticipation when she came home from school, cooing delightedly when she nuzzled his cheek.

The stress of Tony's habits and lifestyle took its inevitable toll on my own health. Unwilling to share any more sordid details of our lives than were already apparent to those around us, I kept all the emotional upheaval inside, determined to stay strong for the children. My doctor recognized the volcano ready to explode inside me and decided it was time for a frank discussion.

"Lydia, unless you find a way to let off steam, your children will not have a mother." His eyes looked deeply into my own, as though willing me to spill out all the bottled-up pain, fear and anger that seemed to pose an even greater danger than Tony. I knew he was right. Unless I found a different way to cope, my children would lose the only parent capable of caring for them.

Within weeks, Tony accepted a new position six miles away but still on the reserve. Each new posting meant another move, this time to another section house without electricity. Every day he drove Lilia back to Morley so at least she could stay in the same school.

One day inspectors from Calgary attended the school, learning from the teacher that a white child was enrolled in her class. They stopped at our house for a visit and, while not actually criticizing the education our daughter was receiving, they cautioned us against leaving her there. The school used a curriculum different from the regular public system and they felt that when we moved again, Lilia would fall far behind other classmates her age.

What now? Neither of us was willing to gamble with our child's education but was it worth sending her away? We discussed it for hours, weighing the benefits against the disadvantages, leaning first one way, then the other. Finally we concluded that if we could find a suitable place for her to live in Calgary we would enroll her in a school there. One of Tony's

CPR colleagues introduced us to a couple who offered to let her live with them. She would stay there during the week and Friday, after school, return home by train.

Besides her physical care, there were other issues that concerned me. *Who would she talk to about her day at school? Who would admire her worksheets and listen to her read? Who would tuck her into bed with a story and prayer?* The lady of the house had her own children and though I knew she would take care of Lilia, some things were a mother's territory. Her *own* mother.

Lilia's new guardians accompanied her on the bus ride downtown to the train station a few times to show her the way but soon she was left on her own. I knew she could find her way, but knowing that my little girl, despite her nine-year-old confidence, was walking four blocks alone to the bus stop gave me many sleepless nights. Each time she arrived home alive and well I breathed a silent prayer of thanks, already dreading Sunday night's return appointment. When she waved forlornly to me from the coach, I fought back tears, trying desperately not to add to her sadness with my own. I timed every moment of her journey, anticipating when she would arrive at the station, how long she might have to wait for the bus, and then the dreaded four-block walk in the dark.

Eventually other arrangements became necessary. *What about a convent?* My friend's suggestion had possibilities. There she would be cared for by resident nuns without the added worry about buses and trains. We visited the convent and decided that this was more suitable than private room and board. I noted all the clothing requirements: tunics, blouses, shoes and even socks, all uniform in color and style.

I previously thought convents were places where girls went in response to some mysterious call and was amazed to see that boys made up a large portion of the student roster. Some of the children lived there as guests of the government, removed from their homes and parents for a variety of reasons.

Lilia disliked the food at the convent and refused to eat much of what was prepared. Strict rules governed mealtimes, rigidly enforced by vigilant nuns. The children must eat everything on their plates, not even allowed to trim fat from meats. I could hardly blame her for resisting, but at the same time, I was concerned about the gaunt pallor already evident in her face after only one week. Fearing for her health, I tried to encourage her to adapt to her new environment rather than continually making comparisons with home. I recognized Suzanne, a girl from a community where we had lived for a short time, who had been taken from her abusive parents. Once thin and sad, she now bounced with energy, her cheeks full and rosy. I often heard her laughter in the hallways.

According to her roommates, Lilia never laughed. She rarely complained during our weekly visits, but they told me that she cried every night after bedtime. I tried to comfort her as best I could, hoping that soon we could live together again.

To my surprise, one day I noticed that other girls wore Lilia's clothes. Since my childhood, I was repulsed at the idea of anyone else wearing my clothes, and felt the same about my daughter's. The nuns were surprised when I protested. After all, the girl had lots of clothes, implying that she should be happy to share them with everyone. I resented being made to feel selfish for wanting her to be the sole user of a wardrobe which had cost me dearly.

A month later, she was limping. Closer inspection revealed a dirty open sore on her foot, already showing the first signs of infection. Did they not have bandages here? Lilia told me that she had reported it to a nun, but nothing had been done. I had not come equipped with salve or bandages and showed Lilia's foot to the sister, demanding to know why it was left untreated. Her look suggested I should mind my own business, but she did as I asked, cleaning the sore and applying a bandage.

A week later the sore was still festering, showing more signs of infection. This time I was prepared and bandaged it myself, making no attempt to conceal my anger. If there was no improvement by my next visit, there would be consequences! I had no idea what those might be but the implied threat achieved the desired result. Lilia's foot, with proper attention, healed even to my satisfaction.

There were other concerns. Each time we came, Tony and I brought treats for all the children and when they saw us, they rushed to see what we carried in our load of boxes and bags.

"Where's Lilia?" I asked one of the girls when I couldn't see her blonde hair flying to meet us amidst the throng of girls. The treats were for *her* to share with her friends.

"Over there," the girl pointed and I looked again. It was definitely my daughter, but what had happened to her hair?

"I wanted short hair so the girls cut it for me," she answered simply. Her hair was shorter, but to say that it had been cut was to stretch the truth. *Chewed* was a more appropriate description of what had happened to her. I remembered the times we had given our blonde baby a brushcut to make her hair grow thicker. I could have done a better job with my eyes shut!

And where were the nuns while all this was happening? Did they have *no* control over the children under their care? The sister in charge, by now anticipating a weekly problem during my visit, just shrugged. "The girls did it and we only found out after it was over."

Was I expecting too much? There were, after all, many children to supervise and it would be difficult to monitor each child one hundred per cent of the time. *Was I an over-protective mother, feeling guilty about leaving my child's care in the hands of strangers?* She was doing well in school but would anyone, anywhere, ever make this situation feel *right?* I agonized over each question, trying to be honest with myself.

Three months after Lilia entered the convent, one of the nuns died. The open casket rested in the chapel and, with other nuns present, the children were summoned to the room for songs and prayers. Lilia was afraid to look at the body and refused to go in, hiding behind the door instead. A nun repeatedly motioned for her to come in too, but she just trembled and shook her head.

After they were finished praying and everyone left the room, the nun dragged Lilia forcibly back into the chapel, making her kneel in front of the casket. The door closed behind her and Lilia was left alone.

I was both pleased and curious when I received an unexpected letter from Suzanne. As I read it, my pleasure quickly turned to horror, both at her description of this event as well as Lilia's subsequent nightmares. Every night the dormitory wakened to her screams.

I made an immediate appointment with Sister Mary, the senior nun, without waiting for the usual weekend visit. The time for polite requests and explanations was over. I was a mother on a mission and cared not a whit for their rules or procedures. That they could do this to a child was despicable. Even some adults shrank from seeing a dead body. How could they force this on a frightened little girl? What were they thinking? I was even angrier when I realized that the nuns were well aware of Lilia's nightmares, but felt it would pass if not given too much attention. I decided that some things were too important to sacrifice for education after all.

"I know why you're taking her out." Sister Mary's tone implied that this episode was not *really* the issue. "You're not Catholic."

Something snapped inside me. Perhaps what I had previously interpreted as indifference about their supervision of my daughter's activities had an altogether different explanation.

"This has nothing to do with being Catholic! I brought her here because I thought a place where people prayed and lived close to God was a safe place for a child! You didn't take care of her when she was hurt, and never seemed to know what she or the other girls were doing. And now you lock her in a room with a dead body!"

By this time I was shouting at the black-robed nun with the patronizing smile. I reminded her that I had faithfully trained Lilia in the church's catechism as I had promised the priest when she was born. How dare she so smugly transfer blame to me!

Sister Mary's belated attempts to placate me made no difference now. Their neglect of my child left me with no alternative. I would take her away. Now.

Lilia told me later how she had knelt in front of the casket, too terrified to move, staring fixedly at the dead nun — who she was certain had breathed. She promised herself that no matter who died, she would never look at another dead person as long as she lived.

I knew she believed in God, but the experience left Lilia with a cynicism about the church in general, and nuns in particular. She saw little relationship between a loving heavenly father, and how his representatives treated her on earth.

The nun's reference to my non-Catholic status reminded me that I needed to prepare myself for eventual conversion to the Church, that is, if I ever found Mama and Papa and they gave me their blessing to do so. Living in the mountains gave me little opportunity to take the required catechism classes or even to attend services, although I managed to meet with the priest in Banff several times. He assured me that I would be a good Catholic because I genuinely desired to understand the faith and to build on the foundation laid in my childhood. In fact, he admitted that often he didn't know how to answer all my questions.

"Why do Catholics pray to Mary?" This was one of the biggest differences that I knew between Lutherans and Catholics. I had been taught that although Mary was the mother of Jesus, she was an ordinary human being.

"No, Lydia, we don't pray *to* her. We ask her to pray for *us.*" He tried to keep his answers to my questions simple, knowing that my growing English vocabulary probably did not include many theological terms. I wanted to know about the sacraments, the weekly practice of communion, and the ceremony of baptism for children, always comparing each explanation to my early training. The basic beliefs, apart from their special attention to Mary, seemed very much the same; the Bible was the Word of God, and many of the ceremonies and songs I remembered from when I was a little girl. In Germany, I was already drawn to God's presence in the Latin liturgy that flowed from the altar into the deepest corners of my soul as I knelt in worship. Succeeding years had not dulled this sense of awe, even without regular church attendance.

We resumed room and board arrangements for Lilia, both in Calgary and then in Lake Louise, with weekend commutes to our various homes in the mountains. This time, friends drove her to the train station. Knowing that she was not alone on dark city streets eased my fears for her safety, even though the sadness in her eyes continually tore at my heart. I sometimes wondered if she was treated differently than her hosts' children, but she never complained. Later she told me how the others were allowed to go downstairs at night if they were afraid of the dark while she was told to stay in her bed. At meals, the other children could refuse to eat bread crusts while she was forced to finish every crumb.

Tony's frequent bids for new positions ensured that we usually stayed in one place for only weeks or months at a time, but at least we always had access to free transportation. If Tony's assigned section was not an official train stop, we flagged it down, although by now the crew knew when to expect Lilia on the platform. My most frequent prayer remained that someday soon we would be able to live together again. I could not imagine both my children living out their childhoods under strangers' roofs, even for the sake of an education. There must be a better way.

24

The best solution was to buy our own home. Bouncing from one dilapidated section house to another was no life for a family with school age children, and I determined to end my daughter's misery along with my own. Calgary seemed the logical place to invest, with easy train access to any place Tony might be assigned.

We recruited a realtor to show us all the houses available in our price range and close to a school. I had a detailed list of what my own home would contain, and so far, everything he showed us was missing some "must haves." After visiting some show homes one day, I finally had the answer. We'd build a new one! We chose a vacant lot, eventually agreeing on one of the developer's plans which allowed us to modify it according to The List. I could hardly believe that my dream home was only months away .

To save money, I painted and decorated the house myself. After years of turning dilapidated section houses into homes, however temporary, adding the final touches to a brand new house was sheer pleasure. The final result could have graced a magazine cover and I was proud of my efforts.

Once the interior was complete, I turned my attention outdoors. Piles of dirt left from the basement had to be levelled in readiness for loads of rich black topsoil. Mama would be so amazed to see the rolls of sod that transformed dirt yards in Canada into instant lawns. I thought of her as I knelt in the newly dug flower beds, inhaling the earthy fragrance and wishing that she could share this adventure with me. I could almost hear her directing me where to plant the tiny seedlings, still safe in colorful packets scattered around my grubby knees. In June, 1957, everything was finished.

Despite my frustrations with Tony's job, there was one benefit which I thoroughly enjoyed; our whole family could travel on a pass throughout Canada and the United States. Every year we took a vacation to some new destination.

When I watched Tony playing with our children, relaxed and happy, during these weeks away from home and work, it was hard to remember the dark side of our lives. He was once again the charming, attentive man I had married. As he explained to them the changing landscape outside the train, I recognized for myself the teacher he must have been. I ached for him. Compared to his well-established career, my own thwarted teaching ambitions were a minor sacrifice. I wondered how differently our lives might have been if he had been more patient about leaving Germany. Perhaps if this love of his life had been restored, he would have no need for bottled comfort.

In July, 1957, we travelled to Windsor, Ontario, where I finally met my Aunt Mena. We had a joyful visit, each of us searching the other for a resemblance to Mama, both in face and manner. She was hungry for every detail I could provide of her family's life in Nikolevka and I could hardly finish one story before she had a dozen questions about other people and events. We parted, each promising the other that if we heard *anything* about *anybody,* we would share the information immediately.

Lilia started school in September and, as planned, I was there to see her off in the morning. In the afternoon I met her at the door when she came home to tell me about her day. I was the one who tucked her into bed at night and thanked God that the days of sending her away on the train by herself were over.

My dreams of settling into my home failed to include some very expensive realities. Besides the monthly seventy-five dollar mortgage payment, there were new and unfamiliar bills: natural gas, telephone and electricity, each with its own hook-up fee. Tony paid ten dollars per month rent at the section house where he lived during the week, returning to Calgary each Friday. Every Sunday night he took with him the best of our grocery budget in meals which I prepared for him in advance, leaving little in my own cupboard for the children and me. I kept telling myself that since he was working to support us, it was important that he eat well, but our own monotonous diet of noodle soup and milk, supplemented only by vegetables from my garden, was increasingly difficult to accept. It was hard to cook good meals for him, knowing that we would not be able to enjoy them too. By November, I made the difficult decision to rent our house and to rejoin Tony, who was once again stationed in the mountains.

Our new tenants, a young couple with two children, agreed to a reduction in the rent in return for my retaining a room in the house where Lilia could live during the week. I looked after her groceries and laundry, and on weekends she again travelled by train to be with us. I was nervous about leaving her with total strangers but they seemed like nice people and I was reluctant to disrupt her life any more than necessary. She was happy in school and doing well so I tried to keep a positive outlook and encouraged her to do the same. After all, things were slowly improving. At least now we had a house to call our own, even if we couldn't live in it together for now.

My discouragement at this change in plans was offset a few months later when I received a letter from Aunt Mena enclosing a letter from my uncle in Siberia! Unknown to us, he had been on the same train as my parents. Now that I finally had an

233

address, I lost no time in writing to him. He forwarded my letter to Mama and Papa who lived in Udtzar. Papa answered immediately. The letter was short, and in recognition of mail censorship, gave little information about their lives. They had heard that I had left my home in Pyatigorsk, but didn't know if I was alive or dead. I could hear his voice through the carefully penned lines, telling me that they always prayed for me and whenever there was a birthday or any celebration, they set a place for me at the table. I cried at the thought. I would pay any price to occupy that chair even once.

If I could not be there, sending gift packages was the next best alternative. I made a beautiful table cloth and pillow shams with pink roses for my mother, crocheted with real crochet cotton, unlike the thin thread we had used at home. I knew she would smile about the pillows, remembering my teenage impatience with needlework. I sent Papa a shiny metallic picture of the Last Supper, praying that it would escape the authorities' notice.

Not wishing to overshadow our mail-order reunion with sadness, it took Papa a few letters to tell me that Reinhold had frozen to death in a snowstorm. *My big brother was dead?* How could that be? He was so strong and, I always thought, the most likely to survive whatever hardships might befall my family. For years I had stubbornly believed that someday they could all come to Canada. It was hard to accept loss of that hope for even one of them. I sat for a long time, tears spilling down my face onto the thin paper.

Try as I might, my memory's version of Victor's and Heinrich's adolescent voices refused to sound as adult as their letters indicated. *My baby brothers — married? With children?* Victor's wife sent unintentionally amusing letters, reporting

234

various family misdemeanors including her sister-in-law Luba's greediness. She had so openly admired the things I sent that Mama invited her to take them. I was unsure why she tried to involve me in petty in-law rivalry, but I declined to participate in a long-distance feud. Having learned the true value of family and the pain of separation, I wanted to shake them, to tell them to live peacefully and to take care of each other. *Things* were temporary and easily destroyed. Family was forever.

We traded photographs and there were few letters that did not contain some record of family events. They apologized for the quality of their small black and white snapshots compared to my colored pictures. I hardly noticed in my eagerness to see them again.

There is no aging process in memories, and even though I expected seventeen years and the ravages of life in Siberia to make a difference, I was unprepared for a current picture of my parents. They seemed so frail, smiling up at me from the glossy print, but they were still very much Mama and Papa. I wondered what my photos said to them. *Would Papa look into my eyes and say, "My little bull's character has changed?" Would Mama know how much I cherished the diary that she gave me and how it hurt me to destroy it?* I remembered to tell Mama how her underpants had decorated my walls and wished I could be there to hear her laugh.

Amidst the excitement of finding my family, I experienced the frustrations of being a landlord. When we brought Lilia back to the city after the Christmas break, the house was empty, the tenants gone. There were more surprises. A collection of bills cluttered the countertop — gas, electric, telephone — all with an ominous *FINAL WARNING* stamp. I was stunned at the tally. Two hundred seventy-two dollars must be paid within ten days or all services would be disconnected. There were also miscellaneous items missing from our storage boxes in the basement: a pair of Tony's shoes; a child's cape that I had brought from Germany and had allowed the woman to use for a portrait of her little girl; a collection of dishes.

At the time, leaving the utilities in our name had seemed the simplest thing to do rather than pay new hook-up charges in the hopefully near future when we could move in again. Our tenants took full advantage of our trust, happily chalking up hours of long distance telephone visits under our name. But they had promised to pay the utilities! Where was I going to find that kind of money?

This called for legal advice. For once, understanding the subject matter was more important to me than practicing English, and I contacted an attorney who was fluent in Russian. He shook his head when I finished my story, incredulous that we would be so gullible. The important thing now was to find the culprits and to recover the money which I had borrowed from friends, hopeful that we could repay them before too long. If at all possible, I hoped to resolve it without going to court.

A few weeks later, our lawyer reported that although he had located the couple, they were unwilling to co-operate. Our only hope was court action. We reluctantly agreed and the date was set. When he also proposed visiting their home with a search warrant for the missing property I was adamant that this was not a matter for police involvement. God knew what they had done and would hold them accountable in his time and way. The lawyer shook his head in disbelief, although he respected my wishes. Did anyone actually believe that God might be interested?

Confident of winning, our lawyer brought all our unpaid bills and copies of receipts to court, hoping that this appointment with justice would cost the defendants more than if they had co-operated in the first place. Predictably, the couple first tried to pass blame to each other for failure to pay a month's rent. Then came the surprising accusation that Tony had touched the wife inappropriately. Neither of these carried any weight with the judge, but we were all taken aback at a sudden outburst from the woman whom I entrusted with my daughter's care.

"Why should we have to pay rent to a DP?" The venom in her voice shocked everyone almost as much as the judge's gavel crashing on the table. He did not tolerate this kind of talk in his courtroom.

"I could charge you right now with discrimination," he said, each word heavy with warning. "It doesn't matter *who* owns the house. If it's not yours, you pay for the privilege of living in it." He motioned for the couple to sit. Turning to me, he asked how much I now charged new tenants for rent. When I told him it was one hundred fifty-five dollars per month, he pointed out to them just how much they had saved compared to actual value. Both of them looked down, fidgeting uneasily under his contemptuous stare. Then it was over. They were ordered to pay all costs, including our legal fees, for a total of three hundred eighty-three dollars. Their lawyer packed his briefcase in obvious disgust, leaving the room without a backward glance.

Like us, they had difficulty producing that sum of money at a moment's notice. Payment arrangements of seventy-five dollars per month were negotiated, to be made at our lawyer's office. On one visit the woman, who had apparently learned little from the experience, grabbed the money and the receipt back from the startled secretary, racing out of the office as fast as she could go. Building security officers easily intercepted her, returning her to the office where the lawyer awaited her with some advice. Since she had two small children, he agreed to keep her out of jail, but she should think very carefully before attempting anything like this again. And, he added, he felt very sorry that her children had to grow up with this kind of mother.

One of her children didn't grow up at all. She was hit by a truck while crossing the road to school and I felt very sad. Although I knew that I was not responsible for the tragedy, I remembered my words that someday God would hold them accountable. I wished I had not said them.

25

Papa's letters contained little information about their journey to Siberia; he believed that the past should remain in the past. Rather than dwell on the unchangeable, it was better to make the most of the present, and to prepare for the future as best one could. Mama, even without all my questions, knew that I craved to know what had happened to them after they boarded the train. Risking the wrath of communist censors, she described their journey in vivid detail. Her letter took me back to the familiar railway platform, tears streaming down my face as I waved goodbye to a white hanky flapping from a freightcar window......

The train made a slight detour en route to Siberia, directed rather to the German battlefront. Before reaching it, officials mounted dummy machine guns on top of the cars, hoping to invite a German bomb attack on the train. The Russians planned to respond with carefully staged "outrage" that the German army had killed hundreds of German citizens. The ploy failed and when it became apparent that the enemy would not be seduced, the train continued on its way.

The entire journey lasted several months with numerous changes in trains, and weeks spent in a vacant school awaiting the next stage of resettlement. By the time they were loaded onto open platform cars for the final phase, it was winter and bitterly cold. Each car was equipped with a sanitation bucket and a heater, which proved to be no match for the bone-chilling temperatures. Papa shared the carpet pieces with other travellers and they all huddled together to preserve what little warmth they had. Scarves over faces were as much a defense against the bucket's stench as from the wind's icy blast.

The food supplies brought from home had long since been depleted. Knowing Mama and Papa, I was certain that as long as they had anything to share with their fellow travellers, they would gladly have done so, even if it meant having less themselves. By the time they were exposed to Siberia's brutal winter conditions, their only food was the bread and water provided on the train.

At every stop, workers unloaded at least twenty starved and frozen corpses, carting them away to an anonymous grave. The remaining passengers watched in silence, each somber face reflecting the same thought: Will I be next? Prayers of gratitude marked each stop where our family remained intact. They always remembered me too. Without any means of knowing whether I was alive or dead, they reminded each other that distance and circumstance alike were no obstacle to God. Wherever I might be, he was there too.

When they arrived at their destination at a remote station, dogsleds waited to take them the remaining one hundred fifty kilometres, finally depositing them in the middle of a frozen wasteland. Each family was given a pick, shovel, tripod and kettle, and minimal fuel, as well as forty kilograms of wheat and three litres of oil per person. With a smirking invitation to build a shelter any way they could, the Russian escorts left them to their fate.

Survival meant immediate action and they set about building a snow house in the bitter cold, digging through two metres of packed snow before reaching the frozen ground below. Undernourishment made an already difficult task even worse. Papa especially struggled with the unaccustomed manual labor, but eventually a shelter emerged. The carpets which used to decorate their house now lined the icy walls of their igloo, this time with a more practical purpose. If Eskimos had lived this way for centuries, perhaps they too could learn new skills.

Some in their makeshift little town who had survived the journey now collapsed, as much from a lack of will to go on as the harsh *conditions. Life and death alike was stripped of dignity, and without meaning or hope, there was no reason to continue the struggle. The meager diet of cooked wheat built scant resistance to ailments considered minor under normal conditions, a growing pile of frozen corpses a grisly reminder that life was fragile. Extreme cold preserved the bodies until spring when officials visited the settlement, and with a generous application of kerosene, turned the stack into a blazing mass funeral pyre.*

Mama's letter listed as many names of victims as she could remember, identifying relatives, friends, neighbours and former classmates. I stopped reading, clearly picturing each of them going about their ordinary lives on the streets of Nikolevka. Out of all these people, why had I been singled out for a different journey that ultimately brought me to Canada, no part of which I would have chosen for myself? I thought back on all the years of wondering what had happened to my parents and brothers. Perhaps the agony of not knowing had, in fact, been a blessing, allowing me to concentrate on the urgency of events in my own life.

Victor, at age sixteen, had trained as a machinist before leaving Nikolevka and now worked in an armaments factory in the Ural Mountains. Education for German exiles was not a communist priority and Heinrich, thirteen, was recruited along with other young people to work underground in a coal mine in Kisilevsk. Knowing that both their sons were housed and fed eased my parents' unhappiness at their being sent away. Although the boys were supposedly allowed to write letters home, none ever arrived.

Eventually Mama and Papa received permission to move to Kisilevsk as well, followed by Victor. Both my brothers married local girls and built a house big enough for all of them to live together. Papa was delighted to find some musical instruments and even more delighted that, after an initial period of rusty playing technique, he could still fill the house with melody.

Mama too was reunited with her greatest passion. Flowers blossomed in abundance around their house and local citizens gathered to marvel, not only at the colorful display but at her determination to create it. The constant struggle against poverty in a hostile climate left little time or energy for pleasure and beauty.

My parents' request to move back to the Caucasus was denied. In 1958, Victor visited Nikolevka with strict orders from Mama to bring back all the seeds he could carry, that is, for flowers rather than vegetables. If she was barred from returning home, the best of home must come to her.

Victor's visit to our old home bore other fruit. Knowing of my unsuccessful attempts to contact Grunya by letter, he visited her in Pyatigorsk. Yuri, now twenty, was serving his mandatory army duty and she was home alone. Confronted by my brother, who was no longer the reckless teenager she remembered, she confessed that, yes, she and other relatives had indeed received my letters, but had agreed to return them unopened to the post office. She shrank from Victor's anger, admitting that her actions had been selfishly motivated by fear that I would, even at such a distance, take Yuri away from her. The post office had subsequently turned the letters over to the KGB, yet even when confronted by officials who forcibly read them to her, she still had not replied. Neither did she share any news about me with my son.

Intimidated by Victor's threat to tell Yuri how she had withheld information from him, Grunya finally agreed to talk to him herself. I received Yuri's first letter within weeks.

My fears that he might forget me proved groundless, even without pictures or other mementos which had been destroyed by the police within hours of my flight from our home. I learned that the authorities' search for me had made it dangerous for anyone to have my photograph. Yuri's questions about what I looked like had to be satisfied with verbal portraits. But neighbours and friends had kept my memory alive for him over the years. I squirmed when I read what they told him about me, uncomfortable with the glowing descriptions. His godmother, who lived across the street, often sighed as she looked at him, always remarking on his resemblance to me. At home he would sit in front of the mirror, staring at his reflection and wondering how his male features might look on a woman. His memories as a five-year-old were unhelpful in recreating any mental image of me now.

When Victor told me about Grunya's rejection of my letters, I was certain that she had poisoned my son against me, perhaps as the traitorous German portrayed in KGB records. Again, I was wrong. She had always told him that I was the best mother he could have wished for, and that I left him only because it seemed the safest choice for both of us. She even told him that our Russian neighbours all loved me and that he should be proud of me.

Only after we had exchanged a few letters did Yuri mention his father. Contrary to the impression given to us by the Russian army, Alexander had survived the war but sustained multiple wounds which were stitched together in a Romanian hospital, where he was left behind when it was all over. His physical wounds healed, however severe amnesia rendered him homeless, without history or identity. Eventually they sent him back to a Russian hospital where his cousin, in a chance meeting, recognized him.

The doctors recommended that she take him back to his home, reintroducing him to friends and relatives and showing him favorite places from his childhood with the hope that a familiar setting might restore what was lost. They gave him an accordion, and his fingers instinctively found the right combination of keys, forming long-forgotten chords and melodies. A less happy but powerful memory came with a visit to the place where his brother was killed by a train. Over a one-year period, Alexander's life was slowly returned to him. He remembered his son, which led to memories of his son's mother. Me. And he wanted me back.

Nothing could be simpler in Yuri's mind than for me to sell everything that tied me to Canada and to return home. As gently as I could, without leaving the impression that I did not wish to see any of them again, I explained that there were many complications with that idea, not the least of which were my husband and children. Yuri reluctantly agreed, recognizing that I would probably be arrested immediately upon arrival in Moscow. Even after all this time, I could still be sent to Siberia. It was better for us to plan that someday he could visit me instead.

26

Summer, 1958. When Tony nearly choked me to death by squeezing a poker against my throat, I knew it was time for me to leave with the children. Without even packing a bag, I called Lilia, grabbed Stanley's hand and started for the main road. I didn't know where we were going or how we were going to get there; my only goal was to put as much distance as possible between me and my drunken husband. He *was* capable of killing me and all the *sorries* in the world would still leave my children without a mother. Rage fuelled my pace, and Stanley, his short legs at full gallop, had difficulty keeping up. Behind me, Tony swayed against the door frame, calling for me to come back. I kept walking, eyes fixed resolutely ahead.

"All right then, I guess I'll just die right here." I turned around to see him staggering onto the railway track, where he lay down between the rails. Tony was at his theatrical best, but I ignored the performance. Enough was enough. I had survived bullets and bombs; I would survive the bottle too!

The train's whistle stopped me in my tracks. Lilia and I heard it at the same time and looked at each other in terror. Both of us knew that if Tony sat or lay down while drunk, sleep usually followed immediately. In any case, once having lost momentum, he had no strength to move himself, even if it meant the difference between life and death.

She raced back to him and I followed as fast as I could, still dragging Stanley by the hand. "Get up! Get up!" she screamed at him, mindful of the train's whistle now dangerously closer than before.

"Leave me here," he said, "your mother is leaving me and I want to die." We both knew this wasn't true. To a devout Catholic, killing oneself was a mortal sin. Besides, tomorrow he would have forgotten the entire episode, genuinely wondering where we were and why he was alone. By this time the train was in sight, its whistle blowing frantically as the engineer saw our drama unfolding, knowing that he was unable to stop in time. Lilia begged Tony to move, alternately pushing and pulling his dead weight. I arrived huffing and puffing, just in time to add my strength to hers as, with a mighty heave, we rolled him off the tracks moments before the train roared past. We collapsed in a soggy embrace, Tony lying in a heap on the grass beside us, mumbling incoherently.

I began to tremble as I realized that I had come within seconds of losing my husband. Whether I liked it or not, Tony depended on me as though he was a child. I would never be able to face the guilt of even indirect responsibility for his death. If I left, Tony was very capable of destroying himself. If I stayed, he would likely destroy me. I was caught in alternate traps of love and duty, incomprehensible to my friends who could not understand what held me in this destructive relationship. But stay I must. I was all he had.

September, with its constant reminders that a new school term was underway, presented an especially difficult time for Tony. In his moody silences and vacant stares, I knew he was reliving a classroom scene with rows of eager young faces, all reflecting a passion for life and impatience to live it. Tony had loved that role and the challenge of finding new and exciting ways to impart knowledge to his students. Some of the stage plays he had written came to Canada in our trunk, along with pictures of him with his students. The war had interrupted a fulfilling career which already included seven years as a principal. I knew he regretted his impatience to leave Germany. Neither sugar beets nor the railway, or even his family came close to filling the void left in his life.

Even after everything we had endured as a family, I still loved him. When he was sober, he was a delightful companion to me and a concerned father to our children. By now, however, I was under no illusion about the permanence of this state. Alcohol's grip on my husband would not be wished away.

Christmas and Easter were often painful holidays. If he was sober, Tony enjoyed them as much as the children and I loved the sound of their delighted shrieks as they "helped" him by tearing the wrapping off his gifts as well as their own. But I could never be confident that he would be with us, or if he was, would he share, or spoil the occasion? As we hung ornaments on the tree one night when Tony was celebrating elsewhere, Lilia asked me why I always cried during times that were supposed to be happy. How could I describe the bitter-sweet flood of long ago Christmas Eve memories, when my whole family would laugh and sing as we decorated the tree? Papa was as excited as the rest of us; *nothing* could have kept him away from his family. I desperately wanted the same for her, but her daddy was gone.

When he returned early one Christmas morning, he was in a surly mood, although, thankfully, not drunk. "Here's your Christmas present!" He threw a package at me with wild aim, and it smashed into the wall instead. I left it where it fell to the floor until Lilia brought it to me. The blue velvet case was soft to my touch, its hinged closing mechanism now permanently bent. A beautiful garnet necklace with matching earrings sparkled up at me when I pried it open. I closed the box without commenting. What good was expensive jewellery without the love that made it special? We went through the festive motions of a turkey dinner, but I felt only a sad hollowness inside.

Easter was the same. I tried to revive the special traditions of my childhood, but without Tony's presence or participation, my own enthusiasm carried a false ring.

After I began to receive mail from my family, Tony withdrew still further. During my years of writing endless letters to the Red Cross, friends and acquaintances from Pyatigorsk, searching for someone, *anyone*, who could tell me what had happened to Yuri and my family, Tony stubbornly refused any attempt to contact his brothers. His reluctance baffled me. They were a close family and as far as we knew, everyone still lived in the same place. Finding them should be less difficult than my own search had been.

Finally he admitted that he was afraid for them — that they might be arrested and thrown into prison (or worse) if the authorities knew where he was. I had never thought of that possibility in my desperation to find my family, and I doubt it would have changed anything. The ache of longing for my loved ones outweighed the fear of consequences and I was certain that they shared my willingness to risk.

When envelopes with foreign stamps arrived in our mailbox, Tony seemed happy for me, although he rarely asked questions or expressed interest even though the letters were addressed to both of us. My excitement at the miraculous long-distance reunion with Mama and Papa never waned and I scarcely noticed that he always became very quiet and withdrawn, staring morosely at the television. Each letter provided an excuse to drink more than usual.

As much as I dreaded Tony's vicious tirades, sometimes they provided a more truthful picture of what was going on inside than he ever admitted while he was sober. I finally realized how deeply he resented my success in finding my family.

"Nazi! Fascist! You think you are *so* clever!" My attempts to ignore the name-calling and accusations only increased his determination to provoke me. It was futile to reason with him when he was like this. Perhaps later I could remind him that I had always encouraged him to write even one letter — that I even offered to write it for him.

To my surprise, he finally wrote it himself. I prayed that he would receive an answer, fearing what might happen if his one attempt did not produce results. One day the blue and red airmail envelope which usually meant a letter for me, had his name on it! *Thank you Lord!*

The news was both good and bad. His oldest and youngest brothers were killed in the war, but his other brother was alive and married with children. He gave Tony's address to an aunt who began to write us letters, frequently referring to her belief in God. I marvelled at the bond created between total strangers who, though separated by oceans, knew instant kinship through shared faith.

There was no definite information about his wife and children. She was believed to be dead and they had heard that his son and daughter were in Latvia but had lost all contact with them.

Even with the sadness contained in the letter, Tony came alive with new vitality and wrote back, anxious to get acquainted with what remained of his family all over again. As in mine, there were now in-laws and nieces and nephews that he had never met, with years of events to recapture, frustrated by limitations of pen, paper and photographs.

Shopping for overseas parcels became a regular activity for both of us. We knew that consumer goods in Russia were scarce with minimal choice and we bought things that were practical and of good quality. My family appreciated all that I sent to them, although concerned that I might be depriving my family on their behalf. The cost to me was small compared to my pleasure in preparing the packages. Knowing that those I loved would handle the items was in itself comforting, although every time I sealed the boxes I wanted to send myself along for a visit.

Some in Tony's family were less appreciative. His niece, a young woman of about twenty, informed us that the fabric we had sent her could be purchased locally and that she would prefer an angora sweater with sequins and a matching scarf, hat and gloves. I was appalled at her audacity, but for Tony's sake priced the articles requested, asking him later if he really wanted to spend over three hundred dollars on things which we could not even consider buying for our own children. He didn't, and sent his niece a terse letter. Her eventual reply was scathing. Why had her uncle married a German who, after all, was responsible for killing her people?

27

In May, 1960, Tony successfully bid for a job in Benalto, a few miles west of Sylvan Lake. With every move to yet another section house, I thought longingly of my well-equipped dream home back in Calgary. At least this house had electricity, I consoled myself. But more important, we now lived within walking distance of a school. I had never reconciled myself to seeing Lilia only for week-end visits, a constant reminder that I was missing out on most of her childhood. Now she would come home every day.

We arrived in Benalto a few days ahead of our furniture and stayed in the town's only hotel. I introduced myself to Catherine, owner of the little coffee shop, and was amazed a short time later when she knocked on my door. Could I please help her? The cook had quit, leaving her alone with fourteen hungry construction workers waiting to order lunch. I was up to my elbows in laundry, but she looked so desperate that I washed my hands and hurried down to help.

Then she offered me a job! I was flattered, but hesitant. What did I know about cooking in a restaurant? She waved aside all my protests. It was just like cooking for a family — a big family, that is. Other than cleaning restrooms in the park, I had never considered working outside my home. But why not? To my surprise, Tony agreed. Catherine's son, Jerry, was Stanley's age and the boys already enjoyed playing together. Our house was conveniently located across the street so if he needed me, I was close by.

Catherine was also a German and we became good friends as well as co-workers. She taught me both how to operate the equipment and to prepare the food. Together we planned lunch and supper menus and she gave me free rein in the kitchen, even letting me cancel the standard order for buckets of pie filling from our Edmonton supplier. When fresh fruit was readily available in the grocery store, why use something with artificial flavoring?

I quickly settled into a daily routine of making seven pies and up to eight dozen doughnuts. The workday began at six o'clock in the morning, preparing for the mid-morning onslaught of local farmers and business people with a pie-and-coffee habit. Why did all these people come here when they could eat at home? This was yet another baffling Canadian custom but definitely good for business. When someone commented on the new tastiness of our pies, I felt rewarded for all the extra peeling and chopping. In the afternoon, hungry school children crowded into the coffee shop for ice cream, pop and milk shakes.

Besides local customers, the coffee shop also provided bag lunches for construction crews working in the area who lived upstairs in the hotel. For supper, ravenous after a long day of hard work, they usually ordered T-bone steaks on company expense accounts. The cash register's steady chime was music to my ears.

Catherine was right. I soon became adept at juggling multiple orders on the grill, topping up endless coffee mugs, and ringing through the bills. I quickly learned names and looked forward to "my" regulars who came by for a daily dose of banter with their coffee. My heavily accented English invited questions about where I came from and how I had landed in their little corner of the world. Catherine's subtle cough reminded me that other chores awaited me. I loved to talk, especially when I had such an appreciative audience. Ever since learning that my parents and son were safe, it was easier for me to share stories from my past without becoming overwhelmed with sadness.

With each of our moves, I wondered if any of my precious overseas mail might be lost, and was reassured every time a new letter answered questions from my last writing. I was delighted when Yuri told me that he planned to be married to a wonderful girl with golden hair and a heart to match. And he wanted my blessing. Despite several years of letters and photographs, I still thought of him as my little boy. Now he was getting married. I suggested that his grandmother should have this honor as she had loved and raised him as her own son. His reply was immediate — and heartwarming. We had been separated by war, not choice. He had always loved me and would wait to marry until I blessed him.

As always, I cried when I received his letters. Of course he had my blessing! I only wished I could deliver it personally and meet Raisa, the girl who shared my son's affections. The wedding card with the bride and groom and congratulatory message which I translated into Russian was a poor substitute for being there but had, nonetheless, said what was in my heart. Yuri told me later that they had framed it and hung it on the wall.

Catherine wanted to be completely free of the business and suggested that I buy it from her. It was an interesting thought, but with Tony's here-today-gone-tomorrow work life, any longterm business investment was out of the question.

"Then run it for me. I don't want to have anything to do with it." One way or another, she was determined to make me responsible for the coffee shop. There were still many things I needed to learn about ordering meat and other supplies but I knew I was capable of doing it.

I loved my new responsibility, especially when the first day's cash totalled four hundred-one dollars. She stared at me in amazement. Her highest daily total until now was two hundred-seventy dollars. She immediately assumed that her employees had cheated her and I cautioned her against making hasty accusations. One of Papa's admonitions still rang in my ears: Before we said anything that could hurt someone else, we should think about it one hundred times before the words left our mouths. Once said, they could never be taken back. Besides, I preferred to blame the temperamental cash register.

Our move to Benalto had one serious drawback. Easy access to a bar resulted in a long-dreaded change in Tony's drinking habits. While he had previously limited his alcohol use to weekends, now it was convenient to stop by the hotel after work nearly every day for a 'little relaxation.' When the shouting started next door, I could be reasonably certain that it involved Tony.

Inevitably, my coffee-shop customers realized that the drunk regularly ejected from the hotel tavern was my husband. An efficient small-town grapevine ensured that Tony was known by reputation long before many people actually met him. Rather than going home, he often came to the restaurant, staring at other customers and making rude comments in a deliberate attempt to embarrass me. If children came to buy candy and happened to look at him, he grabbed them and threw them outside. I tried to stay positive, assuring others that Tony meant no harm. I saw skepticism on their faces, but they were too polite to argue. My bruises told their own story, but unless I wanted to charge him with assault, my friends could only watch helplessly from a distance.

Even with all the problems in my marriage, I still wanted a church-sanctioned wedding ceremony. I had held firm in my determination to remain Lutheran unless, or until, Mama and Papa gave me their blessing to become Catholic. After we had exchanged a few letters I finally took courage and asked the question. I explained that my husband was Catholic and I had promised to raise my two children in the Catholic faith, but that the church's sacrament of marriage was withheld until I too embraced that faith. In a way it seemed strange that I, a grown woman with an ocean between me and my parents, still needed their permission, but I sensed their appreciation of my willingness to wait, even if it never came. Their separate letters gave me an unreserved blessing, concerned only that Tony share my belief in God.

They often expressed relief that I had again found someone with whom to share my life. I deliberately omitted any mention of Tony's abusive treatment. We had all known enough sadness and I was reluctant to add a new burden that they were powerless to change, but which would cause them endless worry.

According to the new certificate, our marriage was revalidated on February 4, 1961. Both of us could now fully participate in all the rites of the Church.

On March 8, 1961, we became Canadian citizens at a ceremony in Red Deer. We studied the questions diligently in advance, but I was still afraid that we might have misunderstood something. I remembered the formidable portrait of Adolf Hitler glaring down at me the last time I changed citizenship. I had travelled many miles since then. This time, a judge presided as we declared our allegiance to Canada and promised to obey her laws.

Benalto was a small community with close ties that still opened to welcome outsiders. Lilia joined Girl Guides and a club at church. Stanley enrolled in Cubs and played hockey. In spring, our backyard became a Friday afternoon classroom for children preparing for their first communion. They came to town from neighbouring farms and the priest taught them their catechism. I was busy with the restaurant, but still found time to participate in church and community events. Except for Tony's drinking, life was wonderful.

Mealtimes were often tense. Tony had no patience with childish squabbles and expected Lilia and Stanley to behave like stiff little soldiers at the table or he would smack them across the forehead with a fork. Even when he was drunk, if the children began to eat before the blessing was asked, he fiercely reprimanded them before slurring into a long prayer himself, usually in Latin.

I could never reconcile his Jekyll/Hyde flip-flops between sober religious devotion and drunken dissipation. He always removed his hat, crossing himself in reverence when passing a church, but hours later might twist my arm behind me until I was dizzy from pain. He insisted that every morsel we ate be blessed with eloquent thanks to God, but curses and foul language flowed with equal ease. Hearing my Lord's name brutalized this way tore at my soul. How could someone, who not only grew up in the church, but served God's people at the altar, desecrate with his mouth all that was holy?

"How can you shout at your children and pray at the same time?" I knew the question would have no effect on him, but needed to ask it anyway. Tony's faith in God had at one time been very real and personal, yet now seemed impotent against the growing pull of alcoholism threatening to destroy all of us. For me, faith was crucial to survival.

On good days, Tony enjoyed playing ball with Stanley or laughing and talking with Lilia and her friends. I knew it was only a short reprieve, but found the fantasy of a permanent change impossible to resist. His evident love for them brought a lump to my throat and I dreaded seeing their love for him choked by fear and loathing in his next rampage. They knew that by tonight the joking and fun could change to curses and violence, sending us to friends' houses for refuge, or just to the back yard where we huddled together on an old mattress behind some bushes. When silence from the house told us that he had fallen asleep, we could safely go to bed ourselves. Sometimes Tony conducted a door-to-door search for us, and the children dreaded the embarrassing whispers and curious glances at school the next day.

I was especially concerned for Lilia. Now a self-conscious teenager, she invited friends home only if she was certain that her father was away. His behavior was always unpredictable, with the risk that he would humiliate her by shouting at them or throwing them out of the house. I now saw more anger than fear in her face when he hit me and knew that a father-daughter showdown was inevitable. Nonetheless, I was shocked when it happened.

Lilia came home late one evening to find Tony on a drunken rampage, hitting me and shouting obscenities. Picking up an empty milk bottle, she slammed it over his head, broken glass flying in all directions. Blood streamed from his scalp as he lunged after her, momentarily forgetting about me. She escaped outdoors, easily outrunning him and he came back inside, the shock of the blow defusing his rage. He sat quietly slumped in the chair as I tended to the cut on his head, trying to remove the tiny shards of glass imbedded in the wound.

This incident signalled a change in their relationship. Lilia no longer hid from her father, returning Tony's violence with force of her own. When she sent a flowerpot crashing through the window, I knew that I must not underestimate my daughter's pent-up anger.

One evening when a friend was visiting, Tony grabbed a handful of Lilia's hair, pulling harder and harder as she screamed, finally fainting from pain. I was hysterical, desperately trying to make him loosen his grip, succeeding only when I bit his hand as hard as I could. With a yelp, he let go, yelling and cursing. "You see what she does!" he shouted loud enough for the whole block to hear. "You can be my witness in court!"

"If I'm anybody's witness, it will be Lydia's!" The man was horrified by the incident, hardly knowing what to do or say.

Tony now felt justified in hurting Lilia physically, even though his attacks until this time were limited to words. The day after their fights, I could see the hate and misery in her face as she looked at her father sitting in silent remorse at the table. I knew the questions churning in her mind, having asked all of them myself many times. Was he *really* sorry for what he had done? Why couldn't he change? Why did we have to live like this?

The tension between Lilia and Tony escalated when boyfriends started to call. I already suspected that no one was good enough for his little girl, and feared for both of them if Tony decided to take action against her Special Someone.

"You stupid DP! You think you're a teacher but you're just a drunk!" Denied permission to go out one night, Lilia went on the attack, knowing intuitively where Tony was the most vulnerable. This evening he was, for once, sober and the words found their painful mark. He stared at her and then slowly went to the bedroom where I heard drawers being pulled open and shut. I was rarely angry with her but the stricken look on Tony's face made me weep. He returned, clutching a sheaf of papers his hand which he lay in front of her. He was crying too. One by one he showed her his certificates from university and Russian schools where he had taught. There were letters from his students and photographs of them together.

Lilia had regretted the words as soon as she'd said them and apologized. They hugged each other and, for the first time in months, just sat and talked. Moments like this were a brief taste of the change I longed for, but I was learning to accept each day, each hour as it came. The Bible seemed to agree, at least according to a recent passage I'd read about "each day having cares enough of its own."

I had my own conflicts with Lilia's social life if my work schedule at the coffee shop coincided with her plans for an evening out. Stanley was too young to be on his own, and even if Tony happened to be at home, I never considered leaving our son alone with him. If Lilia wanted to go out, she had to take her little brother with her. Most of the time I gave in to her wishes, but on this point I remained firm. Stanley was delighted with these arrangements, especially if it meant a car ride. He happily waved at everyone from the back seat, undaunted by Lilia's muttered threats if he should even *think* of stepping out of line. Her friends, including the boys, accepted an annoying little brother trailing along more readily than she did.

To save time, I made the daily quota of doughnuts at night in my deep fryer at home. I was hard at work one evening when Tony arrived home in a foul mood, angry at the bartender for evicting him when his behavior interfered with other customers. He was even more belligerent than usual, and I could feel him looking for a way to provoke me. I stood at the table, making sure that each ring was cooked to golden perfection. Perhaps if I avoided making eye contact, he would leave me alone. He watched me for a few moments in silence, then, without warning, suddenly shoved the fryer against me. Hot, sizzling fat poured down the front of my dress, some splashing up into my neck and face. I screamed, trying to push it back onto the table before I turned my back, frantically pulling away from the searing grease soaking through my clothes.

He did it again, this time spilling the fat all over my back and legs. My shrieks echoed down the street as Lilia, also screaming hysterically, raced across the street to the hotel to find help. Within minutes, the entire neighbourhood descended on our house, everyone wanting to help but uncertain what to do next. Someone pulled off my nylons, peeling off burnt skin with the stocking. They brought me to the nearest hospital in Eckville and the doctor advised that I had third degree burns. Even a mole in my chin, described in my official immigration documents, was burned off without a trace.

The hospital staff cleaned me up and slathered a new salve over my body that the doctor assured me would minimize scarring. By this time I was in shock, unaware of anything said or done to me.

Tony was not allowed to visit me that night. The children stayed with our friends, who were determined that they be kept away from their father. He came the next day, aware that someone had reported the incident to the RCMP.

Tony was, as always, remorseful — and this time desperately afraid. In fact, even in my clouded awareness, it seemed as though what *might* happen to him was of much greater importance to him than what *had* happened to me. He pleaded with me to tell them that it was an accident rather than a deliberate attack. He reminded me of my own fears that he might someday go to jail and lose his job. He touched my hand in an all-too-familiar gesture, followed by an equally contrite declaration that I could have recited verbatim. He would never, *never* do anything to hurt me again. He *loved* me. I turned away, refusing him any reassurance that I would protect him from the consequences of his actions. Any illusions that this time he really meant what he said were scorched from my heart as my skin from my body.

A new thought filtered through the heavy fog of pain medication: I no longer needed to protect him out of fear for my own financial security. I now earned more money than he did. What's more, I had learned to manage it, proving once again my ability to learn new survival skills. The tables had turned; *Tony needed me more than I needed him.*

I knew that the RCMP officers were not deceived by my account of how Tony had accidentally fallen against the table. How did I explain the burns to my front *and* back? Were there *two* accidents? They looked at each other, no doubt recognizing all the typical signals shared by other bruised and battered women who refused to press charges against their abusive spouses. How could I explain why being responsible for sending Tony to jail by telling the truth seemed a greater sin than the lie that guaranteed his freedom?

I stayed in the hospital more than three weeks and even then the doctor was reluctant to release me, fearing for my safety. He kept me there longer than necessary under the pretext that there was still a risk of infection. Lilia and Stanley came to see me every day, wrenching my heart with their tears. I couldn't even hug them, my body still painfully sensitive to touch. They wanted me to come home.

My hospital stay gave me ample time to reflect, my thoughts always circling back to the same questions: *Why should I allow my husband's destructive habits to stand between me and my children — our children — and my responsibility to protect and care for them? If he actually succeeded in killing me, what would happen to them? Did my marriage vows endanger the ones I loved most?*

My parents were worried. Usually I wrote to them immediately after receiving their letter, but weeks went by before I could even hold a pen without excruciating pain. Sparing them the details of Tony's previous assaults, I told them of this one, explaining why I was unable to write sooner. Their next letter arrived in record time, before I had decided exactly how to answer all the questions which I knew would pour from its pages. Too much graphic detail at such great distance served no useful purpose.

My response was a delicate balance of truth and understatement: Tony had started drinking after we arrived in Canada, with no signs before I married him that this might happen. Sometimes he was happy, sometimes angry and rude. But *always* sorry. I neglected to mention my cynical outlook on Tony's unproductive repentance. It was better to leave them a window of hope, even slightly ajar, than to worry constantly about my welfare.

Papa's concern was channelled into prayer, both that Tony would change and that I would be protected from further harm. He encouraged me to do everything possible to keep my family together. We already knew how easily circumstances could separate us, but it should never be our choice. I looked at my arms and legs, still raw and tender. So far my best efforts didn't seem to be working.

Tony was free to read any of my letters from Russia, and was predictably angry when he read the questions and comments that told him they knew what he had done to me. I saw no point in hiding anything from him. When he was sober, he admitted the truth in what they said. When he was drunk, it made no difference.

Even without charges, Tony did not escape the incident unscathed. The CPR superintendent from Red Deer visited him one day with the news that, despite his awards for good workmanship, they were forced to move him to another worksite; the town of Benalto wanted him gone. A job posting at Hector, back in the mountains near Lake Louise, was his only option.

When Tony told me of the pending move, I had some news of my own: He would go to Hector by himself. I was finished living in section houses and the children and I would move back into our house in Calgary. I wanted a normal life for what remained of their childhoods, without weekend commutes. He alone was responsible for disrupting our lives as a family, and from now on I refused to share his exile. Perhaps this would motivate him to seek help.

Despite past failures, I still determined to make him see that strangers were not obligated to tolerate his rudeness and violent behavior. Until he learned to treat others with respect, they would ostracize him, leaving him alone. And, as I well knew, *alone* was not a nice place to be. My lecture was a noble, but futile gesture. Tony had no will to change, either for the sake of family or job. I feared for him. He was like a lost little boy needing his mother, and I was sending him away to fend for himself. For a brief moment, the old pattern of guilt and responsibility threatened to weaken my resolve, but I pushed it firmly aside. It was time to consider my children. They needed me too.

"Mom, why do we have to live this way? Why don't you divorce Dad so that we can make our own life?" Lilia and Stanley were familiar with the subject of separation and divorce, often talking to me about their friends from broken homes, and the bitter conflicts which preceded the actual split.

I reminded Lilia of a visit to Calgary when she was a little girl when we had seen drunks sprawled beside the sidewalk. A stab of premonition had pierced my soul, almost as though I was searching for my husband's face, unrecognizable under a week's stubble and his striped workman's hat draped over one eye. How many broken hearts and homes were represented in that pitiful collection of derelicts?

Lilia remembered it well and I asked her if this is what she wanted for her father. Did she want to see him lying on the street when she passed by, unaware that she was even his daughter? She slowly shook her head, the prospect of seeing him cold, hungry, and homeless more than she could bear. Our doctor had told me that until Tony decided to change, there was little anyone could do to help him. If I abandoned him, his fate was certain.

To my amazement, *I* was the one served with divorce papers. Tony had visited a lawyer and the paper in my hand was the result of his advice: He should divorce me on the grounds that I had been previously married and was guilty of bigamy!

I was dumbfounded. My previous marriage had never been a secret from Tony or anyone else. Though we had not been married in the church due to my unwillingness to become a Catholic, we had discussed it with the German parish priest at great length. He assured us that after a period of time without contact during wartime when missing persons could be presumed dead, there was no possibility that either of us was entering into an illegal union. I wondered how my first marriage, with its indefinite conclusion, was different than Tony's. In both cases our spouses had disappeared. Neither of us had been unfaithful, and with no prospect of a reunion, we had mutually decided to continue with our lives — together.

But perhaps those distant facts were irrelevant, given the present state of our relationship. The children evidently thought we would be better off without Tony. Maybe they were right. He had initiated the divorce and I would not contest it.

When our case reached the court for a hearing, I simply relayed the facts as they had occurred. The judge shook his head in disbelief that anyone, after all this time, could possibly raise such an issue as grounds for divorce. A future court date was set at which time our relationship would officially end.

As I walked down the street following the hearing, I felt curiously calm and detached. I had felt every wave of emotion, from overwhelming joy to wrenching despair, from tender love to burning hate, throughout my marriage, all of it bearing me slowly and surely to this point. It was all going to be over soon. The cycle of pain and blame would be finished. I need never endure Tony's accusations again. No more trying, trying, yet never managing to avoid the slap of open palm, the iron grip of twisting fingers. No midnight flights into the safety of darkness. Freedom to build a new life with my children and friends. Behind me, I heard Tony's lawyer calling his name.

"Lydia! Lydia!" Evidently Tony had other plans and I turned around to find him running after me. "I don't want a divorce! I don't want to leave you!" He insisted over and over again that a divorce had never been his idea. After a few beers and fuelled by one of Tony's dramatic stories, one of his drinking buddies had urged him to go see the lawyer. One thing led to another and before he knew it, we were both in court and his marriage was about to end. I stared at him, suddenly aware of how pathetic he was, unable to keep his promises, unable to accept responsibility for his own actions, unable to be either a husband or father to me and our children. Yet even now, I was unable to desert him.

28

June, 1964. A variety of tenants had occupied our Calgary home while we continued to move from section house to another. The same realtor who had first worked with me looked after all the arrangements, including rent collection. I was confident that our property was in good hands and saw no reason to check it occasionally myself. It was seven years since we first moved in and I was impatient to reclaim my home. More than one surprise awaited me.

Clumps of gravel covered the lawn which I had spent hours landscaping to perfection, weeds choking out what little grass remained. Kitchen tiles were strewn about the backyard, amongst other litter and debris. If the outside of the house was any indication of what I might find inside, I knew it would be a while before we could plan to move. I hesitated at the door, steeling myself for the worst.

A nauseating combination of stale cooking and rotting garbage odors met me inside, nearly cutting off my breath. My house was in ruins. The drapes sagged against the wall. All the closet rods were broken and, as I already expected, holes gaped in the floor where the tiles had been forcibly ripped away.

"What kind of people did you rent to?" My neighbour had seen me arrive and now stood in the doorway demanding an explanation. I was speechless as I viewed the shambles of my home. Without waiting for an answer, she launched into a vivid description of how our tenant used the backyard as a toilet. Besides the devastation before me, I shuddered to think what damage had been done to our reputation in the neighbourhood. Seeing my genuine horror, she eased the attack, no doubt remembering the hours of work I had invested when we first owned the house. I made an immediate telephone call. Someone owed *me* an explanation!

The realtor was skeptical, certain that I must be exaggerating. The tenants had regularly paid the rent and as far as he knew, there was no cause for complaint. Yes, he remembered the condition of the house when we entrusted it to him. The results of my work in painting, varnishing and restoring the house were most impressive, as were my decorating abilities. Rather than attempt a description, I insisted he come see for himself what remained of my investment. My English vocabulary was inadequate to express my outrage, but Tony's eloquent Russian said it for both of us, although I thought it best to withhold an entire translation. The realtor, intimidated by my anger as I pointed out the mounting evidence of his neglect, made little clucking sounds of apology, trying vainly to transfer blame away from himself. He conceded that it was definitely in bad condition, shaking his head in disbelief. I had little money to start again.

But *start again* was a recurring theme in my life and I set to the task of rebuilding my home, this time determined that nothing and nobody would remove us from it again. I had proved to myself that I was capable of earning a living, and felt an invigorating sense of independence return to my spirit. Over the years I had allowed Tony's destructive choices shape our lives and it was time to be free of their consequences.

The house was finally habitable by August. During the week, Tony lived in a section house, returning to Calgary on weekends. From Monday to Thursday I enjoyed a normal routine of homemaking and looking after my children. I renewed old friendships and made new ones without fear of uprooting them in a few weeks or months. Lilia and Stanley settled into school, and I was always home when they returned each afternoon, often accompanied by hungry friends. Replenishing the cookie jar for them was a pleasant chore and they filled the house with noise and laughter.

Weekends told a different story. As Friday approached, a familiar sense of dread settled into my chest. I could hardly eat for knots in my stomach. Tony was coming.

His train arrived downtown at eight o'clock in the evening, but he only returned home hours later, announcing his arrival to the entire community. Angry shouts, slamming taxi doors, and squealing tires drew curious neighbours to peer through blinds already closed for the night. I sometimes wondered what the driver had endured on the way to our house. In this state, fumbling with a key that refused to engage the lock infuriated Tony, and I either left the bolt off altogether or opened it before he reached the top step and tried to crash through it. I tried to imagine being greeted with "Hi Honey! I'm home!"

At times my cynical sense of humor helped me to deal with my anger, but as long as we shared the same roof, I saw no end to my fear of his violence. He vented his rage at some imagined insult by hitting me or twisting my fingers until I screamed with pain, leaving me to nurse a collection of black and blue marks that never quite went away before a new set was inflicted. Our children's bruises were emotional and I prayed for God's protection as their father cursed at them, always in Russian. The Saturday morning ritual of empty "never again" promises meant no more to them than to me.

While I did not condone Lilia's instant readiness to retaliate, I felt better knowing that she could hold her own with him. Stanley was different. He was a timid little boy, his face mirroring every pain and passion in his heart. When Tony chose to spend time with him, Stanley's eyes lit up with expectation, all earlier hurts forgotten. *Please, dear Lord, let him remember this moment,* I prayed as I watched them happily assembling a miniature railway together. *Please, dear Lord, help him to forget,* I prayed as Tony later smashed it to pieces.

Against our advice, Lilia decided to quit school, enrolling in a hair styling program instead. To our distress, she was more interested in a busy social schedule than doing something useful with her life. I knew how important it was for a woman, married or single, to be able to support herself, and did not wish my daughter's roof or daily bread to depend solely on someone else's ability to provide it for her. Anxious years of wondering if my husband would eventually drink himself out of a job made Lilia's apparent apathy about developing a livelihood difficult to accept. We argued constantly. I was especially frustrated when she refused Tony's offer to buy her a beauty salon. How could she so easily turn her nose up at something which others worked years to possess?

Lilia did work as a stylist but her girlish ambitions had not included elderly ladies and their love of finger waves. After a few months she decided it was time to move on.

Tony and I both cried when she announced that she and a girlfriend planned a hitch-hiking visit to their boyfriends in Toronto. We begged and pleaded with her, even calling on the police to keep her in Calgary. They could offer only sympathy. Lilia was now eighteen years old and legally capable of making her own decisions.

Her letters insisted that everything was fine, but all my prodigal daughter really wanted to do was come home. Independence in a big city teeming with action quickly lost its glamour for penniless teenagers. Eventually she and her friend were charged with vagrancy, supposedly accomplices of a male friend who was arrested for theft. Fortunately, he spoke up on their behalf, assuring the judge that they knew nothing of his activities and were innocent of wrongdoing. The judge suggested that Toronto was no place for them and urged them both to go back to Calgary. The police gave them a ride to the outskirts of the city and from there they were on their own. Lilia called me from Winnipeg and asked me to send enough money for both of them to come home by train. To my dismay, the experience had not been the eye-opener I'd hoped for and a few months later she embarked on another adventure — marriage and motherhood.

When Debbie was born, Tony and I were as excited and proud as new grandparents can possibly be. Both of us gravitated to baby departments in stores, hardly able to choose among all the tempting frills and laces displayed for doting grandmas and grandpas who suddenly have more money than sense. I had forgotten how fast babies grow, and bags of new baby things regularly trailed home with me from shopping centres. Danny arrived a year later and we started all over again. Within two years, Lilia's marriage ended and she was on her own with two small children.

I decided to look for a job, especially when I heard that a hotel restaurant in our neighbourhood was hiring. Any expectations that my happy experience in the Benalto coffee shop might be repeated were dashed immediately. The owner, despite all promises, refused to pay me for both additional hours worked and increased responsibility beyond what was originally agreed. Over my protests, she salvaged leftovers from customers' plates with no qualms about adding them to a new order. Three months at this job were more than enough.

Why not check at the General Hospital? According to a friend, such a big place must surely need a regular supply of workers and my restaurant experience could be useful.

Unfortunately, the dietary department had no openings but I was directed to *Housekeeping*. The woman in the personnel office reviewed my qualifications, amazed that with a university degree I was applying for such menial work. I didn't want to be reminded of the hours of study I had completed only to clean toilets!

And toilets *were* part of hospital housekeeping, together with washing walls and disinfecting rooms. Cleaning empty rooms was tolerable but after a day of working in rooms occupied by people who were desperately sick or dying, I wanted to quit. I reluctantly allowed the supervisor to persuade me to come back, particularly when she promised that I could move to different floors away from the sadness of serious illness and death.

My hours were, at times, unpredictable and I struggled with wanting to be home on weekends, especially for Stanley's sake. He was afraid of Tony, who taunted him about being a "Mama's Boy." Perhaps that was my fault for being over-protective, but he lacked the same independent spirit that now earned Lilia a grudging respect from her father. To my husband, fear was an invitation to attack. I dared not leave them alone together.

Stanley served as an altar boy at church and liked me to be there on Sundays. On weekends when I worked, I tried to attend at least one Mass but it never quite made up for those I missed. He worked diligently at learning the Latin liturgy and I thought I would burst with pride as I watched him assist the priest. I was pleased when he told me one day that he wanted to become one himself.

I did not share Tony's delight when the company transferred him to their main station in Calgary. The weekday peace and calm in my home was precious to me, and I was reluctant to replace it with the chaos that accompanied him like a chronic storm cloud. I never knew what might happen while I was away at work if Tony was left by himself.

He discovered that he could just as easily satisfy his thirsty cravings without tavern companionship. Taxis delivered his favorite brand, conveniently ordered from the comfort of his home. I was furious and finally delivered a set of my own orders to the taxi company. Under no circumstances, regardless how often Tony called them, were they permitted to bring liquor to our address or I promised to call the police. They were so zealous in following my instructions that one day when I actually needed a taxi, they were reluctant to respond.

Undaunted, Tony recruited any passerby to bring him a bottle. One young man returned shortly with the telltale brown bag as requested, and, together with the change, delivered a lecture about the risks of trusting total strangers with money. I could have spared him the effort. When it came to alcohol, no price was too high for Tony, no risk too great.

I thought of a devious plan which gave new meaning to the term "mixed drinks." Whenever Tony brought home a bottle of whiskey, I waited until he had fallen into his customary stupor when I poured half the remaining liquor into another bottle, filling both of them with water. The next time he thought he'd run out, I could produce the second bottle before he had a chance to re-visit the liquor store. There were no complaints so I felt free to continue. Barring a miracle, I knew that Tony was destined to drink himself to death. By diluting the poison, perhaps I could buy him a little more time.

Our neighbours were well aware of Tony's habit and I knew it was only a matter of time before someone in our area would be directly affected by it. Andrew, our neighbour's son, was Stanley's friend and became an unwitting target as he visited our house. One day when I was at work Tony hit him and while there was no actual injury, Andrew's father reported it to the police.

By now Tony was well known to the district police detachment and one day they called me in to discuss the situation. The message was clear. If Andrew's father pressed charges, Tony would go to jail and lose his job. They emphasized to me the seriousness of any charges relating to child assault and then suggested that *I* take the blame instead! I stared at them in disbelief. Could they be serious? I protected Tony from the consequences of his actions toward me, but was he *never* to be held accountable for his behavior toward anyone else either?

Regardless of his anger against Tony, Andrew's father immediately dismissed all thoughts of pressing charges when he heard this recommendation. He, along with many others on our street, wondered why I chose to stay with a man who treated me so shamefully. With little to encourage it, my hope that someone somewhere might influence change in him remained alive, even though I had long ago accepted that neither I or our children provided any incentive. Our doctor referred us to a treatment centre where we could work with counsellors.

Since Tony's version of events was fuzzy at best, I described life in our home, sparing no detail of his drunken rampages.

"Is this true, Tony?" The counsellor looked to him for verification.

"Yes, it's true." Tony's voice was predictably contrite. "But I don't know why I do it and I'm sorry." I thought the words before he said them. His pleading tones were part of every guilt-filled aftermath, but any commitment to change was easily forgotten within the hour.

They gave him a prescription of pills that would dull his desire for alcohol, and asked us to come back in a week. The medication seemed to work, however when it was time to have the prescription refilled, he balked. "They're just after my money," he insisted, ignoring my pleas for him to continue. The relatively small cost of eliminating a very expensive habit was, in his mind, nothing short of piracy.

I continued to go by myself for a few weeks, but resented each appointment. Tony was the one who drank, not me. Why should I make this effort on his behalf when he refused even to come with me? They assured me that I also benefitted by learning better ways of coping. If their prediction was accurate that Tony would only come to his senses after landing in the gutter without job, home, or family, it would be too late for all of us.

For all his failings at home, Tony was a good worker with many awards recognizing his years of service to the CPR. During a time when many of the section houses were closed, operations consolidated in main centres, and workers laid off, Tony's boss ensured that he remained employed, transferring him to an inside position rather than working on the tracks. Mindful of the company's intolerance for drunkenness on the job, I watched him like a hawk in the morning before he left for work. Occasionally I called the office if it seemed that his condition warranted some extra time at home.

275

29

All my earnings were earmarked for renovations to the house. We took out walls, installed new windows and rejuvenated the exterior walls with new siding. At the same time, I was deeply concerned about Lilia's living conditions. Sometimes I went with her to look at advertised suites which seemed attractive and affordable, at least on paper, but were usually dark and dreary with the telltale odor of mildew in the threadbare carpeting. I shuddered at the thought of Debbie and Danny growing up in such a depressing environment.

Why not develop a suite in our basement? Perhaps living so close together was only a short-term solution, but eventually we could rent it to someone else when she made more permanent arrangements. We drew a floorplan and settled on one contractor's quotations for materials and labor. Everything was set to proceed, pending a city inspector's approval. His visit changed everything. To meet bylaws regulating basement suites, the house would have to be raised and the foundation increased by two feet. After all the dingy hovels we had seen advertised recently, I could hardly believe that *we* were facing such rigid requirements. I envisioned floor to ceiling cracks in my newly decorated walls as the house was suspended in midair. We had budgeted for renovations, not a new set of costly repairs. Now that the idea of expanding my home to include Lilia's family had taken root, I determined to see it through, even if it meant buying a different house.

Once again a realtor shuttled us from one property to another, enthusiastically promoting the merits of each. Without knowing exactly what I was looking for, I was nonetheless confident that I would recognize the right house when I saw it. I did. It had a high foundation and big windows on the lower level — just right for a suite, and big enough for a family. This would be my thirty-first move in nineteen years and I was ready to settle down.

We enjoyed having our grandchildren close by and spent hours playing with them. When Lilia eventually married Ed Cragg, I was sorry to see them move to their own home, even though I was pleased that the children would again have a father. A few years later, Jason was born, completing Lilia's family.

After five years at the hospital, my back injury was an inconvenient surprise. We were instructed to lift mattresses only with an assistant but I was left alone to cope with an emergency at the end of my shift. Surely, just this once, I could manage by myself. A crunching sound from my back accompanied by shooting pain told me otherwise.

Instead of returning home, I was admitted as a patient, my left leg completely paralyzed. X-rays and myelagram showed that a disc in my spine was damaged, applying pressure to the sciatic nerve. After three weeks of bedrest in hospital my doctor suggested that I try working again, though cautioning me against any heavy lifting.

I tried to be careful but a few weeks later, the pain returned. Additional tests revealed more damage than originally diagnosed; two vertebrae and three discs had to be removed, replaced with bone grafts from my ribs. Doctors were vague about my recovery time or even *if* I could plan a life of normal activity.

My first concern was for the impending move. Four years of accumulating possessions in a house resulted in more complicated packing than we had ever done before. Whatever the longterm results of the surgery might be, the doctor guaranteed that I would have very limited (if any) mobility by our possession date.

I also knew that a hospital stay of *any* duration was too long to leave Stanley at home with his father. The nuns at his school shared my concern and one of them visited me with a suggestion. *Why not enroll Stanley in the Don Bosco Home?* "You can be assured that he will be well cared for." Her tone was reassuring, but my only idea at this point was for him to live with Lilia. As though reading my mind, the nun continued, "Lilia is too young for the responsibility of a teen-age boy. He needs adult supervision."

I knew she was right. Of course Lilia, at twenty-two, *was* an adult but a fourteen-year-old, even a quiet boy like Stanley, needed more authority than a big sister could provide.

The boys' home was run by Catholic brothers and although I wanted to believe that my son would receive good care there, Lilia's experience at the convent made me wary. I hesitated, unwilling to begin a process which painful experience had taught me could carry lasting regrets. But a decision must be reached quickly. The registration process was complicated, involving the Department of Welfare and social workers. If all arrangements were to be completed before my surgery, I must act immediately.

There were endless papers to sign, the last of which committed him to the home for a whole year. I had expected this to last only until I recovered, but surely not an entire year! Tears welled in my eyes, blurring the fine print which transferred Stanley from my home to theirs. I had been so certain that my days of leaving children in someone else's care were over. Why did circumstances always dictate that being with me was not in their best interests? This pattern, begun in Russia, had followed me to Canada.

Stanley accepted the plans without protest, but I felt his sadness the day I took him to his temporary new home. At the top of the stairs an Inuit boy greeted us like long lost friends. He looked healthy and vigorous, and I felt reassured that at least my son would not go hungry. In fact, Stanley turned to me and declared firmly that he was going to like it here. He had met a new friend even before reaching his room, and as far as he was concerned, things could only get better. My heart felt surprisingly light as I left him.

Four painful weeks after my surgery I was free to go home with a list of not-to-do's including stairs, housework, and laundry. I was under strict orders to leave all the packing for our move to others. I also had two weekly appointments for physiotherapy.

I was a spectator in my own life, directing Lilia and other friends as they dismantled my house. Anything occupying space without being useful found its way to the garbage. To no one's surprise and everyone's relief, Tony was made no effort to become involved. With all the mess and upheaval, there was no time or energy to deal with his unpredictable antics. Christmas, my favorite time of year, passed with a minimum of fuss. I appreciated each gift of cookies and other food that friends and neighbours delivered to our door, unable to indulge my own traditional frenzy of baking and decorating. There was time to think. To remember.

I wished that just once I could spend Christmas with Mama and Papa again. *Did Papa still read aloud the story of Jesus' birth in Bethlehem with shepherds and wise men coming to worship? What had happened to the big Bible and the colorful pictures?* When I closed my eyes I could almost smell the fresh-baked aroma of Christmas treats from Mama's kitchen. Now I would be happy just to watch her transform flour and butter into mouth-watering delicacies as she talked to me. But here I was, living like a cripple while others waited on me so that my newly fashioned framework could heal. Inactivity, combined with physical pain and nostalgia, made it difficult not to feel sorry for myself, although I was determined to keep my melancholy from dampening the spirits of those around me..

My surgery and convalescence interfered with previous plans to visit friends in Milwaukee and New York. The doctor shook his head when I asked about travelling; a journey like this, before the healing was complete, would ruin the results of my operation. Although the railway passes were free with no money lost, Tony refused to postpone the trip, preferring to go by himself. Our friends' disappointment that he had come alone changed to shock at his explanation.

I only discovered his creativity in a subsequent telephone conversation with my friend in Milwaukee. In a voice quavering with tears, she demanded to know how I could change this way. I was mystified by her question. "How have I changed?" I demanded, searching my mind for any major offenses in recent memory. "You haven't even seen me for a long time."

"Tony told us you didn't come with him because you were running around with other men!" I nearly dropped the receiver, uncertain that I had heard her correctly. *What was she talking about?* Finally recovering my voice, I set the record straight, complete with Tony's unwillingness to wait until I could safely travel.

When I confronted him later he just shrugged. "I had to tell them something." Tony loved to play a victim role, regardless of the likelihood of being caught in the lie. What made this story even more difficult for me to accept was that he had been sober when he told it.

It happened so slowly that I was unaware of the process. *I had lost my fear of Tony.* His noise and bluster no longer sent me scurrying on futile attempts to appease him. I easily evaded his blows. A sharp word from me now stopped him short, whereas years of appealing to his sense of decency with logic and reasoning had only increased his violent grip on my life. But the delicious new freedom growing in my soul did not mean that the war was over. As though sensing that he was losing the ability to control me through force and intimidation, Tony's tactics changed.

He demanded that I stay close to him at all times while he was home. Even if I was in the next room, he became angry and vengeful, often wreaking havoc in my kitchen. One day I came in from the garden to find hot water overflowing the sink and Tony lying drunk on the linoleum in a greasy mass of melted butter and lard, which was slowly inching its way to absorption in the livingroom carpet. The fridge stood open and empty, its contents spilled or broken on the floor. A pot containing a whole chicken scorched on a red hot element — yet another addition to the trash bin.

It took the better part of the afternoon to mop up the mess. I saved the ruined remnants of food in a bucket to show him later, groceries that must now be replaced at needless expense. "I'm sorry, I'm sorry. I'll never do it again." His eyes begged for understanding when I confronted him with the collection of broken glass and cartons swimming in a disgusting soup of juices, ketchup and miscellaneous leftovers. He explained, however, that it was really my fault for leaving him alone.

My house became my prison. I feared leaving Tony alone, even briefly, never sure what form of chaos awaited my return.

One memorable evening, desperate for normal adult conversation, I left him in front of the television, bottle at hand, while I visited a friend who lived nearby. Walking home a short time later, I noticed that the air was curiously clogged with dust, realizing when I turned the corner and saw the fire engines and people clustered on their balconies, that it was smoke. And it was coming from my house! I began to run, my heart hammering in my chest.

I pushed through the crowd of curious spectators in front of the house. Water hoses aimed inside Tony's bedroom window. He lurched against the front doorway, struggling with a neighbour who was trying to drag him outside. I was thankful that Tony cursed only in Russian, sparing our audience any direct understanding of his loud objections to this intrusion. But even excitement from the fire could not keep him awake for long and he was soon sleeping peacefully, oblivious to the commotion around him.

My worst fears were realized; he had fallen asleep with a burning cigarette in his fingers. Every night I waited until he was snoring, checking for live cigarettes before allowing myself to fall asleep. The one evening I treated myself to a short visit away from home, it nearly cost me everything. Smoke from the smouldering mattress had alerted neighbours before an actual fire erupted and although it was extinguished even before the fire department arrived, they doused the room liberally with water, ruining furniture otherwise undamaged, then throwing it piece by piece onto the lawn.

Hot coils from the mattress had imprinted onto Tony's skin and he wakened hours later wondering why he was covered in bandages. The inevitable litany of remorse when he saw the broken furniture and soggy carpeting meant nothing. Tomorrow night it could all happen again.

I faithfully attended physiotherapy sessions, but my doctor was unsatisfied with my progress and it was nearly a year before he allowed me to discontinue treatments. Stanley's year at Don Bosco was almost over and I looked forward to having him with me again. He had often visited on weekends, sometimes bringing friends with him, although like Lilia at the same age, he was always concerned about how Tony would treat his friends.

To my surprise, when I talked about him moving back to our house, he didn't want to come. He lived in a comfortable room and enjoyed being surrounded by friends without fear of attack or embarrassment. Help with schoolwork was readily available if he needed it. Even the food was good. Best of all, the next summer's schedule of events included water slides, horseback riding and trips to the Shuswap Lakes. I suspected that the prospect of living under the same roof as his father again made boarding school preferable to his home. While I could understand that, I still missed having him there every day, but reluctantly agreed to a six-month extension.

The new school year had barely started when one of the brothers called to ask if Stanley was there. He and his best friend had disappeared and no one knew where they had gone. I panicked. Stanley, while still gentle and soft-spoken, had lost most of his childhood shyness, acquiring in its place a keen sense of adventure and I had no idea where this might take him. The brother learned from some of the boys that Stanley and three of his friends had been panhandling downtown. No one knew why.

I took a photograph of Stanley to the police station and told them to find him. "You know, Mrs. Oushal," the officer's voice was kind, "hundreds of kids run away from home every day. The only way we have a hope of finding them is if they get into trouble, or," he hesitated, "something happens to them." I forced this possibility from my thoughts.

Two long weeks went by. Every time the phone rang, I rushed to answer it, hoping for news. Finally one day it was him! I was weak with relief, happiness at hearing his voice outweighing my anger at him for putting me through weeks of sleepless anxiety. He was calling from Montreal and needed me to wire money for the busfare home.

I waited impatiently for him and grew anxious all over again when he failed to arrive home exactly according to my schedule. The day after I had expected him, I was sitting out in the yard with Lilia when I saw him walking down the street, safe and sound. Hugs and kisses over, it was time for questions and answers, mine and his respectively. He told me about how he and his friend had ridden their bikes to Chestermere Lake one day and met a busload of young people from Vancouver en route to a rock concert in Eastern Canada. The invitation to go along proved irresistible and they hopped aboard with no thought of any turmoil at home caused by their blossoming independence.

Stanley told me how they had been approached by some police officers in Montreal and questioned about where they were from and what they were doing there. To my annoyance, an official check of their names with Calgary police had raised no alarms and they were free to do as they pleased. But my son was home again and this was all that mattered.

"Let's go to Banff."

Stanley's suggestion sounded like a good way to spend a Friday. Tony was working and now that I was able to be active again, a spontaneous outing felt like a celebration. Feeling a delightful sense of new freedom, I packed a small suitcase. If one day of fun needed an encore, I wanted to be ready. And why not take Debbie too? She was excited about a train trip with Grandma and Uncle Stanley; at age five, going somewhere without Mommy seemed like such a grownup thing to do! Lilia agreed and with a quick note to Tony, we were on our way.

My spirits always rose on a trip to the mountains. I enjoyed the thrill of anticipation as the train wound its way through the rolling foothills, finally shielded from the open prairies by towering peaks on all sides. A delicious sense of homecoming filled me as I settled back to enjoy the scenery which was new with every twist and turn of the track. I was momentarily transported back to the Caucasus and the magic of its trails and flowers.

Debbie was a good audience for my stories about "when Grandma was a little girl." I also told her about living in these mountains with *her* mommy and the trips we had made to Calgary just to buy groceries. She could hardly imagine the luxury of a trip like this every week instead of a quick drive to the neighbourhood supermarket. Between my stories and Uncle Stanley's teasing, the time passed quickly and before we knew it the train had pulled into the station.

We enjoyed the hot springs in Banff and ate supper in a nice restaurant before returning to the train station for the trip back to Calgary. A westbound train to Vancouver pulled in first. Stanley and I looked at each other. We were having so much fun that it seemed a shame to cut it short. Debbie was wide-eyed with excitement when I asked her if she would like to go on a longer ride and even to sleep on the train. Without further discussion we hopped aboard. My railway pass had seen little action during my convalescence and I was more than ready put it to good use.

For two days we revelled in the lush beauty of Vancouver parks and seashore. I had never seen such a profusion of flowers and greenery — and eaten so many ice cream cones and hot dogs. Stanley thought it was great fun to share his name with a famous park and we spent hours there, walking the seawall and exploring forest paths. I almost forgot that we were in the middle of a very big and busy city. I was a child again, yearning to swing from the trees and regretting the years' adjustments to my body that kept me securely anchored to the earth.

We had already come this far so why not visit Vancouver Island? The ferry to Victoria churned its way through channels separating wooded islands, far removed from all the noise and commotion of the city. We stayed outside on the passenger deck, enjoying the salty spray on our faces. I could see cottages perched high on hillsides and fantasized about coming here by myself with a big bag of books and food, a feast for mind, soul and body. I would never tire of this combination of adventure and retreat, of mountains and sea with their ever-changing personalities through day and night, sun and storm. Far behind us on the mainland, Mount Baker rose in majestic grandeur, shimmering in shades of pink and gold from the setting sun. A week ago I could hardly have imagined this total abandonment of worry and concern. This time belonged to me. To us.

After a few days of exploring Victoria's shores and shops we still wanted more. We decided to make this an international excursion and my CPR pass transported us to Seattle, again by ferry. By now we had been away for a week and I decided that it was time to go home to my now frantic husband.

Lilia tried to calm him, assuring him that I could take care of myself and was not likely to be lost, especially in Banff. After all, I had friends there and had probably decided to stay longer. I suspected that he was not so much concerned with my welfare as resentful that I had left him on his own. *Too bad*, I thought happily. Who was hurt if my trip to Banff had taken a slight detour? This was the most fun I'd had in a long time.

30

I always looked forward to Christmas, especially after moving into our new house. Cheated out of one year's fun by my back injury, I determined to make up for lost time. Tony spent hours choosing the perfect tree which now stood tall and elegant in the corner, resplendent in decorations that I had painstakingly packed to withstand the voyage from Germany. It was a work of art.

Crash! I was downstairs talking to our tenant and we both raced up the stairs, stopping short at the devastation before us. The tree sprawled lengthwise across the carpet, decorations flung throughout the room, under chairs and table. A drunken Tony stomped on it, as though relishing the crunching sound of shattered ornaments underfoot. What eight days of violent ocean had not damaged with so much as a scratch, my husband accomplished in less than a minute. One by one the delicate baubles, irreplaceable in Canada, were reduced to brittle fragments. I was terrified that the lights, still bravely twinkling, would start a fire or that he would sustain a severe electric shock. Unable to interrupt his rampage, we watched helplessly until his energy was spent and he dropped in his tracks.

I checked his feet, dreading the need to clean gashes infested with tiny splinters of glass. To my amazement, none of the shiny jagged edges clinging to his woolen socks had penetrated the fibres.

For the first time, I left him lying at the scene of the crime. In fact, I promised myself that he would never again wake up in the comfort of his bed where I usually deposited his dead weight after a tour of destruction. This area of service was over. For all I knew, the years of dragging, pushing and pulling him may have been the real causes of my back injury, needing only a hospital mattress to complete the process.

The next day he vaguely remembered knocking something down, his "sorries" interspersed with sorrowful kisses to my hands.

Stanley finished his final six months at the school but decided to find a job instead of completing his diploma. I was concerned when he moved into a downtown suite with his girlfriend. He seemed too young to be on his own and I worried about the kinds of people he might choose as friends. My fears were confirmed when I learned that he was in jail, charged with drug-trafficking.

"Did you do this?" I searched his face when I asked the question. As far as I knew, Stanley had always been truthful with me and I was certain to know if he was lying now.

"No Mom, I didn't." His eyes held mine.

"Then what are you doing here?" Was he guilty by association? Was he mistaken for someone else?

"I don't know. But I didn't do it." I believed him but was determined to find out the rest of the story. Unlike Stanley, the police officer who arrested him could not look me in the eye. I suspected him of lying as he told me about some photographs that proved Stanly was involved.

The photo showed only a head of blond hair but no facial features in a street crowd of young people. The police officer, who had been part of a sting operation, rarely lifted his gaze from the floor. The money and dope had changed hands through a crack in a door down the hall from Stanley's room. The detective had caught a brief glimpse of blond hair and this was enough for him to arrest Stanley. The judge decided that guilty or otherwise, a six-month jail term for Stanley would teach other "rotten apples" the consequences of dealing in drugs. The case was closed.

I knew little about dope but had a keen sense of justice — or in this case, the lack of it. If Stanley was guilty as charged, he deserved the sentence, but nobody should be locked up merely as an example to others. I would not sit idly by, waiting for my son to emerge from jail a true felon. I found a lawyer with more interest in my case than the court-appointed attorney had displayed. A few days later, Stanley was free.

At age sixteen, he became a father. His girlfriend was unable to look after the baby and Monti was raised by his other grandparents with frequent visits to our house as well. I had never known Stanley to take an interest in babies, and watching him with his little son, I felt a tug at my heart. I remembered how he used to try to climb all over *his* father as he lay on the couch and how Tony would brush him off. I had warned him that someday he would wonder why his boy stayed away.

Debbie, Danny and Jason thought their Uncle Stanley's visits were a special treat and he spent hours playing with them at Lilia's house. He often talked to me about meeting her friends, and there was no greater thrill than a ride on their motorcycles. I was afraid of the powerful machines that I heard roaring up and down the busy street nearby, but was reluctant to spoil his enjoyment of male companions who might in some way make up for the lack of fatherly attention in his life.

Stanley was always fascinated with motorcycles. As a little boy, he raced down the road on his bicycle, revving his imaginary Harley to a mighty roar, an obsession I vainly hoped he would outgrow. To my dismay, he had to have one. A *real* one. I always promised myself that I would never contribute to the purchase of something so noisy and dangerous, but since he wanted to use his own money, what could I say? And not just any motorcycle would do. It had to be a Harley Davidson, the biggest, noisiest beast of its kind. He wanted to be a true "HOG" (Harley Owners' Group). Tony was no help, boyishly eager to hop onto the bike with Stanley for a ride.

The day he came home with a colorful crest sewn onto his new leather jacket was the first time I seriously questioned these new friends' influence on my son. His tone was casual, as though joining a motorcycle club was the most normal event in the world. Mine was not.

"Why do you have to join a club just because you have a motorcycle? What if you're injured? Or killed? And don't they fight a lot? Do you know what you're doing?" My voice raised in pitch and volume with each question until I was shouting at him.

Stanley had predicted my reaction and tried to soothe me, patting my arm as though *I* was the child. Being in a club just meant travelling to other cities in large groups, putting their bikes in shows, and sometimes taking holidays together. And, of course, having fun. All the members had jobs and there were very respectable people in the club: accountants, lawyers, and business men. My fears, according to Stanley, were groundless.

Lilia's reaction was even stormier than mine, reinforcing my misgivings. After all, they were her friends and if *she* objected, there must be a good reason.

"You're not like them, Stan!" I heard her pleading with him. "There's more to these clubs than you know!" Stanley listened patiently but his decision remained the same. Did it matter if some of the members looked a little rough and scary? Even though he was their youngest member, everyone was happy to have him there and treated him well. If some of them got into fights, it didn't mean that he had to get involved.

He took his new membership seriously, investing all his time and money in transforming his motorcycle with chrome and paint, a custom design now emblazoned on its sides. He devoted every spare minute to cleaning and polishing the surface to a glossy sheen, always checking for a stray particle of dust that might dim its lustre. This was the first in a succession of machines in front of our house, each one bigger and better than the last, each a masterpiece in colorful artistry.

Stanley was anxious for me to meet his club friends, bringing them to the house for meals or just to visit. At first I was guarded, uncertain what to expect but they were polite and well-spoken, even removing their shoes at the door. Gradually I relaxed enough to enjoy their company.

Although Stanley expressed no further interest in the priesthood, God remained in his thoughts and conversation, even with his new peer group. To my surprise, one of his favorite topics for discussion was the second coming of Christ. Hal Lindsey's book, *Late Great Planet Earth,* travelled on numerous club trips, circulating among members whose curiosity was piqued by Stanley's enthusiasm. He often invited a group to our house for a meal and I enjoyed listening to their theological debates as I prepared food in the kitchen, amazed at the ease with which he integrated his faith and friends. Even more amazing was his acceptance among men, many much older than him, who not only tolerated his religious quirks, but seemed genuinely interested for themselves.

"Mom, you have to come see this!" From the excitement in Stanley's voice, I knew it must have something to do with motorcycles. It did, although I was uncertain why he thought I might be remotely interested in a car and motorcycle show. I looked at Tony, comfortably sprawled in his recliner in front of the television, bottle within easy reach. This should be a father-son event; I was a foreigner in a world of chain drives, shovel heads, pipes and deckers. What if I said something to embarrass him? Reluctantly, I let him persuade me. If he wanted me to share this part of his life, why should I hold back? Many boys his age hardly acknowledged that they *had* mothers. Five-year-old Monti, who idolized his daddy, came with us. He already shared Stanley's passion, full of animated questions about this and that model in a conversation which left me far behind in mechanical dust.

I was too stunned by the display to be concerned about whether I looked out of place in this crowd of experts. Million dollar cars from all over Canada and the U.S. gleamed under powerful spotlights, safely cordoned off from admiring (and sometimes sticky) fingers. Every vehicle entered in the show was custom-designed, limited only to its owner's imagination and budget.

Then I saw it — the real reason Stanley wanted me to come. His bike, which I now accepted as a normal part of the landscape at home, posed regally beside a huge trophy. First prize! Now I knew why he was so insistent that I see for myself that he was number one in North America! The pride in his face made me forget how much I disliked motorcycles and all they represented. *Number one!* I wasn't sure whether kissing the champion was acceptable protocol at events like this but did it anyway. It wasn't every day that a mother saw her son crowned King of his class. Monti jumped up and down, hardly able to stand still long enough to have his picture taken beside the winning machine. The glow on his face promised that someday *his* bike would stand there too.

To my surprise, Stanley decided to complete his high school education as well as a truck driving program, with the dream of someday owning his own rig. Tony tried to discourage this, pushing him to drive for the CPR where all vehicle maintenance was covered by the company. For Stanley, the independence and pride of ownership was uppermost and at age nineteen, he became the youngest trainee in Alberta to pass the licensing exam. Within a few months he owned his own truck, with or without his father's blessing.

31

January, 1972. Every time an airmail letter with Russian stamps appeared in my mailbox, I settled into my favorite chair ready to enjoy yet another one-sided paper visit. The letters from Victor and Heinrich arrived together, their news sadly identical. Papa was dead.

I had known this day would come. He was, after all, eighty years old but my mind still protested a futile *not yet* over and over as I read on, moving the flimsy paper away from the tears spilling onto my apron. He had been sick for only a week, at first insisting that he was able to eat meals at the table with everyone else. The last four days, he did not leave his bed and there he died on Dec. 28, 1971.

Hundreds of people came to his funeral, following the truck bearing his coffin to the cemetery. My brothers told me how people in Kisilevsk had loved him, just as I remembered from my childhood in Nikolevka. Wary of trusting anyone in a system rife with betrayal, people were drawn to Papa's quiet strength and wisdom like a magnet. There too, he had held a position of leadership in the community.

The envelope contained a picture of Papa resting in the casket. Lying on his chest and clearly visible was the picture of the Last Supper which I had sent to him years before. He was buried with it.

I shared my brothers' concern that Mama would be lost without Papa. Even when I was small, I recognized that my parents shared a special bond of friendship, realizing as I grew older that this was not an automatic part of marriage. Their relationship deepened throughout the hardships of Siberia, surviving difficulties under which weaker marriages fell apart. In the last few years, their letters to me reflected a joyful playfulness, like children who never tired of each other's company. Now she was alone.

My brothers' faithful reports told that for nearly a year she was listless and sad, scarcely eating and sitting quietly for hours at a time. One of her grandsons came to live with her, helping her around the house after school. Her letters to me were full of the past, mostly of Papa and how much she missed him. Sometimes the need to be with her, to hold her hand and to comfort her was almost more than I could bear. She had always been there for me when I was growing up and now she needed me to be there for her. It wasn't right that I should be so far away.

Victor and Heinrich tried to cheer her up by painting the house and installing new windows for added brightness. She allowed them to do everything but showed little interest. They were rapidly running out of ideas and planting her garden was their last resort. But, they told her, she would have to look after it or everything would die. To their relief, she emerged from her shell, blossoming together with the flowers that still attracted both neighbours and total strangers to her yard.

Despite revived interest in life, her own health was failing and my brothers were concerned by her refusal to co-operate with the doctor's prescribed diet. She loved fatty foods and as long as she was alive, defied anyone to tell her that she could not eat them. She insisted that she would die according to *God's* timetable, not the doctor's, and in the meantime, life *and* food were meant to be fully enjoyed.

Nearly five years after Papa's death, on Sept. 23, 1976, Mama followed. She was eighty-five.

The first time they were lost to me, a hope that someday we might be reunited sustained me throughout months and years of longing. After finding them, I still longed for the day when I might meet them at the airport and they would come to live with me. With each letter over the years I held fast to that dream, but now they were both gone. There had been no last good-byes or *God-bless-you's*, no chance to ask forgiveness for being stubborn. No opportunity to introduce them to their grandchildren. Or to look after them in their final illnesses.

The familiar stabbing pain of separation tore open old wounds with fresh intensity. For now, the assurance of meeting them again in heaven was a cold comfort.

32

Yuri's and my letters always kept alive the hope of seeing one another again. As much as I longed to revisit my homeland and all that was dear and familiar, he cautioned me against it. The authorities were never too busy to deal with anyone whose allegedly subversive activities had jeopardized the Motherland. *It didn't matter that I had helped Russians,* I thought with a flash of my old rebellion. I was, however, unwilling to risk another term in a KGB cell. Instead, we planned that he would visit me in Canada. I contacted the Russian embassy for all the necessary paperwork which I sent to him. He received it and told me that he would soon apply for his visa.. That was the last time I heard from him over a year. My imagination could not rest, subjecting poor Yuri to every imaginable form of KGB interrogation and torture. The least gruesome possibility was that he was forbidden to write to me again. I shed many tears worrying that I had inadvertently brought disaster on my son, even at this great distance.

The telephone call at four o'clock one afternoon took me by surprise. The operator asked if I would accept a long distance call from Montreal and although I could think of no one who might be calling me from there, I accepted. The caller spoke to me in Russian but I didn't recognize the voice. When he said "Yuri," I nearly dropped the phone. When he said that he was in Montreal and would arrive in Calgary the next day, words failed me and my heart drummed wildly in my chest.

How should I prepare for him. Where would he sleep? What should I cook? Where should we take him? What could I buy for him? I couldn't concentrate on anything for more than seconds at a time and was grateful for Lilia's help. She and Stanley were excited too, hardly able to imagine a new brother, despite hearing about him for years. The photo album story was coming to life with Yuri's arrival!

July 18, 1977. We arrived at the airport early, unwilling to risk any possibility that he might arrive with no one there to meet him. I brought along his most recent photograph, lest my eagerness send me flying to embrace a total stranger. I need not have worried. The last person off the plane matched perfectly the picture in my hand — and heart. *Yuri!*

We threw our arms around each other, squeezing thirty-four years of longing into a joyous flood of tears and laughter. Passersby smiled, sensing that this airport meeting was more significant than most. I was oblivious to everything but my son and the miracle of this reunion. The last time I'd hugged him, I knelt on the frozen ground so that I could look fully into his face. Now he bent toward me.

My family watched from the side, feeling suddenly awkward about this part of my history, often talked about but with no personal connection to them. We finally stopped hugging long enough to really look at each other. Yes, there was a definite resemblance. In our excitement, we had overlooked bringing a camera but an acquaintance at the airport obligingly snapped a few Polaroid shots. Yuri's amazement at cameras capable of instantly developing their own films was the first of many delightful 'capitalist' discoveries.

Except for the language barrier, Lilia and Stanley soon felt that they had known Yuri all their lives. Watching their frustrating and often hilarious attempts to communicate in sign language, I could not resist a dig of I-told-you-so. As school children, they were ashamed of the old country languages and instructed us to speak only English around their friends. All my attempts to continue the foundation of Russian and German laid when they were small were ignored in their need to conform with everyone else. They now regretted the lost opportunities to learn Russian. Lilia was at least able to understand some of our conversation but gave up trying to speak on her own. I was delighted to be indispensable in my role as translator. No matter how much we talked, there was always more to ask. I wanted to know all about Raisa and my grandchildren, poring over a new supply of smiling photographs specially taken for this visit.

I felt sad when he talked about his father. Alexander seemed unable to build a new life for himself, preferring to dwell on the past and always carrying a picture of me in his pocket. Although he'd lived with a woman for many years, she refused to marry him because he always called her *Lydia*. After their fourteen-year-old son was murdered by hoodlums, Alexander started to drink heavily and eventually she left him. A sad and broken man, he had once again moved in with his mother.

Every outing with Yuri was an adventure, whether it was a trip to the mountains or to the grocery store. He was amazed at the abundance of meat and produce, which we took for granted, and the ease of shopping for it. He was fascinated by shoppers pushing heaping carts along aisles with their dizzying array of choices. It all seemed so simple here compared to the endless hours of waiting in line for just one item at home.

I often felt as though *I* was seeing my country for the first time. He marvelled at all the paved roads, even in the country. Did people *really* own their own lots and houses? *And* farms? With all the equipment needed to run them? A daily shower was sheer luxury with an endless supply of hot water that gushed with a twist of a tap.

I wanted to pay for his visit, but with an inheritance from his Grandmother Grunya, who died just before his visit, he covered the cost himself. There were other issues to be dealt with before he was free to leave Russia. He had to sign a form promising to return. Raisa had to sign a form, giving her husband permission to visit his mother. Even his co-workers had a meeting to see if this journey met with their approval. Twelve out of thirteen voted in favor, the lone hold-out certain that Yuri would choose to stay in the Decadent West.

To my surprise, Tony was on his best behavior for most of Yuri's visit. Only once did we stay at Lilia's for night when he showed all the familiar signs of becoming drunkenly violent. If possible, I wanted to spare Yuri any painful memories of Tony's shameful behavior, although he already knew that my life held its darker moments.

The two-month visit passed quickly. We took him to Banff and Lake Louise, showing him various section houses along the CPR line where we had lived. We introduced him to barbecuing and I prepared favorite dishes for him to try. We shopped for gifts that he could take back to his family and items of clothing which were in short supply in Russia. I tried to ignore the underlying reality that his visit was drawing to a close — that once again we would occupy separate worlds, connected only by letters. I longed to keep him safely within reach, though recognizing that he was lonesome for his wife and sons.

To our surprise, Tony's suggestion that Raisa also visit was met with an emphatic *no!* According to Yuri, if Raisa set foot in a Canadian shopping centre she would never return home to Russia, regardless of expiring visas or waiting children. It was best for her to hear about it from him with no thought of experiencing it for herself.

I shared his reluctance for a tearful scene at the airport but when the time came, we both wept unrestrainedly. Only God knew if we would ever meet again.

Two years later, he wrote to let me know that Alexander was dead. With no will to curb his drinking habit, his health gradually deteriorated. One day they found him lying in the street where he had fallen. Alone.

I dreaded Tony's retirement, but my years of vigilance were rewarded; he reached the end of his CPR career without being fired and now qualified for the company pension. With little to occupy his time, I feared that he would plant himself in front of the television and drink himself into an early grave. I envisioned myself constantly on guard against his damaging escapades, with no time to relax or to spend with friends. His doctor shared my concern.

"Tony, you have always worked hard and have strong muscles. If you just sit around and drink now, you won't live long." He was blunt and straight to the point. "Your body needs exercise. Find something to keep yourself busy. Work in the garden. Mow the lawn. *Move.*" I agreed with the message but wished he would refrain from making specific suggestions. Tony's efforts in the yard or garden always required remedial action.

He ignored all advice and as I predicted, rarely moved from his chair, a bottle always nearby. After six months of inertia, he decided that it was time to fulfill a dream. He wanted to be a security guard, to wear a uniform that, in his mind, conveyed prestige and authority. The dream, however, did not include tangling with villains in dark alleys. In fact, he flatly refused any posting where he perceived an actual threat to security. His assignment to various courthouse entrances suited him perfectly as he directed people arriving for their appointments with justice.

I was relieved to see him interested in something again and enjoyed hearing his stories about the job, although I questioned whether the tax bite made it worthwhile. I especially appreciated the strictly enforced rules about alcohol use, but Tony's enjoyment of working with people seemed to outweigh his need for the bottle and he hardly needed my watchful eye. Even at home, he seemed less interested in drinking and we often spent evenings going to parks or playing cards with friends. I dared to be cautiously optimistic, even at this late stage. Perhaps we still had time to rediscover some of the fun of our courtship.

Tony was eventually assigned to a building housing bonds and various other forms of paper wealth. The place bristled with electronic security and employees entered the heavy glass doors only with special identification cards. Tony sat at a table equipped with an emergency call button.

"Open the door!"

"Open it yourself." Tony hardly looked up, assuming that the man standing in front of the table was a worker too lazy to look for the necessary card. Besides, he was here to provide polite guidance to public inquiries, not to take orders from high-handed employees.

"*I said, open the door!*" The man's tone became menacing. A knife pointed at Tony's throat convinced him that the gentleman's business was serious. The training sessions had stressed that there should be no heroics in the event of such a confrontation, for which he was grateful. He edged slowly toward the door with one eye fixed on the knife still aimed at his neck, hoping that his furtive stab at the emergency call button would go unnoticed by the 'visitor'. Within minutes police surrounded the building.

After the initial shock, Tony enjoyed the celebrity status resulting from his dramatic brush with crime. He never wearied of telling the story, his role in the happy ending gaining more importance with each repetition.

As I'd feared, tax time brought the disheartening news that he owed the government over two thousand dollars. He had ignored my misgivings, insisting over and over that retired seniors were exempt from paying income tax. Bearing in mind that much of his information in the past had come from an adjacent bar stool, I remained skeptical. Being right gave me no satisfaction this time. As much as he enjoyed his job, he rejected the idea that the government benefited more than he did. After a few months he quit, resuming his post in front of the television, bottle conveniently by his side. Once again, life became an unpredictable series of surprises.

33

Within five minutes of Tony's return home one Sunday afternoon, two policemen rang the doorbell.

"Is your husband here?" My heart sank. Tony had been drinking but surely not enough to attract police attention.

"Does he own a little gun?" Was this a joke? What was the man talking about?

"No he doesn't."

"Maybe a sawed off shotgun?" I looked at Tony who studiously avoided eye contact with me.

"We don't have *any* guns in the house!" Where were all these questions leading us?

The policeman approached Tony but continued talking to me. "Someone reported that he pointed a gun at a lady in a restaurant and threatened to shoot her." He motioned to Tony who tottered unsteadily to his feet as the officer searched his pockets.

"Here!" he said, pulling a little silver gun-shaped lighter from Tony's pocket. Could he be serious? They were indeed serious, waiting for me to respond. All this furor over a lighter?

"Lady," he said, holding the lighter in his palm, "I was a soldier in the army. We saw 'harmless' little guns like this all the time. Only they killed people." He saw skepticism on my face. "I have a collection which I'm happy to show you if you are interested. And this one looked real enough to the people in the restaurant!"

With a warning about stupid jokes, the officers left our house. At least no charges were laid — this time.

A few weeks later Tony's imaginary firearm surfaced again. He had been drinking and showed all the usual signs of becoming violent. I decided to wait it out the backyard, hoping that he would soon fall asleep. Through the open window I could see him moving around, unfortunately showing no indication of winding down. I noticed him talking on the phone and moved closer to listen. From the tone of his voice, it sounded as though he might be talking to the police!

"Who are you talking to, Tony?" I stood inside the doorway, ready to bolt if necessary.

"Here. Talk to them yourself." He handed me the phone. I took it, careful to watch his every move in case he saw this as an opportunity to hit me while my attention was elsewhere.

"Are you the lady of the house?" It *was* the police.

"Is everything okay? Are you hurt?" What *was* he talking about? Why did the police always take so long in getting to the point?

"Your husband called us and told us that he had shot you." *Oh Tony, what now?* I could hardly believe that my husband would deliberately involve the police in one of his pranks.

"Perhaps you could go outside and let everyone know you're alright." The voice was calm but I panicked. *There were police out there too?* He assured me that my house was surrounded but if I showed them that I was alive and well, they would leave.

I went back outside and saw police cruisers clogging our street. The SWAT team, complete with dogs, circled our house, ready to move if necessary. Most of them left as soon as I let them know my husband's idea of a joke, but the job wasn't quite over yet. They took Tony, shouting his entire repertoire of Russian curses, with them for a night in jail.

I spent the entire next day in court waiting for his case to be heard. The judge sharply reprimanded him, pointing out how he had wasted the court's time and warned him to mend his ways. I appreciated the judge adding his voice to mine. Perhaps Tony might listen to someone with authority who could add uncomfortable weight to an old message. He was duly penitent, hardly daring to raise his eyes to the judge. I had no reason to think his change of heart would last past the exit sign.

My role as Tony's guardian and defender took its inevitable toll. On Mother's Day in May, 1983, I experienced a sharp pain in my left side during a special family dinner at Lilia's house. My hand went weak, unable even to hold the fork. They rushed me to a clinic where a check of my pulse and blood pressure showed that I belonged in a hospital. After eight hours of intravenous, I was free to go home. This was an early warning — a dress rehearsal for a heart attack.

"I've met the girl I'm going to marry." Stanley had just returned from a club trip to a little town in British Columbia and was eager to share his news.

Lilia and I hardly reacted to his announcement. He had always received a lot of attention from girls and it was unlikely that a weekend visit to a place called Lumby narrowed the field to one. But it had.

He saw her carrying a tray in the tavern. Their eyes met and the rest was about to become history, at least according to Stanley. My son was definitely smitten and when I met Carol, I understood. She looked much younger than her twenty-one years and at twenty-eight, he endured much teasing about robbing the cradle. They were married in July, 1983, with many club members present at the wedding, their gleaming Harleys an unusual presence in the church parking lot.

Carol told me that Stanley had talked to her about Jesus the first time they met. He did not become a priest, but his devotion

307

to God outlasted his service as an altar boy and he loved to talk about his faith to anyone and everyone. His fellow club members affectionately referred to him as *the Preacher* or a *Jesus Freak*. Carol decided to become Catholic before they were married, although I cautioned her to be sure this was her own conviction rather than something she did for Stanley.

34

July, 1984. Splatters of blood covered the bathroom. My heart pounded as I raced to Tony's room. What was wrong with him?

He tried to wave aside my concern, attributing the beets he'd had for supper for the telltale red in the bathroom. The grayness in his face told me that something other than a second helping of beets had caused a problem here. All I could think about was that the clinic nearby was open late and that I must get him there as soon as possible. I pulled him to his feet and he tottered unsteadily for a few moments, his breathing labored. Finally he regained his balance, leaning heavily on me as we slowly walked the short distance to find help.

After a quick examination, the doctor sent him for an immediate blood test. She told me later that he was in desperate need of a transfusion, hardly believing that he had managed even the walk from our house to the clinic. Lilia came immediately and drove us to the hospital, where a blood transfusion returned the color to Tony's face.

After several days he returned home, though still without a specific diagnosis. In my heart I knew that alcohol was the ultimate villain. He recovered without further incident and though I watched him anxiously for a few weeks, there was no recurrence. Just when I was ready to relax, I noticed that he was unusually pale one night as he lay in bed reading.

"What's wrong, Tony?" I asked, remembering his untouched plate at supper. He stared at me without replying and it was a few seconds before I realized that he couldn't speak. I called 911 and a team of paramedics took him to hospital. This time the verdict was swift; Tony had suffered a stroke and there was only a fifty-fifty chance that he would live. Doctors suspected that a series of smaller strokes before this had caused irreparable damage.

We stayed by his side in constant vigil. He was unable to talk, move, or in any way acknowledge our presence and I doubted that he even recognized us. I talked to him anyway, telling him anything I could think of, mostly about our family. Tubes radiated from his body, keeping him hydrated, fighting infection and helping him breathe. He was so pathetic lying there, pale and helpless. Was this the man who for most of our married life had terrorized me and our children? Like melting snow, I suddenly felt years of anger and resentment dissolve as I stood by his bed, knowing only that despite all reason and logic, I loved him.

To everyone's surprise, Tony began to recover, first showing signs of recognition and then saying a few words. Gradually he even learned to walk again. His confident stride was gone but each halting step was a gift.

Before his illness, I had planned and paid for a trip to Germany which I now felt duty-bound to cancel. My family, with the doctor's support, thought otherwise. It was time for me to look after myself. Tony was improving and had the best of care; if there was cause for concern, an eight-hour flight would bring me back to his side. GO! The verdict was unanimous and in September, 1984, I went to Germany with a friend.

Despite my concern for Tony, I had a wonderful time seeing a new side to the country which for a short time, had counted me as one of its citizens. I visited Kassel, the city where Lilia was born, near where the camp used to be. It was now a thriving town with no traces of the war remaining. Freight trains now carried normal cargo with no sign of bedraggled refugees peering out of tiny windows. I saw no military uniforms on the streets and no one burst into my room at night or checked my suitcases. I wondered how differently my life might have turned out if we had remained here. Would I still be a "Dumb Russian," or would I have finally blended in with everyone else?

When I returned home a month later, Tony was at the airport with Lilia to meet me. His brush with death gave him a new interest in life. It also erased all interest in alcohol and cigarettes. The man I married once again shared my life and I often thanked God for bringing him back to me. Lilia and Stanley became acquainted with the father they'd seen in brief glimpses during their childhood. His grandchildren looked forward to coming to our house without fear of angry outbursts. He was always ready for an outing to a park, a trip downtown or a walk in the fresh air. We visited with friends, playing cards and laughing until the early morning hours. Life was good.

In November, 1984, Tony suffered another stroke, complicated by an intestinal disorder requiring surgery. The prognosis was doubtful, again with only a fifty-fifty chance of survival. For four-and-a-half agonizing hours I waited, together with our priest, to know the results. Finally a nurse emerged from the operating room and waved at me. The smile on her face was all the reassurance I needed.

He had survived the operation but the doctor was still anxious. They had removed two feet of small intestine and installed a colostomy, assuring me that eventually it could be reversed if everything healed properly. It didn't. The doctor's face was grave as he told me that infection had set in, that instead of healthy pink healing tissue, the wound had turned black. Another operation was his only hope.

After this surgery, Tony retained only two feet of small intestine. The doctor told me that if the infection recurred, there was nothing more they could do for him. I practically lived at the hospital, reluctantly allowing Lilia or my grandchildren to drive me home after eleven o'clock for a few hours of sleep before returning the next day.

I was almost afraid of what I might see in the faces of those caring for Tony, looking for signs of forced cheerfulness or any other indications that all was not well. They were all cautiously optimistic when day after day, the wound remained pink and free of the dreaded infection. For a month his only nourishment flowed through a tube into his veins but one day the doctor greeted me with a big smile, holding a milkshake out to me. Tony could eat! The tubes were disconnected and he no longer resembled a laboratory project. They were even able to reverse the colostomy.

Once again God had spared him and after a four-month hospital stay, he was able to come home. It was a short reprieve. In June, 1985, he had another stroke, and although he survived it, we reluctantly agreed that Tony now needed care beyond what I could safely provide at home. When he could be discharged from the hospital, we took him to a nearby nursing home, sadly aware that he would live out his remaining days there.

I visited him every day, wheeling his chair outside as often as weather permitted. His greatest delight, however, was when Christie, our first great-grandchild, was brought to him. Although too weak to hold his "princess," he loved to stroke the baby-soft cheek when Debbie laid her across his stomach.

For the first time Tony and I talked about dying and what that meant for whichever one of us went first — and for the one left behind. He had two wishes: not to die alone and not to be cremated. His speech was slow and labored but regardless of how hard it was to communicate, he was determined to resolve outstanding issues.

Tony's memories, which for years blurred behind an alcoholic haze, now haunted him with agonizing clarity. Sometimes he silently grasped my hand, tears trickling down his cheeks and I knew he was watching himself hurting me, as though in a torturous film for which there was no *off* switch.

"I'm *so* sorry. Please forgive me." The words were the same as I'd heard on countless morning-afters, though now the opportunity for restitution was gone. I had already forgiven him, realizing as I stood by his side after the first stroke that the slate was wiped clean. The Lord had simply asked me to give him the load of pain and resentment I carried beneath the obligation of "'til death us do part." I did, and it was gone, forever removed.

Sensing that time was limited, Tony made his peace with Lilia and Stanley too, asking their forgiveness for the pain he had caused, and for his failure to be a father who cared for and protected his children.

He died on September 4, 1985, with all of us by his side. Stanley asked him if he could see Jesus and he smiled in response. My eyes never left his face, which seemed instantly thirty years younger, as though to reassure me that death was restoring what life had taken away.

Though Tony had been away from our house for several months, it was now strangely empty without him. I did not share the relief tactfully expressed by some of my friends at his passing. Their concern for my welfare was a deeply ingrained habit that the past year of Tony's sobriety had not erased. It was surely time for a new start. How could I explain that I missed my husband — that I was not yet ready to enjoy my new freedom as they seemed to expect?

I was thankful that Tony had always allowed me to look after our business affairs, unlike other widows who struggled with each detail of banking, insurance and investment. In fact, I recognized that the God who had known me as I was being "knit together in my mother's womb" had included a stitch of independence which propelled me through childhood and served me throughout every phase of my life. He would provide everything I needed to get through the next weeks and months of adjusting to life on my own.

Lilia and Stanley, together with their families, helped to fill the void. My grandchildren often came to visit, their antics restoring laughter to my life. It was impossible to be sad when they were always clamouring for hugs and attention. Bedtime, as well as waking up to an empty house, was difficult for me but I dedicated time at each end of the day for prayer and this eased the suffocating pain of loneliness.

I sent a photograph of Tony in his casket to Yuri, describing the changes in his life that had taken place, and how we had been able to fulfill his wish not to die alone. Yuri wrote a comforting, yet wistful letter back, comparing his father's lonely death in the street to Tony's, surrounded by people who loved and cared for him.

My involvement with the Catholic Women's League had continued ever since Sonya had signed me into membership back in Lacombe. While our frequent moves between section houses had made active participation impossible at times, I appreciated knowing that I belonged to this supportive sisterhood. Now I was free to devote more time to helping with their various projects, including food and clothing for the homeless.

Tony and I had enjoyed day or weekend trips with the CPR Club and although it felt strange to participate in their activities without him, I went along at every opportunity. A Hawaiian vacation in February, 1986, was something to look forward to and I added my name to the list.

Those plans changed in January. As I walked home from an afternoon of playing cards at a friend's house, my feet suddenly became lead weights, barely obeying my will to move forward. I struggled onward to my house, pulling myself along the fence for support, finally crawling up the cement stairs. Excruciating pain squeezed breath from my lungs. Even turning the key in the front door needed more strength than my fingers could muster. It had taken me an hour to walk three blocks.

Stanley and Carol lived in the basement and heard my cry for help. He raced up the stairs and after one look at my face, dialled 911. The paramedics arrived within minutes and one checked my vital signs while the other alerted the hospital. No one listened to my feeble protests and I was belted onto a stretcher and hoisted into the ambulance. I could faintly hear the siren's wail clearing the streets, and regretted all the fuss. A pill or two would surely have been enough!

I was in the intensive care unit for six days with only my family allowed to visit. It was my turn to sprout tubes from every conceivable opening. When I was finally declared fit enough to be transferred to a regular unit, the seriousness of my condition was evident in my doctor's face. He scheduled me for an angiogram, showing me on the monitor how the dye passed through my veins to my heart, as well as the blockage that interrupted its circuit. There were two such places and he explained that two double bypasses were necessary to correct the situation. He also explained that the chance of it being successful was a scant fifteen per cent.

I hardly needed to think about it. On God's calendar, my lifespan was already fixed. As long as he had a purpose for my being here, no heart attack would remove me. And no frantic medical tampering would increase my life by so much as a day.

35

When a tense rivalry developed among motorcycle clubs for territorial supremacy, many bikers, including Stanley, withdrew their memberships, turning in their crests and other insignia in an attempt to avoid the escalating violence. He and Carol moved to Salmon Arm, British Columbia to distance themselves from club activities. The lifestyle held many happy memories but it was time to think about what was best for their family.

Stanley's enthusiasm for his trucking business remained strong. Next to Carol and daughters, Danielle and Raelyn, the open road was his greatest pleasure.

December 10, 1991. Stanley had no way of knowing that morning when he waved good-bye to Carol that he would never see her alive again. "There must be some mistake," was his first response that night in Vancouver when the phone call came advising him to come right away. It must be someone else lying in a Kamloops hospital in a coma. She had been fine in the morning with no hint of illness. He could see her standing in the picture window holding eleven-month-old Raelyn with Danielle, age four, at her side.

It all happened very suddenly. She and her mother had enjoyed a busy day of Christmas shopping, including a visit to a photographer for new portraits of the children. That evening she developed a severe headache that literally blinded her. Trying to stay calm, she instructed Danielle to dial Grandma Rona's number.

"I'm dying. Please look after my children!" Her voice was weak from pain. Trying to stay calm, Rona tried to reassure her that everything would be fine, but both children were crying in the background and it was apparent that *nothing* was fine. Then all she heard was silence.

"Carol! *Carol!*" There was no response. Now frantic, she called Carol's neighbours who soon found her unconscious on the floor, two frightened little girls huddling beside her.

Dazed by the swift turn of events, Rona recalled that a year ago Carol had predicted that she would soon die. At the time, she had dismissed it. Why would anyone in the picture of health be pre-occupied with gloomy thoughts of death? She would not allow herself to think about the second part of Carol's premonition: Stanley would die too.

Stanley, despite his worry about Carol, was mindful of my heart condition and called Lilia in the middle of the night. She came to my house immediately. The news stunned me. How could I believe that my happy, vibrant daughter-in-law was, even now, breathing only with the help of a machine?

As quickly as we could organize ourselves, we left for Kamloops, driving directly to the hospital. It was true. She lay there pale and fragile, a respirator hissing air into her lungs. I held her hand, encouraged by the warmth. Surely this wasn't as serious as they had said!

"She wants her organs to be donated for transplanting. That's why they're keeping her alive." The nurse was matter-of-fact, as though discussing the weather. I boiled inside, unable to believe anyone could be so unfeeling. They were treating Carol like a factory of spare parts! It all seemed coldly cruel and calculating.

"Mom." Lilia's arm circled my shoulder. "Her brain is dead. Carol is gone."

Stanley was lost. Carol had been the light of his life and when that light was snuffed out, his spirit seemed to go with her.

I ached for him, wanting to make it better but as I well knew, even a mother's love cannot soothe away grief's searing pain. I prayed that he would find his way out of the darkness. His little girls needed their daddy.

Their care was an immediate concern. As a trucker, Stanley's schedule varied from week to week and it was difficult to predict when he would be home. I stayed there for several weeks at a time, returning to Calgary long enough to look after my house before going back to Salmon Arm. Stanley tried repeatedly to find a live-in nanny but none of them were genuinely interested in looking after children. To them, this position was only a temporary alternative to a *real* job.

I worried about Danielle. At night she refused to stay upstairs in her room unless I was close by, insisting on sleeping with Stanley or on the livingroom sofa. She often awakened screaming, with no memory of it the next morning. During the day I would find her lying on the kitchen linoleum, always in the same spot, eyes vacant and staring. I tried to reason with her, telling her that it was not good to wipe the floor with her clothes. I encouraged her to find a more comfortable place on the carpet or sofa, but to no avail. I learned later that this was where Carol had collapsed.

Counsellors recommended that Stanley sell the house. A home without constant reminders of her mother might be what Danielle needed. He reluctantly agreed, feeling that now Carol was lost to him forever. How well I knew that feeling. Now it was my turn to comfort my son with Papa's view of separation; regardless of time, distance, or circumstances, those we love cannot be truly lost because we carry them in our hearts. *Always.* He listened without really hearing me. After two years, his every thought and action was still for Carol, including developing the new house the way she would have liked.

When Carol died, Raelyn was too young to remember her mother, but the rest of us determined to keep alive for her an awareness that her mommy had loved her very much. I sometimes carried her on a picture tour of my walls, encouraging her to name family members smiling at us from my photo gallery. Her little finger happily pointed out everyone she recognized, however any time she came to Carol's picture, she pulled back, uncertain about this person who everyone referred to as "Mommy," but who never made a personal appearance.

My deepest desire for Stanley was that he would again find someone to share his life, someone who could be a mother to his children. Rona and I did what we could to care for them, but they needed more than even devoted grandmothers could give. There must be someone to fill the void that Carol's death left in their family, to help them all move through their grief — to rediscover joy in living. When a few women showed an interest in doing just that, Stanley maintained a cool distance, appreciating their friendship, yet unable to offer more in return. His heart belonged to Carol.

36

Victor was coming! It was fifty-two years since I had said goodbye to him at the railway station, and I remembered every detail of that parting, his white hanky still waving its sad farewell as the train curved out of sight. Despite the new freedoms of *glasnost* and *perestroika,* he encountered one obstacle after another in making the arrangements.

I bought his ticket, which was eventually returned to me due to an obscure policy requiring him to purchase it in Russia. The documentation I sent to him needed an additional stamp, available only for an exorbitant fee. The rules seemed to change hourly and in my impatience, I despaired that he would ever come. Finally I received his schedule and arrived at the airport with a whole family delegation to meet him. The children, carrying bouquets of roses, were caught up in the excitement without quite understanding the significance of this visitor. A television reporter and camera crew met us there. Family reunions such as this warranted media attention.

Had he changed? Would I know him? He was sixteen years old when I last saw him and despite the recent photograph, this was how I remembered him. As passengers streamed out of the doors, I stood on tiptoe, straining to see the next person to emerge, fearful that a tall stranger might block my view at a critical moment. The flight attendants and pilots emerged, pulling their travel cases behind them. But no Victor.

His problems had continued, even after he'd notified me of his schedule. After all the unexpected delays and red tape, he arrived at the Moscow airport too late for a seat assignment and had to wait for another flight. A day later, he arrived. There were no flowers or television cameras this time, but Victor was here! I would have recognized him anywhere, with or without a photograph. His features were the same and his eyes, still sparkling with mischief as we hugged each other, promised hours of laughter in the weeks ahead.

Yuri's visit had prepared me for some of Canada's novelties for foreign guests and again, I felt as though I was seeing this country for the first time. Like Yuri, Victor was intrigued by a land without dirt roads, even in the country. He stared at row upon row of houses, each with at least one car parked in the driveway. In his eyes, we were all millionaires living in a city of palaces. I tried to explain that very few people actually owned these things outright, that mortgages allowed us to enjoy things as we paid for them. Big houses full of expensive furniture and gadgets rarely meant a pocketful of cash for the people who lived in them. Credit and interest was a difficult concept for someone from a communist background to grasp and he preferred his own version, already looking forward to describing his capitalist Canadian relatives to friends back in Russia.

I tried to balance his view by telling him about the homeless people my church group helped with groceries, meals and used clothing. I described how we arrived in this Land of Plenty with an overseas packing crate, a suitcase and two hundred seventy-five dollars in American currency. Everything I now owned came from years of hard work, cautious investment and diligent saving. Canada was no free ride!

He loved accompanying me to the supermarket where it was so easy to buy things. He could hardly imagine picking out meat and vegetables for himself from such a bewildering display of choices! And if I ran out of sugar a quick trip to the store let me continue cooking with scarcely any interruption. The casual blue jeans and T-shirts he saw everywhere puzzled him. At home, shopping was a dress-up event.

Lilia and Ed invited us to accompany them and a group of friends on a weekend trip to Stanley's home in British Columbia. Victor was astonished at the idea of travelling in a motorhome with a fridge and stove where everyone but the driver could sit at a table enjoying a snack or game of cards during the trip. At night I was ready for bed long before the bonfire was extinguished. Victor was in high spirits, unwilling to miss a minute of fun, and their laughter made me smile in the darkness.

Each day held new surprises for my brother. "What a life you have here!" I heard this over and over again. "You live like the aristocracy!" I realized, with some guilt, how easily we accepted as commonplace a lifestyle that elsewhere meant luxury.

Once again, I acted as interpreter for my children who thoroughly enjoyed getting to know their uncle. As with Yuri, they understood most of what he said but could not be coaxed to try speaking the unfamiliar sounds themselves. I loved to watch them together, making up for all the lost years. Stanley's laughter was music to my soul. *Thank you Lord!* Perhaps Victor's visit could remind him that the road through sadness still held joy. If only Tony could have met him too.

We usually stayed up late at night talking, never running out of conversation. He wanted to know about my life with Tony, correctly reading through years of carefully worded letters that *"happily ever after"* did not describe our marriage. When I saw the look on his face, I was glad to have spared them the graphic details earlier. Again, I hastened to balance the scales, anxious for him to know the kind, generous man I'd married long ago. It was fun to remember the good times when Tony entertained us with his accordion. Or when we danced to Russian folk melodies with no thought for creaking knees or stiff muscles.

I wanted to know everything about their lives since boarding the train. *"What did Papa do? What did Mama say?"* No detail was too insignificant. I wanted to hear again about Reinhold, still finding it hard to believe that my big strong brother had been the only one to die in the frigid temperatures. And Heinrich? Was he still my quiet, sensitive baby brother who rushed to defend me against Victor's teasing?

Papa had told me that he had been injured while working at the mine and Victor provided more details. When a drunk employee had arrived to help pull Heinrich's truck out of the mud, instead of driving forward, he had put the truck in reverse, pinning Henrich's leg against a wall. Even after two surgeries, he walked with great difficulty aided by a cane.

Victor noticed that my former stubborn streak had vanished. I shared with him that after reading their letters, I wondered how I could possibly change myself, eventually realizing after months of fleeing with the Germans, that it had happened without me even noticing. I reacted more patiently in situations where I didn't get my own way and accepted people for what they were, regardless of things that I previously found to be distasteful. Weeks on the road without a bath followed by "Dumb Russian" treatment had shown me the need for tolerance and the injustice of discrimination. I learned the hard way what Papa tried vainly to teach me. Sometimes circumstances beyond our control affect how we look on the outside. Inside, we are all the same, created by God who loves us equally.

The month was over far too quickly and once again we were on our way to the airport, though this time less exuberantly than before. Victor was laden with gifts for his and Heinrich's families as well as photographs of every memorable moment. I wished that I could hear him describe everything to his family who would, no doubt, sit in wide-eyed wonder at stories of houses on wheels and supermarkets where you wore jeans and chose your own meat. I forced away thoughts of *will I see him again?* This visit was a gift to be treasured and enjoyed without worrying whether others might follow.

37

Stanley was seriously depressed. Besides the children, he was interested only being on the road in his truck. It became a refuge where he did not have to see or respond to others' concern for him. A doctor and counsellor both told him that he should quit working for six months, that he needed to deal with the source of his depression. It was important that he begin to let go of Carol and their life together — to build a new life with his girls. He now suffered from blinding migraine headaches which placed him at additional risk behind the wheel.

Unable to face staying at home, he began driving for a logging company, against all medical advice. Once again, babysitting arrangements became a problem and the girls finally stayed with their grandmother Rona in Lumby. While Stanley was relieved to know that they were well cared for, he was unable to see or spend time with them. One night he sat in my living room, tears pouring down his face after he hung up the phone from talking to them. If he stayed home where they were, his grief was compounded through inactivity. The therapy of work, however, took him away from his children for days at a time and he missed them terribly. I cried with him.

Eventually a solution presented itself. Debbie and her husband, Jim, agreed to move into Stanley's house, giving his girls a stable home with their two children, and Stanley the opportunity to see them nearly every day. While Jim had always been eager to live in British Columbia, Debbie was reluctant to leave the security of family and friends in Calgary. I encouraged her to try it, having proven over the course of many relocations that good friendships await, even in the remotest of corners. A one-year trial period seemed reasonable and arrangements were made, including the rental of their house in Calgary and storage of furniture.

Stanley's spirits rose noticeably. The sadness never quite left his eyes but every time I heard him laugh, I breathed a quiet *thank you, Lord.*

July 15, 1995. Debbie and Jim were ready to go, awaiting Stanley's arrival back in Calgary with his truck. While I had encouraged the move, I knew how much I was going to miss having them and my great-grandchildren nearby. Frequent reminders to myself that Lumby was within easy driving distance, and that Danielle and Raelyn would be cared for in their own home, did not dispel the sense of loneliness at their imminent departure. It was all for the best.

A letter from Raisa! The airmail envelope with the familiar Russian stamp was a welcome diversion to my restless melancholy.

By the time you get this letter, Yuri may be gone from this world.

My frantic telephone call later that evening confirmed it. Yuri was dead. My life with him had been so short and full of interruption. Our reunion, after years of wondering if the other was alive or dead, had strengthened the bond that neither time nor distance could break. Now he was gone.

Raisa, her voice choking with tears, shared details of his illness that medical personnel were previously ordered to keep secret. Yuri was a Chernobyl casualty, dying of skin cancer. The vague references to diseases such as eczema or psoriasis were deliberately misleading, and only after his death had they admitted the truth. During the last few months, he had lived in excruciating pain, his skin raw and oozing as though severely burned. She told me of her difficulty in filling prescriptions for various creams and ointments that would supposedly treat his condition. At least one ingredient was consistently lacking in every pharmacy, suddenly miraculously available when additional money was offered. Yuri wanted to protect me from long-distance worry and deliberately downplayed his suffering, both in letters and during our telephone conversations.

After talking to Raisa I sat and cried, grieving again for the little boy I'd left behind and the years of his childhood lost to me; for the grown man who still wanted his mother's blessing before he married and had two sons and grandsons of his own. I wanted to be with them, to meet his family that I knew only through letters and photographs. *My* family.

I didn't want to be alone but it was approaching midnight and I was reluctant to call Lilia or any of my friends. Sleep was unlikely so I decided to call Stanley, who was on his way back to Calgary from Vancouver. He planned to arrive in the middle of the night so I was sure he was getting close. I reached him shortly after midnight.

His voice was cheerful on the phone and and he told me that an RCMP officer had just stopped him after someone reported that his truck was weaving on the highway. He was now just west of Banff after driving for thirteen consecutive hours — too long without sleep, according to guidelines governing the trucking industry. The officer had invited him into the cruiser and lectured him about the hazards of driving beyond the designated limits, for which a five hundred dollar penalty was in order. In the end, he fined him only twenty-five dollars for an incomplete logbook and told him to sleep at least until three o'clock before resuming the last leg of his journey.

"Go ahead and sleep," I urged him. "I'll call you again at three." My news could wait until I saw him in person. If I was going to be awake anyway, I might as well do something useful. He assured me that he would wait until two o'clock, in case the same police was farther down the road, ready to pull him over again. He laughed off my concern. The RCMP were certain to have a change in shift before then and couldn't be everywhere at once anyway. He was excited about everything that was finally working out, and eager to help Debbie and Jim with the last details of their move.

"Goodbye Mom, I love you and God bless you. Take care of yourself." It was Stanley's usual sign-off to our telephone conversations and I echoed it back to him. It was 12:55 a.m.

Nothing prepared me for the policeman's announcement the next morning. He asked if I was alone or if there was someone he could call for me. I managed to give him Lilia's telephone number which I was incapable of dialing myself. Terrified by the sound of my sobs behind the forced steadiness of the officer's voice, she rushed over to my house.

There had to be some mistake. It was someone else's truck, someone else was driving. Any minute now Stanley would run up the front steps alive and well, wondering what all the fuss was about.

But there was no mistake. Lilia's determination to see his body before believing the news was gently discouraged by the medical examiner's office. A while later other policemen arrived, one of them the officer who had stopped Stanley earlier. They had detailed reports and photographs available for us to look at if we were ready to see them. The truck had failed to negotiate a curve in the highway, slamming through the guardrail into a mountain. It had happened at 1:38 a.m. He hadn't waited until two o'clock after all. And now he was dead.

For the moment, I just wanted to know how he was sitting in the truck, how he had died. Had he suffered a long, slow death waiting for help that never came? He had been wearing his seatbelt but was killed by a head injury. They tried to assure me that he had died instantly, that he had not suffered. *How could they be so certain? Who would ever really know?*

The RCMP officer who had pulled him over also came to my house, his face drawn and haggard. He told Lilia and me how he had lectured Stanley for exceeding the number of hours behind the wheel, frustrated by yet another driver who endangered innocent lives in his rush to meet deadlines. Stanley had sat in the back seat of the cruiser and cried. This was a side of my son that few people witnessed. Then they started to talk as one man to another. Stanley told him about Carol's death and his desperate loneliness for her, about his children and the struggle to find a way to be with them. He talked about the incapacitating headaches that kept him from sleeping and the medication that helped him to function.

The officer, also the father of two children, was overcome by remorse for his earlier impatience. While he was obligated to enforce highway regulations, he had felt unusual compassion for this driver who had shared some of the sadness that always accompanied him on the road.

When the call came from the dispatcher notifying him of the accident involving a truck and its lone occupant, his first thought was of Stanley. Surely it couldn't be him! But it was. The emergency team at the scene had collected all the documentation they had found in the cab but he waved it away. He had already seen everything he needed to complete his paperwork.

According to the official report, Stanley had fallen asleep behind the wheel. I suspected a heart attack, perhaps related to his headache medication. In recent weeks he had sometimes complained of severe chest pains, but refused to have it checked by a doctor.

I lived an endless nightmare as one day blurred into the next. Time meant nothing and I ate and slept as directed with little initiative of my own. Media coverage of the accident quickly spread word of Stanley's death and messages of condolence poured in, many from people in various places we'd lived while Tony worked for the CPR. I heard the phone's incessant ringing as through a fog, unable to summon the strength to answer it myself. Stanley's friends from motorcycle club days called from far and wide, all stunned at the news.

Lilia made the funeral arrangements, keeping me posted about details that failed to register. *What did any of it matter? Would any of it bring him back to me? To his children?* How could Danielle and Raelyn, now aged seven and four, go through life without mother *and* father? Stanley's death left a big hole in every heart.

"Where are his feet?" Raelyn and her cousin Lukie stood by the casket in the funeral home. The lid was open, showing the customary top half of the body. No explanation was adequate. They *had* to see for themselves that Stanley was intact — with feet. The funeral director obliged, opening the other half to reveal his legs and feet complete with shoes. Lilia had arranged a Harley Davidson headband to hide the injury. He looked as though he had fallen asleep. *Could it be possible that he would never open his eyes again?*

Holy Trinity Church was packed to capacity. The service began late as more and more people streamed inside, filling every space in the sanctuary, foyer and even the nursery. Motorcycles slotted into every available nook and cranny in the parking lot and on the street, truckers' rigs lined up for blocks. Leather-clad bikers with colorful club crests and insignia crowded into pews alongside proper suits and dresses, oddly united in paying their last respects.

I remember little of the funeral, only that others guided me through the motions. A wall of numbness separated me from the reality of the service. It was easier to remember Stanley assisting the priest at this very altar than to believe that his body now rested in a casket in front of it. I could still see the concentration on his face as he recited every Latin word from memory, and the light in his eyes when he announced his intention to become a priest himself. I wondered if I would be sitting here today if he had pursued that choice.

His former club members rode their bikes in a convoy past my house as a final tribute, their helmets at their sides in a gesture of respect. Overwhelmed by my own grief, I still felt the depth of pain Stanley's death held for this strange collection of people who had briefly shared his life — who I would never have chosen as suitable friends for my son. Big, tough men draped tattooed arms around each other, weeping unashamedly into shaggy beards. One seemed particularly stricken, unable to tear himself away from the casket.

I wished that I could take Stanley home with me one last time, away from the funeral home and public sympathy. There were so many things that had been left unsaid until we could sit down together. *If only* he had stayed off the road like he promised. *If only* he had taken more time off. *If only... If only......*

The burial took place the next day in Lumby where he was laid to rest next to Carol. Friends and neighbours from the town met us at the cemetery for a short service. With Lilia and my grandchildren close by my side, I read two passages from the Bible as I stood beside the new grave; Luke 23:44-49 with its despair in the face of death, contrasted by the message of hope and new life in Christ found in Romans 6:3-10.

Before leaving the cemetery, I paused beside the adjacent marker. Carol Oushal. Soon another gravestone would mark his resting place beside her. The certainty of their reunion, beyond the confines of any grave, comforted my spirit as the casket was slowly lowered into the ground.

I ached for Stanley's children who now lived with Debbie and Jim, although not in British Columbia as first planned. Their house shrank from this sudden expansion in their family and a new, five-bedroom house was built before winter. Danielle, who had never cried or shown emotion outwardly when Carol died, became even more withdrawn after Stanley's death. I feared what might happen eventually if she never learned to express what was going on inside. At night she walked and cried in her sleep, wanting both her mommy and daddy, again remembering nothing by morning.

Raelyn was as vocal as Danielle was silent. She was now the same age as Danielle had been when Carol died, and was uninhibited about expressing her sadness.

"I'm going to take a gun and shoot Jesus!" Her angry outburst was in response to hearing us say that Jesus had taken her daddy to be with him. I realized that what to me was a comforting thought, portrayed him as a villain.

"No, Raelyn, you must not talk that way." I pulled her onto my lap and held her close. "Jesus loves us." I explained to her that Jesus knew her name even before she was born and he also knows when he will take her home to be with him. I told her that Daddy was now with Mommy in heaven and if they heard her saying things like this, they would both be very sad.

"I want to go to heaven too," she announced firmly, going to get her coat out of the closet. I explained that if she went to heaven she could not come back. Only Jesus knew the right time for her to go. Sometimes she sat in the livingroom, crying quietly and hugging a photo album containing pictures of her daddy. My own tears spilled down my cheeks as I watched her, wanting desperately to make it better — for all of us.

EPILOGUE

Each day is a gift to treasure.

I have learned that there is no magic moment when the ache of grief and separation is over, or the wellspring of tears runs dry. There are days when the longing for Mama and Papa still rises so painfully in my chest that even breathing is difficult. I still check my mailbox, unconsciously waiting for the familiar airmail envelope from Yuri. When the phone rings, I hope that Stanley is calling to let me know he will be home for supper. And on a warm summer evening, I want to go for a walk in the park with Tony.

None of these will ever happen again.

But every morning the sun rises, bringing with it a new day, new life. I love the outdoors, and wish that I had the strength to spend more time in my garden. The seasons, with their vigorous cycles of birth, growth, and harvest remind me that there is order in all of creation, including my life.

It has not always seemed so. Yet, when I look back I see that even in times of greatest sadness, confusion, and despair, God was always there. In lice-infested darkness when I felt alone, God was with me. With each good-bye, each graveside parting, he reaffirmed his presence. When I doubted that I would ever belong anywhere, when others "trespassed against me," he was there. The *Our Father,* which Papa urged me to hold in my heart, has sustained me over the years as he knew it would.

God's protecting hand still covers me. Recently I was enjoying the sunshine and a good book in my yard when I decided to get a glass of water. Moments after reaching the house, I heard a crash. A car had smashed through the fence, sending the lawnchair flying across the grass. Was it simple thirst that drew me to safety at just the right time?

God is faithful in his promise to change my mourning into dancing. As I hold each new baby in my arms, my heart sings with the joy and promise of a new generation. My grandchildren and great-grandchildren fill my house with noisy fun and I welcome their visits. They try to "fix" the way I talk (silent English letters still baffle me). I retaliate with Russian words that *they* cannot pronounce. We share holidays and special events, camping trips and visits to the mountains. I am also grateful for special friends, who continue to bless me with gifts of love and laughter.

Lilia and I have a close relationship. I thank God for her, and the comfort and support that she has given me, even as a little girl when her own childhood was clouded by sadness.

With the prophet Jeremiah, I can say, *"Because of the Lord's great love we are not consumed, for his compassions never fail. They are new every morning; great is your faithfulness."* (Lamentations 3:22-23 NIV)